# The Age of Crisis

Alfredo Saad-Filho

# The Age of Crisis

## Neoliberalism, the Collapse of Democracy, and the Pandemic

palgrave
macmillan

Alfredo Saad-Filho
Department of International Development
King's College London
London, UK

ISBN 978-3-030-81607-0 ISBN 978-3-030-81608-7 (eBook)
https://doi.org/10.1007/978-3-030-81608-7



This Palgrave Macmillan imprint is published by the registered company Springer Nature Switzerland AG
The registered company address is: Gewerbestrasse 11, 6330 Cham, Switzerland

*In memory of my friends taken too soon.*

*For my children, light in dark times.*

# Acknowledgements

I am grateful to the Transnational Institute (TNI) and the Department of International Development, King's College London, for part-funding the research work for this book.

Nicolás Águila co-authored Chapters 9 and 11.

# Abbreviations

| | |
|---|---|
| AEs | Advanced Capitalist Economies |
| ARDS | Acute Respiratory Distress Syndrome |
| BJP | Bharatiya Janata Party (India) |
| BLM | Black Lives Matter |
| CDC | US Centers for Disease Control and Prevention |
| COVAX | COVID-19 Vaccines Global Access |
| COVID-19 | Coronavirus disease 2019 |
| DEs | Developing Economies |
| EU | European Union |
| GDP | Gross Domestic Product |
| GFC | Global Financial Crisis |
| IBC | Interest-Bearing Capital |
| ICU | Intensive Care Unit |
| IMF | International Monetary Fund |
| M&A | Mergers and Acquisitions |
| NATO | North Atlantic Treaty Organisation |
| NHS | National Health Service |
| OECD | Organsation for Economic Cooperation and Development |
| PASOK | Panhellenic Socialist Movement |
| PPE | Personal Protective Equipment |
| QE | Quantitative Easing |
| SAGE | Scientific Advisory Group for Emergencies |
| SARS | Severe Acute Respiratory Syndrome |
| SUS | Universal Health System (*Sistema Único de Saúde*) |
| UK | United Kingdom |
| US, USA | United States of America |
| WHO | World Health Organisation |
| WTO | World Trade Organisation |

# Contents

# Introduction

The COVID-19 pandemic was the worst global public health emergency since the 'Spanish' flu that enveloped the world after World War I: a catastrophe following a nightmare. In comparison with the flu's 50 million victims in a world with a population under 2 billion, the number of deaths due to COVID-19 is relatively small; yet, the pandemic produced countless tragedies, traumatised the survivors and triggered the sharpest economic contraction recorded in the history of capitalism.[1]

This book examines three overlapping crises in the current 'age of neoliberalism' from the point of view of Marxist political economy: the crises in the global economy (creeping stagnation, finance-driven volatility, and periodic collapses); contemporary politics (the decline of democracy and the rise of authoritarianism and new forms of fascism) and human health (highlighted by the COVID-19 pandemic). For reasons of space, time and expertise, the book does not address other crises in neoliberalism, for example, those of the food system, water, antibiotics and the environment.[2] This book brings together two strands of my previous research: on neoliberalism and the implications of the Global Financial Crisis (GFC), and on the crisis of democracy and the rise of overtly despotic forms of governance.[3] They provide the context for an original interpretation of the COVID-19 pandemic and its likely implications.

The economic crisis in global neoliberalism is closely related to the escalating crisis of democracy and the (uneven) drift toward authoritarianism in many countries. This drift cannot be reduced to an epiphenomenal or self-correcting slip into unsustainable projects led by self-centred, thieving or megalomaniac politicians, after whose inevitable failure the world will get back to normal. This is unlikely. The rise of overtly authoritarian modes of governance derives from a neoliberal politics of crisis management centred on the manipulation of sectional (exclusionary) resentments in order to shore up the system of accumulation by means of permanent strife, repression, high rates of exploitation within and between countries, and outright plunder. Underlying social divisions have been contained, channelled and deflected by nationalism, racism and violence, often encased within right-wing, authoritarian and populist political forms. These processes became evident with the anointment of Narendra Modi as Prime Minister of India, in 2014, the Brexit vote in the UK and the election of Donald Trump in the USA, in 2016, and the election of Jair Bolsonaro, in Brazil, two years later. Similar developments took place in Austria, Hungary, Italy, the Philippines, Poland, Turkey and elsewhere.

This interpretation of the stresses in global neoliberalism is framed around three paradoxes: (a) the *economic paradox*, by which the achievement of unprecedentedly favourable conditions for accumulation has been followed by declining rates of GDP growth and a deteriorating pattern of employment; (b) the *political paradox*, that the consolidation of neoliberal democracy has ossified the institutions of the state and degraded the structures of political representation, curtailing state capacity to address conflicts of interest and undermining democracy itself, and (c) the *paradox of authoritarianism*, that the economic and political crises in neoliberalism have fostered the personalisation of politics and the emergence of 'spectacular' authoritarian leaders whose policies undermine their own base of support.

The interactions between these crises and paradoxes will open spaces for new forms of fascism. In the meantime, neoliberalism has become increasingly reliant on coercion and violence. This includes the targeted deployment of 'fiscal austerity' backed up by punishing measures against the poor, the underprivileged, the neglected and those who are hard to reach, serve, and provide for; attacks against collective representation;

mounting repression against all forms of dissent, ranging from lynching-by-media to victimisation, interception of communications and persecution by the police, the security services or the military and so on. Escalating repression makes it harder to elicit systemic changes, but it also makes the system of accumulation less adaptable. It is shown, below, that as it became the dominant economic, political, institutional and ideational form of our time, neoliberalism has also become brittle: it is strong but also prone to catastrophic failure, since it sits on an unstable terrain.

The COVID-19 pandemic hit a world already strained by the paradoxes and crises outlined above. Since the pandemic emerged in a context of growing inequalities, deteriorating economic performance and disintegration of democracy, and since it imposed additional stresses onto the system of accumulation, examination of the health disaster can highlight important features, strengths, contradictions and vulnerabilities of global neoliberalism. The pandemic is also likely to intensify the crisis tendencies in neoliberalism, with detrimental implications for economic performance, wellbeing, equality and personal freedoms. Finally, the pandemic will have adverse consequences for the legitimacy of neoliberalism; for example, 'classic' neoliberal policies including privatisation, marketisation, financialisation and liberalisation of trade and finance have been shown to be either ineffective or counter-productive; notions of social solidarity and distribution have gained traction, and established (neoliberal) political systems have lost legitimacy. The crises in neoliberalism can contaminate capitalism itself, since this mode of production has little to offer to the young, the precarious, the marginalised and the poor. Growing awareness of these limits could open spaces for new forms of left-wing political activity.

The pandemic had profound implications for social reproduction and daily life. They range from the sudden disarticulation of the extraction and circulation of surplus value because of the coronavirus and the lockdowns seeking to contain it, to unprecedented state intervention to secure social order and the relations of exploitation, to changes in urban spaces because of the decline of the high streets, the rise of online shopping and the transformations of office work and the service sector more generally. Unexpectedly, the productivity of the dislocated workers was found to be about the same as it was in the traditional office: when the pandemic happened, the technologies required for home working were already available, even if few employers had realised it; in any case, homeworking was not widely trusted. Now that they can reduce drastically the costs of office space, many companies will want to do so permanently, with significant implications for the economy and community life.

At the global level, countries confronted the pandemic in distinct ways, with strikingly dissimilar outcomes. A heterogeneous group of countries, regions and provinces was highly successful, at least initially—among them, China, Cuba, Ghana, Kerala State in India, New Zealand, Senegal, Singapore, Taiwan and Vietnam. Others witnessed extraordinary policy failures culminating in tens of thousands of avoidable deaths, for example, Brazil, Ecuador, Hungary, India, Italy, Sweden, Turkey, the UK and the USA.

In general terms, the most uncompromisingly neoliberal economies were rapidly shown to be unable even to secure face masks and personal protective equipment (PPE) for their health personnel, not to speak of ventilators to keep their hospitalised population alive. These countries were also incapable of mounting coherent policy responses to the pandemic. Instead, several governments attached themselves to (more or less explicit) policies of 'herd immunity', an approach replete with social Darwinistic overtones. Their peoples paid a heavy price for this policy choice. It follows that the crises of public health and the economy were the outcome of the earlier dismantling of, or current disregard for, state capacities, a shocking underestimation of the threat, callous political decisions and staggering failures of implementation, for which reputations must be destroyed as part of a systemic reckoning.[4] In turn, in places where neoliberal ideology was less influential and the 'reforms' of the state, industry and health provision were less advanced, notions of common citizenship tended to be more prominent, welfare states remained stronger and health systems were more comprehensive and resilient. These states also tended to have more policy space and to deploy better coordinated policies. They often could suppress the coronavirus and resume 'normal' life faster and with far less casualties; however, the failures elsewhere would force the 'successful' states to keep themselves isolated from the world to avoid importing new cases of COVID-19.

In summary, the pandemic stress-tested countries, economies and political systems like never before, but the health crisis will not necessarily trigger positive changes in global neoliberalism; instead, the pandemic is likely to intensify the grip of the dominant system of accumulation, regardless of its limitations, contradictions and perversities. Yet, the pandemic can also boost powerful mobilisations to democratise the economy and society. Struggles around the meaning, reach and depth of democracy are likely to become increasingly prominent, because of their immediacy and relevance to our capacity to address the crises to come, especially around climate change and the 'green transition'.

This book includes four parts and eleven chapters. Part I outlines the theoretical framework. Chapter 1 describes the interpretation of neoliberalism and financialisation deployed in the book, and Chapter 2 looks into the forces that can explain the underperformance, instability and crises in contemporary capitalism. Part II examines the relationship between neoliberalism and democracy; Chapter 3 reviews the political forms of neoliberalism, and Chapter 4 discusses the crisis tendencies in neoliberal democracy. Part III turns to COVID-19, arguing that it is a pandemic with neoliberal characteristics. Chapter 5 reviews the evidence around the health crisis, and Chapter 6 outlines the implications of the pandemic for economic policy, politics and ideology. Part IV focuses on case studies. Chapter 7 surveys the impact of the pandemic in the Global North and the Global South, and Chapters 8–11 examine, respectively, the cases of the UK, USA, Brazil and India (the 'Quartet of Calamity'). The final chapter concludes this study. Evidently, the work cuts across different levels of analysis, as it moves from a highly abstract examination of the system of accumulation to country-specific studies.

The book argues that the pandemic is both a symptom of the contradictions and flaws in neoliberalism, and an indictment of capitalism itself. Yet, there is no guarantee that either the health crisis or the political or economic crises will transform the system of accumulation. Neoliberalism has been presumed or even proclaimed dead several times; for example, after the elections of Bill Clinton, Barack Obama, Donald Trump, and Joe Biden; after the East Asian crisis; during the 'Pink Tide' in Latin America; following the GFC and, now, in the wake of COVID-19. Each time, neoliberalism has managed to defeat, absorb or transform its enemies, rivals and alternatives, while addressing temporary setbacks through the deft deployment of ideological pressure, public resources, repression and adaptation. This time, too, neoliberalism will change only if it is confronted by overwhelming pressure.

It is clear that the economic crisis cannot be resolved within neoliberalism, and that the degeneration of democracy must be addressed by broad alliances: the construction of alternatives to the system of accumulation requires the integration of economic and political demands into an ambitious programme for the expansion of economic and political democracy. It has also become evident that pandemics must be confronted through wide-ranging and coordinated policies and the deployment of state capacities to support public health, backed up by ambitious industrial, economic and social policies. If these lessons are learned, we may be in a stronger position to face the more dramatic crises that will hit our species in the coming years. Our future literally hangs in the balance.

## Notes

1. This book was completed in May 2021.
2. I examine some implications of climate change and progressive policy alternatives in Saad-Filho (2021a).
3. See, for example, Ayers and Saad-Filho (2015, 2020), Boffo, Saad-Filho and Fine (2019), Fine and Saad-Filho (2017) and Saad-Filho (2008, 2011, 2017, 2019, 2020a, 2020b, 2020c, 2021b).
4. For the case of the UK, typical in many ways, see Grey and MacAskill (2020).

PART I

# Neoliberalism, Financialisation, and Crisis

CHAPTER 1

# Neoliberalism, Financialisation and Their Consequences

This chapter outlines the theoretical framework and the main concepts underpinning the analysis of the three crises covered in this book, focusing on the concepts of neoliberalism, financialisation and system of accumulation. They are closely related. A system of accumulation is the configuration or instantiation of the capitalist mode of production in specific historical circumstances; neoliberalism is the dominant system of accumulation worldwide, standing in contrast with 'classic' liberalism before World War I and Keynesianism, after World War II. Neoliberalism is underpinned by financialisation, or the dominant role of finance in production, ideology, policy practice and social reproduction. Financialisation has driven the restructuring of the global economy since the 1970s across several dimensions, including new production technologies, patterns of exchange, distribution and modes of work; new social structures, ideologies and processes of political representation and new forms of rule. Outcomes have been complex and uneven both domestically and globally, but they generally include remarkable prosperity for the top layers of society, accompanied by the creation of patterns of poverty and inequality that are typical of the current age of neoliberalism.


A. Saad-Filho, *The Age of Crisis*,
https://doi.org/10.1007/978-3-030-81608-7_1

## Neoliberalism and Financialisation

Neoliberalism has been understood in different ways in the literature (Fine & Saad-Filho, 2017; Saad-Filho, 2017). In particular: (a) neoliberalism as a right-wing political project against the workers and the poor, that was dramatically imposed by governments starting with the dictatorship of Augusto Pinochet in Chile, followed by Margaret Thatcher in the UK, Ronald Reagan in the USA, and many others around the world; (b) neoliberalism as a set of public policies and practices inspired by the so-called Washington Consensus, generally seeking to 'roll back the state' and causing untold damage to the poor; (c) neoliberalism as a more or less coherent set of ideas and ideologies associated with Austrian and monetarist scholars, especially Friederich von Hayek, Ludwig von Mises, Milton Friedman and the 'neoliberal thought collective' fronted by the Mont Pèlerin Society and an array of think tanks, non-governmental organisations, university departments, international organisations, lobbies and media outlets; (d) from a Foucauldian perspective, neoliberalism as a technology of the self-promoting a specific subjectivity, entrepreneurial mindset and mode of (self-) governance, and (e) neoliberalism as the contemporary phase, stage, configuration, or mode of existence of capitalism, distinguished by the financialisation of production and social reproduction.

Although these approaches to neoliberalism overlap to a large extent and are mutually complementary rather than contradictory, the latter is the preferred approach in what follows, since it recognises that neoliberalism is not only, or even primarily, about shifts in ideas, economic policies or power relations. Instead, it is a totality encompassing the economy, modes of labour, resource allocation and forms of international integration; the political system, class forces and relations and modes of representation of interests; the social structure, property relations and forms of exploitation and social domination; and the dominant rules, institutions, ideologies, subjectivities and modes of behaviour.[1] In this sense, neoliberalism is a *system of accumulation*. Across the various features and domains of neoliberalism, state power has been deployed to enforce a finance-driven recomposition of the rule of capital under the ideological guise of 'non-intervention' and 'promotion of the markets'.

Historically, neoliberalism emerged in Latin America in the mid-1970s and, more significantly for our purposes, in the UK and USA a few years later in response to the crises of capitalist reproduction at the end of the post-war boom, especially the disarticulation of the Keynesian social democratic consensus in the advanced capitalist economies (AEs) in the Global North, the paralysis of developmentalism in the developing economies (DEs) in the Global South and, later, the implosion of the Soviet alternative (Saad-Filho, 2007, 2018).[2] The new system of accumulation spread in the Global North through Atlanticism, and in the Global South and the former Soviet Bloc through the policy reforms associated with the Washington Consensus, that were usually driven by balance of payments crises followed by 'conditionalities' enforced by the International Monetary Fund (IMF) and the World Bank.

The most salient feature of neoliberalism is the financialisation of production, exchange and social reproduction. Like neoliberalism, the term financialisation has been understood in diverse ways. The latter include:

> the phenomenal expansion of financial assets relative to real activity; ... the proliferation of types of assets, from derivatives through to futures markets with a corresponding explosion of acronyms; the absolute and relative expansion of speculative as opposed to or at the expense of real investment; a shift in the balance of productive to financial imperatives within the private sector whether financial or not; increasing inequality in income arising out of ... financial rewards; consumer-led booms based on credit; the penetration of finance into ever more areas of economic and social life such as pensions, education, health, and provision of economic and social infrastructure; [and] the emergence of a neoliberal culture of reliance upon markets and private capital and corresponding anti-statism despite the extent to which the rewards to private finance have ... derived from state finance itself. Financialisation is also associated with the continued role of the US dollar as world money.

Historically,

> however financialisation is defined, its consequences have been perceived to be: reductions in overall levels and efficacy of real investment as financial instruments and activities expand at its expense even if excessive investment does take place in particular sectors at particular times; ... prioritising shareholder value, or financial worth, over other economic and social values; pushing of policies towards conservatism and commercialisation in all respects; extending influence of finance more broadly, both directly and indirectly, over economic *and* social policy; placing more aspects of economic and social life at the risk of volatility from financial instability and, conversely, placing the economy and social life at risk of crisis from

> triggers within particular markets ...Whilst, then, financialisation is a single word, it is attached to a wide variety of different forms and effects of finance. (Ashman & Fine 2013, pp. 156–157)

A systemic interpretation of financialisation can start from the subordination of economic and social reproduction to the accumulation of what Karl Marx called interest-bearing capital (IBC).[3] IBC is a general category for capitals seeking valorisation through the truncated circuit M–M' (money that valorises itself without the intermediation of production, with the difference between M' and M being called interest, rather than the more general term 'profit'). In practice, IBC includes not only the capital of banks, pension funds, mutual funds, hedge funds, stockbrokers, insurance companies and so on but, also, the financial arm of industrial capital; for example, large automobile manufacturers, supermarket chains, electronics manufacturers and so on have finance divisions that aim to facilitate sales as well as profit from financial investment, rather than funding production directly.

From a historical point of view, financialisation has been the main driver of the restructuring of the global economy since the 1970s, and it played a key role in the restoration of the US empire after its defeats in Vietnam and Iran and the dollar crisis in the 1970s (see below, Panitch & Gindin, 2012, and the *Socialist Register* 2004, 2005). Typically, in financialised economies IBC (rather than, say, public sector institutions and large-scale industrial capital, as the case in the previous systems of accumulation) controls the main sources of capital across production, domestic commerce, international exchanges and the financing of the state, as well as the intertemporal, intersectoral and international allocation of resources. The latter include the level and composition of output, investment, consumption and government spending, as well as the cross-border processes of production and accumulation. These forms of resource allocation tend to be regulated global conglomerates and international organisations centred in the USA, from JPMorgan Chase and Bank of America to the US Department of the Treasury, the World Bank and the IMF (Panitch & Gindin, 2012; Panitch et al., 2010).

Financialisation does not distort 'pure capitalism', nor does it express a 'financial sector coup' against productive capital[4]; similarly, finance is not merely a parasitic superstructure draining industrial profits or sucking workers' incomes. Instead, in the age of neoliberalism *finance is hegemonic* because IBC commands economic activity and the reproduction of capital as a whole, percolates all manner of social intercourse, and drives policy-making: in summary, neoliberalism is underpinned by financialisation in multiple and overlapping ways.

The extended range, reach, influence and resourcing of IBC has assisted the expansion of finance and financial institutions in a cumulative process taking place, primarily, through the creation of new paper instruments and the explosive growth of markets where these papers are traded. For example, the 'markets in currency derivatives and interest rate swaps grew from almost nothing in 1990 to about three times global GDP in 2006' (Harvey, 2009; for up-to-date figures and analysis, see UNCTAD's annual *Trade and Development Report*). These developments have fostered a semi-autonomous sphere of speculation supporting the appropriation by IBC of an expanding share of the (surplus) value produced. For example, '[t]he profits of financial companies [in the USA] jumped from below 5 per cent of total corporate profits, after tax, in 1982 to 41 per cent in 2007' (Wolf, 2009). This share declined immediately after the GFC, but soon returned to 30% (Klein, 2015).

Even before the GFC, the conventional notion that finance mobilises and allocates resources efficiently and brings growth, productivity and welfare gains for the economy as a whole was untenable, for three reasons. First, the liberalisation of domestic finance and international capital movements failed to trigger faster growth in most countries; in fact, economic growth has tended to falter since the transition to neoliberalism. Conversely, the experiences of rapid growth were largely unrelated to changes in financial regulations and were not normally driven by the expansion of IBC (CGD, 2008). Second, since IBC is directly unproductive its profits are, necessarily, transfers from the non-financial corporate sector and the workers. This implies that the growth of finance can benefit the economy only if it promotes the creation of more value than finance itself absorbs which, patently, has not been the case, since capitalist economies have tended to slow down (see below). Third, since finance is the best-rewarded sector in the economy, its expansion in a context of growth slowdown must have contributed to the polarisation of incomes (see below).

An alternative interpretation seems more plausible: financialisation has boosted the size and profits of IBC, helped to transnationalise the operations of large industrial and financial conglomerates, and supported global neoliberalism through the perpetual threat of capital flight if economic and social policies diverge from the short-term interests of financial market operators. At the same time, the pursuit of financial gains has tended to crowd out productive activities and promote the concentration of income and wealth within and between countries, undermining aggregate profitability, macroeconomic stability and long-term economic growth. These adverse outcomes were compensated, in part, by enhanced extractions from the workers, from poorer countries and from nature, making neoliberalism a system of accumulation increasingly reliant on parasitical impositions as opposed to investment for productivity growth.

## 'Globalisation' and the Restructuring of Production

The approach to neoliberalism in this chapter, as a stage in capitalism driven by financialisation, informs a specific understanding of the contemporary political economy that highlights the transformations in the patterns of growth, investment, production, employment, finance and consumption. In brief, neoliberalism and financialisation underpin the transnationalisation of production and the liberalisation of trade, finance and capital flows, which are usually summarised by the term 'globalisation'. These processes have been supported by banking, regulatory and legislative changes promoting the modalities of (globalised and financialised) production that are typical of the contemporary 'age of neoliberalism'.

These forces have restructured the national systems of production at a higher level of productivity, at least at firm level. They have promoted new technologies, labour processes and employment relations, and brought about new products, forms of production and modes of exchange based on the international integration of circuits of capital at the level of individual firms; that is, the *microeconomic* integration of capital, in contrast with the earlier (macroeconomic) integration of nations through trade based on colonial relations or the exchange of finished products. These transformations were accompanied by the stagnation of real wages and the exponential growth of all forms of finance, debt, and fictitious capital, with significant implications for consumption and forms of social reproduction and community life. These processes have also contributed to a tighter integration of the elites, while the working classes have been restructured globally; workers have also been divided and disempowered by the changes in policies, practices, ideologies, technologies and the law that have accompanied the transitions to neoliberalism.

As a consequence of the restructuring and relocalisation of key value chains and the (closely related) deployment of specific industrial and development policies, some countries have managed to sustain impressive rates of growth under neoliberalism, with Northeast and Southeast Asia to the fore; more recently, China has become the export assembly hub of the world. This is far from, indeed the opposite of, suggesting that neoliberalism fosters either economic growth in countries following the 'right' policies, or an unproblematic 'global convergence'. Instead, neoliberalism creates new patterns of uneven and combined development, in which immense prosperity within and between countries benefits specific social strata (often identified as the financial or other elites or oligarchs, the top 1%, or the top 0.01%), and coexists with new patterns of poverty and its reproduction in areas where it already prevailed.

## Ideologies, Policies and Social Reproduction

Ideologically, neoliberalism and its inequitable outcomes have been justified by a discourse drawing on two principles. In the economic domain, 'competitiveness', followed by its corollaries, 'market efficiency' and 'inflation control', as they are presented in neoclassical, Austrian and monetarist approaches. From this point of view, the financial and currency markets offer the template not only for the functioning of all economic sectors (regardless of the differences between the markets for Treasury bills and those for oil, housing or shoes), but, also, for individual behaviours under neoliberalism. In turn, in the political domain the key principle is 'democracy', in the shallow sense of competition between shades of neoliberalism in a political market regulated by law and policed by the media (Ayers & Saad-Filho, 2015). 'Competitiveness' and 'democracy' underpin the neoliberal vision of the 'good society', guide the norms of conduct supporting the system of accumulation, and have become principles of the 'common sense' of our age.

The neoliberal conceptions of competitiveness and democracy follow from a specific notion of neoliberal subjects and their subjectivity and a typical mode of governance of the public sphere. In this worldview all economic agents, including consumers, workers, capitalists, managers, financiers and the state itself, are expected to conduct themselves in ways that are compatible with the maximisation of the net present value of their assets through practices of entrepreneurialism, (self-)investment, and attraction of potential customers and investors. This individualist conception of self and society is incompatible with the notion of collective interests or demands for common rights or minimum standards of welfare. It follows that neoliberal subjects have no guarantee of security, protection, sustenance or even survival; consequently, the welfare protections enacted under previous systems of accumulation ought to be removed, and the notion of a society of citizens founded on (some perception of) the 'public good' should be displaced by a neoliberal collection of maximising firms and *homo oeconomicus*. This is wholly incompatible with the idea of a *demos* entitled to assert collective sovereignty (see Chapter 3 and Ayers & Saad-Filho, 2020).

The state plays a key role across all the domains of neoliberalism. The state must drive the transition from the previous system of accumulation, build the new (financialised and globalised) legal, institutional and policy framework, and legitimise the transition. This is done by recourse to claims of the superior efficiency of the market and the endless repetition of the mantra that 'the public finances are in a parlous state', leading to the conclusion that there is an imperative to privatise and commercialise public services, roll back the welfare state, shift to means-tested benefits, impose private sector performance indicators on public institutions, repress the opposition, and, paradoxically, cut taxes, especially on the rich. In this way, public policies have dismantled state capacities and public services, reformed public institutions to serve capital in general and finance specifically, and transformed the ideologies and modalities of social reproduction.

Historically, the forms of social discipline associated with neoliberalism have been imposed through five channels. First, the expansion of (neoliberal) capitalism in the AEs and across Eastern Europe, Asia, sub-Saharan Africa and Latin America, leading to the incorporation of hundreds of millions of workers into transnational circuits of accumulation. These processes imposed much greater competition between capitals, countries and workers, and disciplined them accordingly.

Second, a wave of technological innovations, the restructuring of production and the creation of new patterns of employment, together with restrictions to wages, subsidies, transfers, benefits, entitlements and other non-market protections that had been introduced under Keynesian, developmentalist and Soviet-style regimes (see above). They have created mass unemployment, compressed wages and diffused around the world informal, part-time, 'flexible' and insecure patterns of work, with low levels of job-specific skills and rapid turnover.

Third, persistently contractionary fiscal policies, except in moments of crisis, which have been directly responsible for the long-term decline of real investment, productivity growth and output growth.

Fourth, the restructuring of public institutions, ideologies, policies and practices, in order to consolidate a mode of governance supporting the new system of accumulation and shielding market processes from most forms of accountability (Dardot & Laval, 2013).

Fifth, financialisation transformed the structures and processes of social reproduction. In most countries, especially the advanced Anglo-Saxon economies, asset-poor workers have tended to become enmeshed in financial circuits through their bank accounts, overdrafts, credit cards, mortgages, pensions, insurance policies and payments for education, health, and other areas of social provision, as well as clothes, holidays, home improvements and even daily expenses. These expenditures were often financed by 'easy' credit or equity withdrawals through the serial remortgaging of their homes in booming housing markets, drawing working-class families into the speculative logic of asset price inflation.[5] These processes were mirrored, at the top of the distribution of income, by the growth in the demand of the wealthy for personal credit or (depending on individual circumstances) outlets for investment. In all cases, the financial institutions gained scope for selling services to households and for trading new paper instruments. This became especially pervasive in the macroeconomic context of low interest rates between the early 1990s and the mid-2000s.

Under neoliberalism, then, different forms of debt became a powerful tool of social integration, as well as a way of compensating workers for the stagnation of real incomes, the diminishing supply of 'good jobs', and the reduced availability of public housing, retirement benefits, education, healthcare and so on (see below). The transitions to neoliberalism were also normally accompanied by intimations to *consume more*. Under these circumstances, many workers effectively turned their homes, future salaries and pensions into cash machines, so they could pretend to be earning higher salaries in the present.[6] The inevitable pressures for repayment and the threat of losing houses, cars and reputations pushed many debtors to accept strict forms of work discipline, including long hours in multiple jobs with casual or temporary contracts and precarious employment rights, in increasingly stressful conditions.

Consumer lending was not only a form of compensation for lower wages, a modality of integration and subordination of the working class and a source of profits. For the US and UK governments, it was also a key macroeconomic policy tool, because the regulation of consumer and mortgage loans through movements in interest rates helped to maintain economic and social stability in low wage and low fiscal deficit economies. In particular, every time the US and UK economies slowed down (for example, in the late 1990s, after the dotcom bubble, and after 9–11) their central banks lowered interest rates to encourage remortgaging and the accumulation of unsecured personal debt in order to stabilise aggregate demand. This policy arrangement was temporarily successful; for example, the US Bureau of Economic Analysis 'estimated that home equity extractions led to an additional GDP growth rate of 1.5% per year between 2002 and 2007. Excluding that, the US would not have grown faster than the supposedly sclerotic Eurozone' (Marazzi, 2010). These policies have been assimilated to an 'asset price Keynesianism' because, to some extent, private deficits replaced public deficits as the main tool of macroeconomic stabilisation.

The restructuring of production, employment, modes of labour and social and community life outlined above have had profound implications for social reproduction in general, and for the composition, mode of existence, cultures and solidarities of the working class. These developments can be described as the *financialisation of social reproduction*. Together with the restructuring of production and the institutional changes that followed the transition to neoliberalism, the financialisation of social reproduction underpinned a significant increase in the rate of exploitation through the extraction of absolute and relative surplus value.

Their impact can be gauged by the fall in the wage share of national income in most neoliberal countries. For example, the average real incomes for the bottom 90% of Americans fell 9% between 1973 and 2002. In contrast, the incomes for the top 1% rose 101%, and the incomes of the top 0.1% rose by 227%. Similarly, while in 1991 the wealthiest 1% owned 39% of corporate wealth, by 2003 their share had increased to 58% (McNally, 2009). More generally, the *World Inequality Report* shows that, since the 1980s, the top 1% earners have captured twice as much growth in global income as the 50% poorest individuals (Alvaredo et al., 2018). These unequalising tendencies help to explain the recovery of the rate of profit in most neoliberal countries since the early 1980s, despite the underlying lack of demand (Boffo et al., 2019; Saad-Filho, 2011).

## The 'Economic Losers'

It was shown above that neoliberalism, financialisation and globalisation have been associated with large-scale economic restructuring, including the internationalisation of systems of production across work processes, technologies, inputs and outputs, with major implications for international specialisation, patterns of employment and consumption, forms of social reproduction and community life. These shifts have had profound implications for the composition and mode of existence of the working class. Specifically, they tended to create an array of economic 'losers' centred around the skilled working class and radiating outwards as conditions also deteriorated for the informal workers, the traditional middle classes and many other strata, including managers and small and medium capitalists and family farmers.

Millions of skilled and stable jobs and managerial positions were eliminated, especially in the AEs, as entire categories were hit with new (globalised) technologies or suffered large transfers of posts abroad; in the meantime, employment opportunities in the public sector shrunk with mass privatisations and the neoliberal 'retrenching' of state institutions. Most formal workers and professionals witnessed a deterioration in their pay, conditions and welfare protections, and their patterns of employment and work tended to become increasingly precarious and deskilled. Severe losses also hit the informal workers, whose prospects of transfer into the formal sector shrunk drastically, and for pensioners, often at the sharp end of the neoliberal reforms. Similar pressures were felt by an impoverished, vulnerable, indebted and increasingly anxious middle class; almost everyone had to bear the stresses of insecurity, overwork and long-term income decline (Wacquant, 2009).

In most neoliberal economies, including some of the wealthiest countries in the world, formerly privileged social strata found themselves lamenting their inability to realise the material aspirations mandated by the consumption cultures of neoliberalism; they were also unable to bequeath improved material circumstances to their offspring, breaking a generational contract of continuous improvement ('we sacrifice so that our children will do better than us') that had helped to legitimise the hardships inflicted by capitalism since the eighteenth century

(Boffo et al., 2019; Boyle 2013; Roediger, 2020). Inevitably, the 'losers' tend to be politically disenfranchised, since they are structurally separated, disorganised, ideologically perplexed and, consequently, unable to express their grievances through the political system that neoliberalism itself imposed (see Chapters 3–4).

## Notes

1. For an overview, see Boffo et al. (2019) and Dardot and Laval (2013).
2. 'Global South' is shorthand for what used to be called 'the periphery' or 'the Third World': roughly speaking, the world minus the US, Canada, Western Europe, Scandinavia, Japan, Australia and New Zealand. The latter are referred to as the 'Global North', 'the West' or the 'Advanced Economies'. Debates over classification are beyond the scope of this paper.
3. See, for example, Ashman and Fine (2013), Christophers and Fine (2019), Fine (2013–2014), and Fine and Saad-Filho (2017). For a historical overview see Gowan (1999), Panitch and Gindin (2012), Rude (2005), and Saad-Filho (2007).
4. For a contrasting view, see Duménil and Lévy (2011).
5. See Krippner (2005, 2011), Montgomerie (2009), and Panitch and Gindin (2012).
6. This was especially important in the US and the UK. In Italy, personal credit is less widespread, and younger 'precarious' workers tend to rely on their parents' salaries, pensions and—eventually—assets through inheritance. Evidently, both the accumulation of personal debt and the dependence on parental income or assets can only be temporary.

## References

Alvaredo, F., Chancel, L. Piketty, T., Saez, E., & Zucman, G. (2018). *World Inequality Report*. https://wir2018.wid.world/

Ashman, S., & Fine, B. (2013). Neo-liberalism, varieties of capitalism, and the shifting contours of South Africa's financial system. *Transformation, 81*(2), 144–178.

Ayers, A., & Saad-Filho, A. (2015). Democracy against neoliberalism: Paradoxes, limitations, transcendence. *Critical Sociology, 41*(4–5), 597–618.

Ayers, A., & Saad-Filho, A. (2020). The twilight of formal democracy: Contradictions of accumulation and the political crisis of neoliberalism. *Journal of Australian Political Economy, 86*, 230–255.

Boffo, M., Saad-Filho, A., & Fine, B. (2019). Neoliberal capitalism: The authoritarian turn. In L. Panitch & G. Albo (Eds.), *Socialist register* (pp. 247–270). Merlin Press.

Boyle, D. (2013) *Broke: Who killed the middle classes?* Fourth Estate.

CGD (Commission on Growth and Development). (2008). *The growth report: Strategies for sustained growth and inclusive development*. https://openknowledge.worldbank.org/handle/10986/6507

Christophers, B., & Fine, B. (2019). The value of financialization and the financialization of value. In P. Mader, D. Mertens, & N. van der Zwan (Eds.), *The Routledge international handbook of financialization*. Routledge.

Dardot, P., & Laval, C. (2013). *The new way of the world: On neoliberal society*. Verso.

Duménil, G., & Lévy, D. (2011). *The crisis of neoliberalism*. Harvard University Press.

Fine, B. (2013–2014). Financialisation from a Marxist perspective. *International Journal of Political Economy, 42*(4), 46–66.

Fine, B., & Saad-Filho, A. (2017). Thirteen things you need to know about neoliberalism. *Critical Sociology, 43*(4–5), 685–706.

Gowan, P. (1999). *The global gamble: Washington's Faustian bid for world dominance*. Verso.

Harvey, D. (2009). Interview: Exploring the logic of capital. *Socialist Review*. http://www.socialistreview.org.uk/article.php?articlenumber=10801

Klein, N. (2015). *This changes everything: Capitalism vs. the climate*. Simon and Schuster.

Krippner, G. (2005). The financialization of the American economy. *Socio-Economic Review, 3*, 173–208.

Krippner, G. (2011). *Capitalizing on crisis: The political origins of the rise of finance*. Harvard University Press.

Marazzi, C. (2010) *The violence of financial capitalism*. Semiotext(e).

McNally, D. (2009). From financial crisis to world-slump: Accumulation, financialisation, and the global slowdown. *Historical Materialism, 17*(2), 35–83.

Montgomerie, J. (2009). The pursuit of (past) happiness? Middle-class indebtedness and American financialisation. *New Political Economy, 14*(1), 1–24.

Panitch, L., & Gindin, S. (2012). *The making of global capitalism: The political economy of American empire*. Verso.

Panitch, L., Gindin, S., & Albo, G. (2010). *In and out of crisis: The global financial meltdown and left alternatives*. PM Press.

Rude, C. (2005). The role of financial discipline in imperial strategy. In L. Panitch & M. Konings (Eds.), *American empire and the political economy of global finance*. Palgrave Macmillan.

Saad-Filho, A. (2007). Monetary policy in the neoliberal transition: A political economy review of Keynesianism, monetarism and inflation targeting. In

R. Albritton, R. Jessop, & R. Westra (Eds.), *Political economy and global capitalism*. Anthem Press.
Saad-Filho, A. (2011). Crisis *in* neoliberalism or crisis *of* neoliberalism? In *Socialist register* (pp. 242–259). Merlin Press.
Saad-Filho, A. (2017). Neoliberalism. In D. M. Brennan, D. Kristjanson-Gural, C. Mulder, & E. Olsen (Eds.), *The Routledge handbook of Marxian economics*. Routledge.
Saad-Filho, A. (2018). Monetary policy and neoliberalism. In D. Cahill, M. Cooper, & M. Konings (Eds.), *Sage handbook of neoliberalism*. Sage.
Wacquant, L. (2009). *Punishing the poor: The neoliberal government of social insecurity*. Duke University Press.
Wolf, M. (2009). *Is America the new Russia?* https://www.ft.com/content/09f8c996-2930-11de-bc5e-00144feabdc0

CHAPTER 2

# Economic Instability and Crises Under Neoliberalism

This chapter examines the *economic paradox of neoliberalism*, that global neoliberalism has enjoyed the most favourable conditions for accumulation in generations, yet neoliberal AEs have been unable to capitalise on them. The consequence has been the gradual slowdown of their rate of GDP growth, with adverse consequences for distribution, employment, social welfare and the living conditions of the poor in some of the wealthiest economies in the world. The chapter examines these developments and the crisis tendencies springing from them, focusing on the GFC and its consequences.

## The Economic Paradox of Neoliberalism

Neoliberalism and financialisation both created and benefitted from unprecedentedly favourable conditions for accumulation, which drove a remarkable recovery of profitability in the AEs since its lows in the early 1980s (see Chapter 1). These conditions include the West's victory in the Cold War; the spread of capitalism worldwide and the 'globalisation' of production, leading to a dramatic expansion in the global labour force; the liberalisation of trade, finance and capital movements; the provision of unparalleled support to accumulation by competing states; the reduction of taxes, transfers and welfare provision in most countries; the destruction of most nationalist movements and governments in the Global South; the



A. Saad-Filho, *The Age of Crisis*,
https://doi.org/10.1007/978-3-030-81608-7_2

decline of the traditional sources of resistance to earlier forms of capitalism (trade unions, peasant movements, left parties and social movements), and the ideological hegemony of a bogus but vociferous 'free market' capitalism. They have fostered intensified modes of exploitation of the workforce through financial exactions, changes in the law, the restructuring of production, new technologies and means of communication, the compression of wages and the expansion of precarious forms of labour, culminating in the 'gig economy', as well as heavy extractions from the periphery through unequal trade, financial transfers and rents, and the unprecedented plunder of nature.

Despite oft-repeated assurances that the neoliberal reforms would bring faster growth, macroeconomic stability and prosperity for all, the rates of investment and GDP growth have tended to decline, especially in the AEs. Around the world, the episodes of growth under neoliberalism have become increasingly reliant on finance-led bubbles, but these always collapse with destructive implications for accumulation, distribution and social reproduction, and their containment invariably requires expansive, and expensive, state intervention. Examples include the international debt crisis in the early 1980s, the US savings and loan crisis in the 1980s, the M&A mania and the stock market bubbles and crashes in the 1980s and late 1990s, the Japanese crisis and the subsequent underperformance since the late 1980s, the crises in East Asia, Mexico, Russia, Brazil, Argentina and other middle-income countries at the end of the twentieth century, and the dotcom, credit, financial and housing bubbles in the early 2000s, culminating in the GFC and the disaster in the Eurozone (see below).

In this light, it is possible to identify *the economic paradox of neoliberalism*: that the delivery of extraordinarily favourable conditions for accumulation has been accompanied by an astonishing inability to capitalise upon them (Boffo et al., 2019). Rather than thriving on the basis of the extremely propitious conditions that neoliberalism itself helped to impose, accumulation has been hampered by a persistent growth slowdown, volatility, declining real investment, rising inequality and a deteriorating job market. In other words, the system of accumulation has become increasingly unable to elicit productivity growth, even though this is the most important redeeming feature of capitalism. Instead, neoliberalism relies more and more on exploitation and pillage.

The economic paradox derives from the financialisation of the economy, that has created towering and increasingly fragile structures of paper claims on income and wealth (which Marx (1981) called 'fictitious capital'). *Economic growth under neoliberalism is generally driven by the accumulation of fictitious capital*, that is, by the speculative pursuit of financial gain. This modality of growth tends to crowd out productive activities and fuel asset bubbles only loosely connected with the restructuring of production, and that favour the appropriation of profits by the owners of paper assets. Ultimately, financialised accumulation undermines the capacity of the economy to generate new values and the profits needed to service those financial commitments: this is a fundamental contradiction of neoliberalism.

This modality of financialised accumulation is closely associated with other faultlines in neoliberalism. They include deepening inequalities of income, wealth and power; disparities across gender, 'race', jobs and the provision of health, education, transport, housing and other basic needs; new technologies and the globalisation of production that have created patterns of employment devaluing, deskilling and expelling labour power; dysfunctional linkages between finance, industry, agriculture and services; growing vulnerabilities in the balance of payments; the systematic dismantling of earlier systems of provision as well as state capacity to formulate and implement public policies and coordinate and monitor economic activity, and a relentless drive to hollow out the welfare state.

In summary, as accumulation and social reproduction have become financialised under neoliberalism, economic crises have also become financialised: today, crises are typically due to the *overproduction of fictitious capital*, and they tend to be triggered by the collapse of complex structures of paper claims on income and wealth. These crises centred on the overaccumulation of fictitious capital stand in sharp contrast with the crises of disproportion and overproduction of commodities that were typical of previous stages of capitalism.

The welfare effects of the economic slowdown under neoliberalism, and the seemingly inexorable descent of most neoliberal AEs into macroeconomic stagnation, have been partly compensated, at the top of the distribution, by intensified forms of exploitation of poorer people, poorer countries and nature (see above). It is quite different at the bottom of the distribution, where pre-existing deprivations have tended to intensify, while new forms of poverty have emerged in connection with the new patterns of work, pay, consumption, debt, technologies, modes of communication and access to public services and basic amenities. These deteriorating circumstances have been accompanied by a creeping crisis of legitimacy of neoliberalism. In response, neoliberal governments have tended to rely on increasingly authoritarian tools to secure their rule, which has degraded political democracy (see Chapter 4).

## The Global Financial Crisis

The GFC was a direct consequence of the financialisation of accumulation and the extensive restructuring of economic and social life under neoliberalism. In contrast with previous financial crises, the GFC was not initiated by a speculative frenzy around primary commodities (e.g., oil or gold) or luxury goods (tulips, art, or prime real estate), or the overestimation of profits from new fields of investment (South Sea or dotcom). Instead, the GFC was a typically neoliberal crisis: it was caused by the overaccumulation of fictitious capital created by a globalised financial system, and triggered by the default of unpayable mortgages owed by the poorest households in the USA, that had been re-packaged into new types of financial assets traded through channels that did not even exist a few years earlier (Saad-Filho, 2011; Tett, 2009). At a global level, the circulation of titles of fictitious capital had helped to cover the current account deficits in the most financialised AEs, especially the USA and UK, while also generating profits for finance.

These merry-go-rounds required an ever-growing appetite for credit by banks, households and states, to provide an outlet for the complex assets being pumped out by unhinged financial institutions. In the early 2000s, the entire arrangement was viable only while house prices kept rising, since they were fuelling the mortgages, remortgages and equity withdrawals that families needed to support their own (and the economy's) credit-fuelled consumption, as well as the tangled relationships between the USA, China and the rest of the world. Aware of the fragilities of this arrangement, policymakers in the USA and UK did everything they could to support rising prices for fictitious capital and real estate, including incentives for predatory subprime lending in the USA and buy-to-let speculation in Britain, and privileged tax regimes for financial speculation in both countries. The flaw in this strategy was that the success of the macroeconomic policies during the so-called 'Great Moderation' (roughly, between the late 1980s and the mid-2000s) would inevitably lead to the disconnection between, on the one hand, house prices, mortgage debts and consumer loans and, on the other hand, the stagnant wages from which repayments must be made (for example, in 2007 the bottom 40% of UK households already had a negative cash flow, see Saad-Filho, 2011).

This macroeconomic arrangement became increasingly fragile; for example, it could not be sustained if there was a contraction of liquidity or hardening of the conditions for the accumulation of debt. In the meantime, the subsidisation of the US and UK economies by cheap goods and cheap credit originating in poorer countries supported the notion that the finance-driven restructuring of accumulation had been successful, and that the more neoliberal (Anglo-Saxon) AEs were doing better than the laggards (e.g., France, Germany, Italy and Japan). This reasoning helped to legitimise neoliberalism and disguise the fact that the 'success cases' depended on an unsustainable model of debt-led growth supported by low interest rates and misaligned exchange rates. In this sense, the GFC exposed the limitations of financialisation as the driver of accumulation.[1]

This systemic interpretation of the GFC focusing on neoliberalism and financialisation contrasts with other heterodox views focusing narrowly on the decline of real investment because of the easier and higher returns offered by financial speculation, the erosion of effective demand due to low wages and the rising burden of household debt, or the adverse implications of deindustrialisation because of the restructuring of global manufacturing and the relocation of capacity to East Asia in general and China in particular. Although they are undeniable, these processes did not operate in isolation, nor they did directly cause the GFC or its forms of manifestation. Quite the contrary: the GFC was symptomatic of the key features of neoliberalism, especially the impoverishment of the workers and the centrality of finance for economic and social reproduction, while the policies adopted in its wake revealed the dominance of finance both ideologically and policy-wise (see below).

Historically, the locus of the GFC and its reverberations changed over time. At first, the crisis was concentrated on the AEs, with the USA at the forefront, and its immediate impact destroyed up to 45% of the wealth of the world (Saad-Filho, 2011, p. 249), as well as widespread home repossessions, the collapse of production and mounting unemployment. Later, the epicentre of the crisis shifted to the Eurozone periphery, with the Greek drama as its most powerful symbol. Finally, the crisis engulfed the middle-income countries, with striking examples in Argentina, Brazil, China and Turkey.

In contrast with previous instances of economic malfunction, the speculative boom and the crash could not be blamed on 'excessive' wages and benefits, along the lines of neoclassical, Keynesian or 'radical' profit-squeeze views. In the past, these interpretations had helped to legitimise the transfer of the burden of adjustment onto working people and the poor. This time, since working-class activity had been almost completely absent and real wages had been stagnant for many years, the explanations for the crisis had to be located in inter-capitalist relations in general, and financialisation in particular. However, even if finance and its excesses were obviously guilty, the mainstream rushed to argue that finance had to be rescued to prevent an even worse impact upon everyone else.

## The Global Economy After the Crisis

In the wake of the GFC, some of the largest financial institutions in the world were offered unlimited support through ultra-loose monetary policies, symbolised by zero interest rate policies, emergency bailouts, Central Bank purchases of their worthless financial assets and successive waves of quantitative easing (QE). These shockingly expensive rescue operations aimed to rescue the largest banks in the world from the consequence of their own folly. This was claimed to be in the general interest, presumably to avoid even worse outcomes should the endangered financial institutions fail. In reality, the unprecedented forms of state intervention in the USA, UK, Japan and the Eurozone revealed the continuing hegemony of finance, which those states saved at the expense of everything else (Davidson, 2017;McNally, 2011). The DEs, especially Brazil, China, South Korea and Thailand, implemented different forms of state intervention primarily based on fiscal policy, but equally repugnant to the ideologies of neoliberalism.

The sheer size and pervasiveness of the GFC initially overwhelmed the policy responses and the forms of international cooperation that were deployed to contain the crisis and limit its effects. Those limitations reflected the close connections between different types of financial institutions and the complexity of the asset structures built under financialisation. They created severe difficulties to identify the roots of the problem and agree what to rescue, how, by what criteria, to what end and at what cost, and what supplementary policies would be needed.

Despite these difficulties, the policies adopted after the GFC eventually stabilised the global economy and restored the profitability of finance. Yet, the causes of the cataclysm remained unaddressed, while the policies deployed after the GFC created new vulnerabilities. In particular, zero interest rates and QE reduced systemic financial risks, but they also led to the accumulation of debts and created new asset bubbles, especially in the Global South. For an illustration, between the start of the GFC and 2015, the total debt of financial corporations increased by US$12 trillion; public sector debt increased by US$25 trillion (of which more than US$20 trillion in 8 OECD countries), and the liabilities of households rose by US$7 trillion (Dobbs et al., 2015). Moreover, virtually all the gains achieved in the economic recovery were captured by the top income strata: in the USA, *all* the income growth in 2009–2013 went to the top 10% of families, while the income of the bottom 90% fell (Tcherneva, 2015, p. 3).

In the aftermath of the GFC, 'fiscal austerity' was presented as being essential to stabilise the public balance sheet given the extraordinary cost of salvaging finance. In reality, however, 'austerity' served to advance the neoliberal agenda on a wider front through higher and more regressive taxes, lower transfers and the expanded commodification of social reproduction (Albo & Fanelli, 2014). Harsh 'austerity' policies also served to pre-empt the argument that, since finance could be saved by state intervention, perhaps similar support could be offered to housing, health, transport and other sectors with greater relevance for the majority of the population. 'Fiscal austerity' might, then, be called 'socialism for the rich and capitalism for everyone else', justified by paltry ideological arguments that heavy state intervention is essential to protect the free market in general and finance in particular, despite its causal role upon the crisis itself, but the salvaging operation must not benefit the poor directly, and it ought to be funded by cuts to social welfare and the further dismantling of state capacities, rolling out even greater destructions of sociability and new waves of social (re)engineering.[2] The relationships between financialisation, growth slowdown, real wage stagnation, worsening job prospects, cuts to social security and public services, and rising inequality were ignored (Roberts, 2016, 2020).

The containment strategy after the GFC was followed by new forms of accommodation between the state, finance and industry with, for example, states flirting with industrial policy and the provision of infrastructure in order to shower money, loans, paper assets and profitable contracts upon private capital. Nevertheless, after a decade of limited recovery, it became clear that those responses did not deliver a renewal of economic performance on the scale experienced during the 1990s, let alone over the post-war boom. Instead, in the years following the

GFC the global economy drifted into what became known as a 'Great Stagnation', that would be interrupted only by the economic implosion due to the COVID-19 pandemic (see Chapter 6).[3]

In summary, the GFC demonstrated that, first, that neoliberalism had created strong tendencies towards further financialisation and the concentration of income when the economy grows, when it contracts, *and* when it recovers. Second, capital markets are largely useless at delivering employment, technological development, housing or pensions. They are also hugely costly to society, provision is inequitable and they can generate extreme economic instability. These challenges were not addressed in the decade following the GFC, leading to lingering consequences in terms of low GDP growth, investment and employment creation, together with the accumulation of debt, with disabling implications for public sector capacities.

These limited, and limiting, outcomes suggest that neoliberalism can offer no alternatives to the economic model based on high personal indebtedness and high financial profits, either because they are too central to the system of accumulation, or because unwinding household and corporate debts would require improvements in income distribution and the scaling up of public provision of housing, education, healthcare and retirement benefits. They were too disruptive to be countenanced. Instead of changing course, in the aftermath of the GFC neoliberal states tended to deploy increasing levels of repression to enforce policies of 'fiscal austerity', validated through discourses and practices of (selective forms of) nationalism and (more or less disguised) racism.[4] In all cases, the goal was to make the poor pay for the crisis of finance. In summary, neoliberalism was unable to resolve the crisis of accumulation after the GFC, and it continues to have no clear strategy to restore economic dynamism nor to improve the living conditions of the vast majority.

## Notes

1. See, for example, Evans (2015), McNally (2011), Mirowski (2013), Panitch et al. (2010), and Saad-Filho (2008, 2011).
2. 'In the short term defending capitalism means, paradoxically, state intervention. There is a justifiable sense of outrage among voters and business people (and indeed economic liberals) that $2.5 trillion of taxpayers' money now has to be spent on a highly rewarded industry. But the global bailout is pragmatic, not ideological. When François Mitterrand nationalised

France's banks in 1981 he did so because he thought the state would run them better. This time governments are buying banks (or shares in them) because they believe, rightly, that public capital is needed to keep credit flowing' (*The Economist*, 2008).

3. See Eichengreen (2015), Gordon (2015), Summers (2015, 2016) and Teulings and Baldwin (2014); for a heterodox view of this concept, see Backhouse and Boianovsky (2016).
4. In the European Union, the cases of Croatia, Hungary and Poland offer striking examples of this tendency (see Fabry, 2019; Stubbs & Lendvai-Bainton, 2019; see also Berberoglu, 2021 for a global view).

## References

Albo, G., & Fanelli, C. (2014). *Austerity against democracy: An authoritarian phase of neoliberalism?* https://socialistproject.ca/content/uploads/2014/08/AusterityAgainstDemocracy.pdf

Backhouse, R., & Boianovsky, M. (2016). Secular stagnation: The history of a macroeconomic heresy. *European Journal of the History of Economic Thought, 23*(6), 946–970.

Berberoglu, B. (Ed.). (2021). *The global rise of authoritarianism in the 21st century crisis of neoliberal globalization and the nationalist response.* Routledge.

Boffo, M., Saad-Filho, A., & Fine, B. (2019). Neoliberal capitalism: The authoritarian turn. In L. Panitch & G. Albo (Eds.), *Socialist register* (pp. 247–270). Merlin Press.

Davidson, N. (2017). Crisis neoliberalism and regimes of permanent exception. *Critical Sociology, 43*(4–5), 615–634.

Dobbs, R., Lund, S., Woetzel, J., & Mutafchieva, M. (2015). *Debt and (not much) deleveraging* (McKinsey Global Institute Report). https://www.mckinsey.com/featured-insights/employment-and-growth/debt-and-not-much-deleveraging

Eichengreen, B. (2015). Secular stagnation: The long view. *American Economic Review, 105*(5), 66–70.

Evans, T. (2015). *The crisis of finance-led capitalism in the United States of America* (Working Paper No. 51). Berlin: Institute for International Political Economy.

Fabry, A. (2019). *The political economy of Hungary: From state capitalism to authoritarian neoliberalism.* Palgrave Pivot.

Gordon, R. J. (2015). Secular stagnation: A supply-side view. *American Economic Review, 105*(5), 54–59.

Marx, K. (1981). *Capital* (Vol. 3). Penguin.

McNally, D. (2011). *Global slump: The economics and politics of crisis and resistance.* PM Press.

Mirowski, P. (2013). *Never let a serious crisis go to waste. How neoliberalism survived the financial meltdown*. Verso.
Panitch, L., Gindin, S., & Albo, G. (2010). *In and out of crisis: The global financial meltdown and left alternatives*. PM Press.
Roberts, M. (2016). *The long depression*. Haymarket Books.
Roberts, M. (2020). *The virus, capitalism, and the long depression. Interviewed by Ashley Smith*. https://spectrejournal.com/the-virus-capitalism-and-the-long-depression/
Saad-Filho, A. (2008). Marxian and Keynesian critiques of neoliberalism. In *Socialist register* (pp. 337–345). Merlin Press.
Saad-Filho, A. (2011). Crisis *in* neoliberalism or crisis *of* neoliberalism? In *Socialist register* (pp. 242–259). Merlin Press.
Stubbs, P., & Lendvai-Bainton, N. (2019). Authoritarian neoliberalism, radical conservatism and social policy within the European Union: Croatia, Hungary and Poland. *Development and Change, 51*(2), 540–560.
Summers, L. H. (2015). Demand side secular stagnation. *American Economic Review, 105*(5), 60–65.
Summers, L. H. (2016). *The age of secular stagnation. What it is and what to do about it*'. Foreign Affairs, https://www.foreignaffairs.com/articles/united-states/2016-02-15/age-secular-stagnation.
Tcherneva, P. (2015). *When a rising tide sinks most boats: Trends in U.S. income inequality* (Policy Note 2015/4). Levy Economics Institute.
Tett, G. (2009). *Fool's gold: How unrestrained greed corrupted a dream*. Little, Brown & Co.
Teulings, C., & Baldwin, R. (Eds.). (2014). *Secular stagnation: Facts, causes and cures*. Centre for Economic Policy Research. https://voxeu.org/content/secular-stagnation-facts-causes-and-cures
*The Economist*. (2008). Capitalism at bay. https://www.economist.com/node/12429544

PART II

# Neoliberalism and Democracy

CHAPTER 3

# Political Forms of Neoliberalism

This chapter focuses on the political forms associated with neoliberalism. It shows that the transitions to neoliberalism followed different paths but, by the 1990s, a specifically neoliberal form of democracy had become the political form of the system of accumulation. Examination of the key features, contradictions and limitations of neoliberal democracy suggests the *political paradox of neoliberalism*: that the triumph of neoliberal democracy undermined democracy itself, and made the political system and the institutions of the neoliberal state unresponsive to the demands and expectations of large strata of the population. This limitation created political vulnerabilities that help explain the rise of authoritarianism after the GFC.

## Transitions to Neoliberalism

Neoliberal experiences tend to go through three phases that are, inevitably, more logical than chronological and that depend on the country and region, and on economic, political and historical circumstances. Despite the scope for variation, these phases can be divided by the East Asian crisis in the mid-1990s, and the GFC (Boffo et al., 2019).

The first ('transition', or 'shock') phase of neoliberalism invariably emerges in opposition to the previous system of accumulation (Keynesian social democracy in the AEs, developmentalist in the Global South,



A. Saad-Filho, *The Age of Crisis*,
https://doi.org/10.1007/978-3-030-81608-7_3

Soviet-style socialist in the former Eastern Bloc, or whatever else). The transitions to neoliberalism always require aggressive interventions by the state in order to enforce economic 'shock therapy', promote the interests of private capital, foster the transnational integration of production and finance, contain labour and disorganise the left, with little regard for the social, economic, distributional, employment, balance of payments or any other consequences. This phase also requires the re-regulation of the economy along neoliberal lines and the construction of a new institutional framework underpinning the reproduction of the system of accumulation. Four longer-term developments tend to follow: an increase in the share of capital in national income at the expense of labour; the relative, if not absolute, impoverishment of the working class and their escalating indebtedness; the transformation of public policies and the reorganisation of the state itself under 'market principles'; and the shift of mainstream political parties (especially liberal, centrist and social-democratic parties) towards neoliberalism, accompanied by the collapse of left-wing parties associated with (different forms of) socialism (Davidson, 2017; Peck & Tickell, 2002).

The first transitions to what would become recognised as neoliberalism took place in the military dictatorships in the Southern Cone of Latin America in the 1970s, especially in Chile, Uruguay and Argentina. They were followed by transitions in formal democracies such as the UK (through Thatcherism) and the USA (Reaganism); neoliberalism was then imposed throughout Latin America and sub-Saharan Africa by structural adjustment programmes, and across the Eastern Bloc by the transitions to capitalism. This first phase of neoliberalism closed with the imposition of stabilisation policies by the IMF in the wake of the East Asian crisis, in the mid-1990s, marking the transition in that region.

The second ('mature') phase of neoliberalism ran from the mid-1990s until the GFC. Politically, this period was associated with the so-called 'third way', under the leadership of 'centrist' politicians like Bill Clinton, Tony Blair and Gerhard Schröder. This phase saw the stabilisation of the new system of accumulation, the deepening and intensification of the financialisation of social reproduction, the consolidation of the social relations imposed in the previous phase, the institutionalisation of the new modalities of international integration, and the introduction of typically neoliberal (limited, targeted and conditional) social policies to manage the dysfunctions, deprivations and adverse social consequences of the transition, what would become known as 'neoliberalism with a human face' (Boffo et al., 2019). Finally, a limited form of democracy became established as the dominant political form of neoliberalism (see below).

The mature phase also saw the ideological stabilisation of the system of accumulation: neoliberalism evolved from being a fact on the ground (the world as it *is*, following the forceful imposition of the new system of accumulation in the first phase) into the 'common sense' of the age (the world as it *ought to be*); that is, the widespread acceptance that 'there is no alternative' to neoliberalism. This was achieved in different ways, usually including the promotion by the state, private capital and the mainstream media of a neoliberal subjectivity centred on 'individual freedom and initiative'. This worldview was encapsulated in the notion of 'self-responsibility' as the dominant form of ideology and rationality, which redefined the relationships between individuals, the economy, society and the state. Everyone was pushed to adopt an entrepreneurial mode of living, and social intercourse was increasingly subordinated to narrow economic criteria (Fine & Saad-Filho, 2017). Neoliberal ideology was destructive for working-class culture and agency, since it deprived citizens of their collective capacities, valued consumption above all else, placed the merit of success and the burden of failure on isolated individuals, and disabled collective agency by suggesting that the resolution of every social problem requires the further individualisation, marketisation and financialisation of social intercourse. At that point, the space for traditional left political activity had become severely limited, both because the economy and the society had changed, and because most people either no longer believed in such left values as equality, solidarity and distribution, or no longer believed that these aspirations were realistic.

## Building Neoliberal Democracies

The early transitions to neoliberalism were associated with authoritarian political regimes, especially terrorist dictatorships in Latin America, sub-Saharan Africa and Turkey. They were followed by the rollout of neoliberal reforms by constitutional means in most AEs, especially the UK and USA. Later transitions to neoliberalism tended to be coeval with political transitions to democracy, for example, in Brazil, South Africa, South Korea and in Eastern Europe.

Whatever the path of transition, by the 1990s what may be called 'neoliberal democracy' had become established as the typical (hegemonic, though, obviously, not unique) political form of the system of accumulation (Ayers & Saad-Filho, 2015). By that time, most neoliberal countries were democratic at least in the formal (procedural) sense; most non-democratic countries were not neoliberal; and most transitions to democracy, whether from military dictatorship, single-party rule, autocracy or Soviet-style socialism, were articulated with transitions to neoliberalism.

The neoliberal form of democracy is substantively different from the limited male-oriented democracies in the 'core' countries before World War I, the social-democratic compact in the AEs after World War II, or other democratic political forms that achieved prominence in the past. The neoliberal democracies are bounded in historically specific ways. Typically, they include constitutionalism, the rule of law, ideals of 'good governance', an individualistic conception of human rights, political pluralism and the periodic election of political representatives via multiparty elections, as well as a 'market economy' and an 'independent' civil society. In these regimes, political community is understood in terms of nation-states constituted by the neoliberal 'neutral' state, the neoliberal public sphere and the neoliberal individual ('self'). This political model embodies an individualist, formally egalitarian, capitalist, meliorist and universalist conception of self and society, underpinning a procedural democracy that is functionally articulated with neoliberalism.

The 'normal' political process in neoliberal democracies tends to be limited to periodic calls to the ballot box to choose between competing shades of neoliberalism. For example, centrist Democrats versus mainstream Republicans in the USA, moderate Tories (i.e., Conservatives) versus Blairite Labour in the UK, sensible Christian Democrats versus ultra-accommodating Social Democrats in Germany, centre-left versus centre-right in Austria, Canada, France, Italy, Sweden and elsewhere, and so on, in what are, effectively, political pseudo-markets regulated by neoliberal ideology, an aggressive and plutocratic mainstream media and a rigid legal framework enforced by a nominally 'independent' judiciary supportive of neoliberalism (see below). In these countries, regular elections would lead to the alternation in power of political parties espousing marginally different versions of neoliberalism. These shifts would help to fine-tune the system of accumulation, including its core processes of extending the law of value across every sphere of social reproduction under the hegemony of finance, growing commercialisation of social provision and community life, enhanced commodity fetishism, mounting economic inequalities, and penetration of the profit motive into new areas of social intercourse.

Even though the offer to the voters of slightly different versions of neoliberalism is important, a more significant feature of neoliberal democracies is the separation between the economic and political domains of social life and the insulation of economic policymaking from political 'interference' by the majority, whether through elections or in any other way. In neoliberal democracies, despite the appearance of openness and flexibility, the substantive choices about social provision, the composition of output, the structure of employment and the distribution of income are subtracted from the realm of politics and transferred to technocratic institutions bounded by rigid rules, that are, nevertheless, implemented flexibly according to political determinations. Hence, public policy becomes determined primarily by bureaucratic processes, lobbying and 'internal' institutional and other pressures, rather than being set by negotiations and compromises between representatives of competing social forces.

This arrangement tends to exclude economic matters from political debate, curtail the accountability of the public institutions and entrench the supremacy of finance in economic and social reproduction, drastically limiting the scope for democracy itself. The key economic institutions in neoliberal democracies are Ministries of Finance dominated by neoliberal policymakers; so-called 'independent' Central Banks beholden to finance and mandated to control inflation as well as rescue feckless financial institutions; inflation-targeting regimes primed to protect financial asset values, and Treasury departments constrained by maximum fiscal deficit rules, except when it becomes necessary to provide unlimited resources to finance. They are backed up by wholesale privatisations meant to curtail any potential levers for public influence over the allocation of resources and the pattern of growth; floating exchange rate regimes that compel governments to follow the whims of market traders; the legal 'autonomy' of a wide range of public bodies, not least regulatory agencies captured by the corporations nominally under their control, and the use of referenda to bypass representative democracy, which appears to empower individuals at the expense of 'elite' interests but, in reality, serves primarily to allow raw economic power to override legal, institutional and other constraints to elite interests.

At a further remove, economic and social policy were both imposed and monitored by lobbies, business associations, transnationalised financial institutions, treaties and international organisations (e.g., the European Commission, WTO, and so on), and by the stock market and the mainstream media, whose self-serving opinions could shift asset values in dramatic ways. Their authority was underpinned by a nominally independent judicial system tasked with enforcing the jurisprudence that neoliberalism itself had imposed (Brown, 2015; Purdy, 2012). In this way, neoliberalism imposed discipline upon key social agents, with the workers at the forefront, but these institutional structures also served to discipline capital, the state, and even finance, with a growing intolerance to dissent. In the meantime, a barrage of propaganda promoted overconsumption, often funded by borrowing, as the essence of the good life, while the state itself signalled that class-based collectivities would no longer be recognised, and that cash-poor individuals were either 'failures' or 'crooks', severely undermining what remained of social cohesion (Boffo et al., 2019; Fine & Saad-Filho, 2017).

Looking at neoliberal democracy from another angle, democratic states enjoy political legitimacy because they are seen to respect the rights of citizenship and the rule of law. Neoliberal governments have used their legitimacy to validate the transfer to finance the allocative and conflict-resolution functions of the state, and to facilitate the concentration of political, economic and media power. At the same time, states have imposed 'reforms' locking in the institutions of neoliberalism and making it difficult to shift the system of accumulation by constitutional means. Given the diffusion of neoliberal ideology, these regressive outcomes could be presented as effects of the universalisation of democracy (the 'end of history', for Francis Fukuyama). In this way, political democracy helped to secure the legitimacy and institutional stability of neoliberalism and financialisation, as if they expressed the general good (Dardot & Laval, 2013, p. 6; Konings, 2018). As former Fed Chairman Alan Greenspan noted, '[t]he global economy ... requires capitalism's safety valve: democracy' (Davidson, 2017, p. 621).

The changes in social structures, institutions and the law driven by the transition to neoliberalism, and the consolidation of neoliberal democracy along the lines described above, constrained all forms of opposition to neoliberalism; they also drastically limited the space for nominally democratic states to shape policy and find negotiated solutions to the contradictions, conflicts and crises in neoliberalism. At that point, there *really* was no alternative to neoliberalism: ideological domination and institutional rigidity meant that no substantive economic policy choices were available, and there was no need to debate the material reproduction of society.

The growing inability of neoliberal political systems to tackle contradictory demands and conflicting interests shows that, even though they remain formally inclusionary, neoliberal democracies are fundamentally exclusionary at the levels of the economy and human freedom, and they are not geared to the protection of the interests of the weak. Rather, under neoliberalism democracy is substantively hollow, and it serves primarily to legitimise the plunder of resources by the rich. As neoliberal democracy consolidates itself, a lethal dynamic is set in motion against social solidarity and basic equalities of status, condition, prospects, treatment and protection, even though democracy depends on them.

These degenerating outcomes were not merely due to the 'capture' of neoliberal states by selfish financial elites. Instead, the impermeability of the economic domain and the concentration of economic and political power also derive from the material structures of the system of accumulation and the imperative to secure international competitiveness according to the parameters set by global finance (i.e., the US-led 'international community'). For example, the international integration of production and finance inevitably constrains the policy space available to country governments, because globalised production requires international legal and policy harmony and a spiralling number of treaties that curtail the scope for variation in the modes of economic and social reproduction, with important political repercussions.

## Neoliberal Democracy and the 'Losers'

It was shown above that the economic, technological, institutional and legal changes under neoliberalism transformed the modes of labour and the patterns of reproduction of the working class. In brief, the working class under neoliberalism tends to be more segmented, atomised and internationalised than ever before, with consequences for employment, education, culture, consumption and, at a further remove, forms of sociability and sense of collectivity based on shared material circumstances.

Those material and ideological changes undermined the institutions of representation of the working class and their traditional forms of intervention in social life through political parties, trade unions, social movements, community organisations, clubs and so on. These institutions and their rules, processes, demands and modes of struggle became increasingly detached from the lived experiences of the working class, and they gradually lost their social base and *raison d'être*. With the decline in the strength and credibility of these institutions, their members, supporters and voters were turned away, which reduced their relevance still further, in a vicious circle. Over time, the political capacities of the working class under neoliberalism were severely weakened. In summary, as the working class and the wider group of economic 'losers' (see Chapter 1) were socially decomposed, they lost their cultural and ideological identity and it became harder to articulate their concerns, disappointments, fears, resentments, grievances, demands and hopes. The 'losers' became unprotected politically at the same time as the political system tended to become rigid in the neoliberal democracies (see Chapter 4).

The signs were ominous. Around the world, centre-left and centre-right parties haemorrhaged members and voters, and electoral turnout ebbed. As the main political parties converged around neoliberal policies, the disempowerment of the 'losers' morphed into disenfranchisement, fuelling a crisis of representation and sapping the neoliberal claim of 'freedom of choice' in the political domain. In these strained circumstances, the alienation and anger of the 'losers' ended up, paradoxically, feeding individualism and reinforcing neoliberalism.

At the same time, neoliberal discourses became the common sense of the age—that is, widely accepted and unquestioned, because they took the mantle of 'obvious' and unmediated reflections of reality. They were endlessly relayed by a mainstream media that claimed for itself the double role of being the only legitimate channel of representation of the public, and the judge of the collective interest. Over time, social problems and contradictions tended to be interpreted through a prism combining a neoliberal form of 'common sense' with elementary neoclassical economics, which turned collective conflicts into casual disputes between 'honest' and 'dishonest' people. This suggested that societies were not divided along the lines of class or even 'race' or nation but, rather, between 'good people' and 'bad people', with the latter creating trouble either because of their crooked nature, or because of their rational choices given the incentives created by public policy.

This moral universe includes rivalries and ethical conflicts, but it lacks systemic relations of exploitation and structures of reproduction of inequality. In essence, 'our' group of honest insiders is surrounded by a swarm of predatory outsiders, and 'our' values of honesty, self-reliance and hard work are being undermined by corrupt politicians, swindlers wrongly claiming benefits, criminals robbing 'our' property, immigrants crowding 'us' out of 'our' houses and hospitals, and distant countries stealing 'our' jobs. At a further remove, a bloated, costly, inefficient and corrupt state has granted undue privileges to an endless procession of opportunistic interlopers claiming different forms of victimhood. They include the undeserving poor, women, pullulating minorities claiming compensation for their disadvantages, assorted ethnic groups, immigrants, refugees and many other outsiders seeking to embezzle 'our' just rewards and claw their way into respectability at the expense of 'our' traditional roles. Their agenda is unjustifiably accommodated by politically correct liberal states, at the expense of justice, 'tradition', 'culture' and the 'national interest'. It seemed that, under neoliberalism, each person was out for themselves—except for the perception that minority groups were either being given by the state, or were taken by dishonest means, what did not rightfully belong to them.

In other words, the 'losers' can recognise the damage inflicted by neoliberalism and distrust its dysfunctionality, but they are led by politicians, right-wing forces and the media to blame groups at the bottom of society for their troubles. If there is a crisis of provision of health, education or housing, it must be the fault of people even poorer than we are, who are taking what belongs to us; if there are crises of deindustrialisation, unemployment or deskilling, it must be the fault of countries even poorer than we are, and so on.

These misinterpretations of the impact of neoliberalism are grounded on the vulnerabilities of the 'losers' due to the erosion of their sense of collectivity and scope for agency, and the closely related degradation of class cultures and political capacities under neoliberalism.[1] In these circumstances, instead of being channelled through the traditional institutions and modes of conflict resolution, mass frustration tended to be captured by, and expressed through, the right-wing media and far-right political organisations, movements and governments. They have induced the 'losers' to blame 'the other' for the damages inflicted by neoliberalism, with the alleged victims being represented through cultural and religious hierarchies. Stereotypically, in the AEs the 'losers' are imagined as hardworking, morally upright and ethnically privileged male-led blue-collar families, while the opportunistic 'winners' are portrayed through cultural, religious and 'racial' stereotypes against the poor, women, immigrants, non-white peoples, poorer countries, minority religions, and so on, using images steeped in history. They require little explanation: a code word here and a wink there are enough. Everyone knows who is taking advantage of 'us', and how.

It was as if every frustration due to capitalism, neoliberalism, financialisation, globalisation and imperialism could be explained by the misbehaviour, dishonesty and corruption of scheming 'others', aided and abetted by an unfriendly state. These challenges and the litany of woes presumably imposed upon the 'losers' concealed the contradictions, inequalities and forms of exploitation under neoliberalism in a fog of scandalous headlines. In the meantime, the afflictions of the 'losers' were ignored, and they were derided by the media and the institutions of the neoliberal state. Everything seemed to be upside-down, with the undeserving persistently cutting in front of the 'morally upright', in sharp contrast with the misty olden days when people of good character, strong discipline and sharing 'our' values could count on steady employment, rising incomes, promotion prospects, generous pensions and, most importantly, social recognition and self-respect. These advantages evaporated under neoliberalism, and the 'losers' were left behind.

Following the individualistic and 'ethical' lines described above, the perceived malfunctioning of the state and the distortions and perversities of public policy were, inevitably, ascribed to the corruption of 'the politicians', who appeared to be there 'only for the taking'. This was not unreasonable, since neoliberalism engenders specific forms of corruption. In particular, as the policymaking capacity of the state was disabled, money was anointed as the sole measure of success, the commercialisation of social intercourse became a mantra, and revolving doors were put in place between politics, the civil service, unelected advisors, business, finance and the media. In the meantime, the neoliberal capture of the judiciary, the depletion of the political sphere and the demobilisation of the electorate facilitated all manner of electoral irregularities and chicanery, for example, voter suppression, breaches of electoral spending limits, judicial interference in processes and results, and outright fraud. Ultimately a 'pay-to-play political system' allowed moneyed and corporate interests to buy politicians and elections, accelerating the demoralisation of democracy both ideologically and in practice (Ayers & Saad-Filho, 2020).

While corruption is perceived to undermine the economic system from above, the feckless poor and the immigrants corrode it from below, and foreign countries attack it from outside. As the systemic shortcomings of neoliberalism are dislocated towards individual and country-level dishonesty, the failings of the system of accumulation are concealed. It seems that all would be well if the political system is 'clean' and no one cheats on their benefits.

These polarising logics (deserving vs. undeserving, majority vs. minority, insiders vs. outsiders, and so on) have fuelled the individualisation of life under neoliberalism, and pushed political narratives towards the cultural register at the expense of economics (Crouch, 2019). The ensuing nationalist, xenophobic and populist politics obscures the class dynamics of neoliberalism, with debates ignoring economic strategy and distribution, and being taken over by culture, religion, nationalism and racism. In other words, the 'depoliticizing of economics leads to the politicizing of everything else' (Davidson, 2017).

Captured between these pincers, the demands of the workers and the 'losers' drifted towards claims for the restoration of privileges, wrapped in a 'moral' discourse stressing commonsensical ideas of justice, individual merit, level-playing fields, traditional rights, respect and the imperative of honesty in public life. This type of politics is destructive of progressive forms of collective identity; it also gravitates towards the right, since it focuses on pleas for incorporation within the existing system of accumulation, respect for its rules, and revulsion at violations of the dominant order.

These processes are neatly expressed in the convergence of forces against corruption, which is the only legitimate form of mass mobilisation within neoliberalism, and in support of nationalism as the only permissible form of collective identity, even as it slides into racism. *Nationalism* and *racism*, drawing upon superficially shared identities, values, morals and background, and predicated upon the exclusion of the 'other', offer the 'losers' a commonsensical framework to articulate their experiences in concert with the dominant ideology and the lurid narratives found in the mainstream media. Nationalism and racism also allow the losers to reaffirm their self-worth, innate virtues and presumed links with the privileged, which neoliberalism routinely denies, and to recreate a sense of collectivity that was destroyed in other spheres of life. The 'losers' are, then, offered an opportunity to respond to real injuries, address their perceived victimisation by outsiders aided and abetted by a disordered state, and a way to gain something after years of abuse by undeserving 'others'.

## The Political Paradox of Neoliberalism

The consolidation of neoliberal democracy, between the early 1980s and the mid-2000s, buttressed the system of accumulation and reduced the space for opposition. It also created forces undermining the ideological legitimacy of neoliberalism and fostering mass alienation from its political reproduction.

It was shown above that neoliberalism degraded the capacities of the state, hollowed out the structures of collective representation, reduced the scope for political negotiation and made public policy inflexibly hostile to the majority. Inevitably, these processes fed apathy and anomie, corroded the legitimacy of democratic politics, and sapped the credibility of traditional parties, leaders and institutions, both because of their obvious powerlessness, and because of perceptions of corruption in an increasingly commercialised public life. In turn, structural economic limitations implied that the material aspirations validated by the consumption-oriented cultures of neoliberalism could not be satisfied (see above).

These developments conflicted with the ideologies of neoliberalism. These ideologies are based on notions of 'individual rights', 'freedom of choice' and the 'realisation of ambitions', underpinned by the 'roll-back' of a state that grew detached from the experiences of the 'losers'. In addition, it became increasingly obvious that neoliberalism is *actually* based on the state-driven enforcement of a financialised mode of social reproduction, deep economic and social restructuring, imposition of an individualistic subjectivity, and repression of opposition. The corrosion of neoliberal politics was intensified by the flaring of resentments and mutually incompatible demands for 'change', reflecting the worsening position of large numbers of people in mature neoliberal societies, especially after the GFC. As they struggled to navigate these choppy waters, neoliberal states were compelled to deploy shifting and often contradictory combinations of political repression, 'fiscal austerity', demand-boosting policies, conciliatory gestures, propaganda, jingoism and so on:

> [S]tates around the world have been experiencing spiralling crises of legitimacy that generate a bewildering and seemingly contradictory politics of crisis management that appears as schizophrenic in the literal sense of conflicting or inconsistent elements. (Robinson, 2019, p. 176)

Given the disarticulation of the left, these volatile circumstances fostered the rise of anti-systemic forces attached to neoliberalism, but not committed to neoliberal democracy (see below). Gradually, political life drifted towards what Crouch (2020) called a 'post-democratic' condition, in which the institutions of democracy persist but they have been drained of vital energy and relevance.

*The political paradox of neoliberalism* is that the institutionalisation and generalisation of neoliberal democracy undermined the foundations of democracy itself. Ultimately, this paradox was driven by the tensions inherent in the deployment of an *inclusive* (electoral) political system to support an *exclusionary* system of accumulation. This contradiction led to the evacuation of the institutional structures of collectivity and representation, and rendered key aspects of life immune to democratic accountability.

## Note

1. A parallel process is described by Marx (1852).

## References


Ayers, A., & Saad-Filho, A. (2015). Democracy against neoliberalism: Paradoxes, limitations, transcendence. *Critical Sociology, 41*(4–5), 597–618.

Ayers, A., & Saad-Filho, A. (2020). The twilight of formal democracy: Contradictions of accumulation and the political crisis of neoliberalism. *Journal of Australian Political Economy, 86*, 230–255.

Boffo, M. Saad-Filho, A., & Fine, B. (2019). Neoliberal capitalism: The authoritarian turn. In L. Panitch & G. Albo (Eds.), *Socialist register* (pp. 247–270).

Brown, W. (2015). *Undoing the demos: Neoliberalism's stealth revolution*. Zone Books.

Crouch, C. (2019). Post-democracy and populism. *The Political Quarterly, 90*, 124–137.

Crouch, C. (2020). *Post-democracy after the crisis*. Polity Press.

Dardot, P., & Laval, C. (2013). *The new way of the world: On neoliberal society*. Verso.

Davidson, N. (2017). Crisis neoliberalism and regimes of permanent exception. *Critical Sociology, 43*(4–5), 615–634.

Fine, B., & Saad-Filho, A. (2017). Thirteen things you need to know about neoliberalism. *Critical Sociology, 43*(4–5), 685–706.

Konings, M. (2018). From hayek to Trump: The logic of neoliberal democracy. *Socialist Register, 54*, 48–73.

Marx, K. (1852). *The eighteenth Brumaire of Louis Bonaparte*. https://www.marxists.org/archive/marx/works/1852/18th-brumaire/

Peck, J., & Tickell, A. (2002). Neoliberalizing space. *Antipode, 34*(3), 380–404.

Purdy, J. (2012). *The Roberts Court vs. America*. https://democracyjournal.org/magazine/23/the-roberts-court-v-america/

Robinson, W. I. (2019). Global capitalist crisis and twenty-first century fascism: Beyond the Trump Hype. *Science and Society, 83*(2), 481–509.

CHAPTER 4

# The Crisis of Neoliberal Democracy

This chapter explores the limitations and crises of neoliberal democracy after the GFC. It shows that, given the political, institutional and other fragilities of neoliberal democracy, the stresses caused by the most severe economic crisis since 1929 created deep fractures in society, that could not be healed easily. These tensions worsened with the decision of many AE governments to push for 'fiscal austerity'. In this context, the longstanding limitations of neoliberal democracy created favourable conditions for the emergence of 'spectacular' political leaders associated with an authoritarian and radicalised version of neoliberalism. Examination of the circumstances behind the rise of these leaders, and the constraints under which they operate, allows the identification of the *paradox of authoritarianism*, that is, the limitations of democracy spawn 'spectacular' leaders but their rule is intrinsically unstable and it opens spaces for new forms of fascism.

## Neoliberalism After the GFC

The GFC marked the end of the second (mature) phase of neoliberalism and the start of the third phase, distinguished by the need to manage the consequences of the crisis in a context of erosion of legitimacy of neoliberalism. This erosion was due to the widespread realisation that neoliberalism had foundered even in its own terms: it had failed to



A. Saad-Filho, *The Age of Crisis*,
https://doi.org/10.1007/978-3-030-81608-7_4

deliver rapid and stable accumulation, undermined democracy, concentrated income and wealth, imposed unpopular patterns of employment, and triggered an unprecedented economic catastrophe with astronomical costs. It also became evident that neoliberal political systems would tend to respond perversely to these challenges, first by protecting finance and the rich, and, later, by socialising the costs and losses of doing so. In these circumstances, policies of 'fiscal austerity' could be implemented only through the intensification of repression and the introduction of new forms of exclusion.

The GFC was due to decades of neoliberal reforms and expanding inequalities (see Chapter 2). It unleashed destructive tendencies, starting with the loss of millions of jobs, homes and businesses, followed by several years of 'fiscal austerity' justified by the need to pay for the policies that had salvaged finance at the expense of everything else. Coming on top of the crisis itself, austerity had devastating implications for the 'losers', the workers as a whole and the public sector, since it brought real wage losses, welfare cuts, new waves of social engineering, further dismantling of state capacities, and another round of destruction of sociability.

The inability of neoliberal states to address the concerns of the 'losers' in the wake of the GFC reinforced the perception of loss of efficacy and relevance of policies, practices, political parties and leaders that were, previously, taken to be unassailable. In a brief interval, an entire cohort of prominent operators slipped into oblivion: Hillary Clinton, Gordon Brown, David Cameron, Matteo Renzi, Francois Hollande, George Papandreou and many others.

The loss of control by the traditional political elites opened spaces for anti-systemic forces polarised by 'spectacular' authoritarian nationalist leaders and a new generation of far-right movements.[1] In the background, the impression was already growing that solutions to felt problems must lie outside conventional politics (because it is demonstrably ineffective), that they ought to be based on intransigent campaigns (because it is essential to push harder to elicit responses from a rigid system), and that political agency must lie in individual 'leaders' operating outside the existing institutions of representation (since the traditional institutions had been rendered ineffective in practice).

In the meantime, many traditional political parties, especially of the social democratic variety, split, shrunk or even imploded; for example, the French Socialist Party, numerous Italian parties of the centre-left, the German Social-Democratic Party and, perhaps most dramatically, the

Greek socialist party PASOK, whose collapse generated the term 'Pasokification'. While social democracy was diminished and even devoured, mainstream Conservative parties showed greater resilience, partly because they are more closely identified with the dominant ideology, and partly because the right is better adapted at deploying misleading programmes and hollow nationalist slogans to win elections. However, even these parties have been compelled to triangulate towards increasingly strident nationalist and exclusionary programmes, while a new generation of far-right parties and neo-fascist movements threatens their core vote from the right (Hausermann et al., 2021). Given the earlier collapse of the far left, these processes have led to a sharp dislocation of the political spectrum towards the right.

In this context, new leaders and movements—sometimes entirely new but, on occasion already lurking at the margins of politics—gained new appeal and plausibility, as they vouched to confront the neoliberal state, finance, globalisation, the elites, foreigners and so on, in order to support the 'losers' and transfer the cost of the GFC towards 'Wall Street' and the 'fat cats'. However, when in power, their administrations would invariably deepen financialisation, impose more repressive forms of neoliberalism and seek to degrade democracy at every turn. The rise of a new generation of 'spectacular' leaders is, then, one of the consequences of the hollowing out of the technocratic and exclusionary democracies that were typical of mature neoliberalism.

The disintegration of neoliberal democracies became painfully obvious during the Eurozone crisis, when elected governments in the periphery were replaced by so-called non-party technocrats (in reality, experienced political operators committed to the status quo), to make sure that the policies decided in Berlin and Frankfurt would be implemented (Cyprus, Greece, Italy; see Bonefeld, 2017; Nedergaard & Snaith, 2015; Ryner, 2015). Subsequently, an administration elected for its non-mainstream approach was forced to abandon its voters (Greece).

The malaise eventually reached the core NATO countries when Brexit won the UK referendum on 23 June 2016 and, on 9 November, Donald Trump was elected US President. In France, Marine Le Pen reached the second round of the presidential elections in 2017, which were won by Emmanuel Macron, an unconventional politician leading a new party aligned with neoliberalism. Nativist populism thrived in Austria, Switzerland and Scandinavia. Across the Eastern periphery of the EU, far-right politicians prospered on the basis of exclusionary, xenophobic and racist programmes centred on attacking the weakest, especially after the refugee crisis in 2015. These were components of a wider process by which authoritarian governments were installed in several countries by fair means or foul, including more or less ‘clean’ elections (Argentina, Chile, Hungary, Italy, Philippines, Poland, UK, USA), abuses of constitutional prerogatives supported by the security forces (India, Russia, Turkey), judicial-parliamentary coups (Bolivia, Brazil, Honduras, Paraguay), and military coups (Egypt, Thailand), with escalating pressures on Nicaragua and Venezuela.

Through their ingrained anti-leftist discourse and practice and senseless support for a zombie ‘third wayism’ past its sell-by date, liberals and some sections of social democracy have failed completely to comprehend the journey of the ‘losers’ towards the right. Accompanied by much hand-wringing and incredulity, mainstream politicians and their pet academics have often reproached those who have lost out for their cognitive impairment, moral failure or both, while refusing to admit that those individuals and communities were responding, however perversely, to their lived experiences under neoliberalism, the impact of its economic and political crises, and the regressive changes under the new system of accumulation:

> After decades in which nominal working-class parties clearly represented capital more effectively than labor, workers around the global have turned to nationalist populists. For all their proto-fascist tendencies, at least these leaders are able to successfully appeal to working-class interests, even if only in rhetoric. (Z. Levenson, 2020)

In the UK, for example, the liberal intelligentsia was shocked and incredulous at the Brexit result. Yet, as Winlow et al. (2017, pp. 201–202) have documented, not so anyone with any recent first-hand experience of:

> the old working class’s precarious existence ... [and the] hardening attitudes ... festering sores and open wounds of those sections of British society that had suffered the worst effects of neoliberal restructuring ... [W]hen you’re plagued by debt, and when your job is insecure and poorly paid. If you don’t know how you’ll pay the rent next month, or how you’ll afford to feed your family, optimism recedes and darker emotions come to the fore.

The political crisis in neoliberalism and the rise of ‘spectacular’ leaders is, then, neither an aberration nor a reversible abnormality due to stupidity.

This is also not only about the election of Donald Trump (who received several million votes less than his rivals, Hillary Clinton and Joe Biden), Brexit (that won at the margin, and without any possibility of agreement about what the vote was *for*), the election of Jair Bolsonaro in Brazil (whose victory owes as much to chance as it does to the media-induced frenzy against the Workers' Party), or the rise of authoritarian neoliberal leaders elsewhere. As Achcar (2021) rightly put it:

> [H]owever significant Donald Trump's defeat in the latest US presidential election was … [h]is loss occurred not because of the disaffection of his supporters but *despite* a huge increase in their numbers (11 million more voters) at a time when, unlike 2016, there was no possible illusion about what Trump represents and, therefore, hardly any ambiguity in the sense of voting for him. At the global level likewise, there are presently no signs of neofascism waning: The continuing popularity of figures such as Jair Bolsonaro (until very recently, at least), Narendra Modi, or Viktor Orbán does not portend any withering away of the far-right pandemic in the foreseeable future.

The crisis of neoliberal democracy is the outcome of its success in the previous phase of neoliberalism, a by-product of the failure of financialisation and the delegitimation of neoliberal ideologies, and a consequence of 'austerity', the intensification of repression, and the emergence of new forms of exclusion in the wake of the GFC. This is, then, a systemic crisis of great import for the system of accumulation, and it cannot be 'fixed' through attempts to restore third-wayist neoliberal democracy. That ship sailed years ago.

## Authoritarian Neoliberalism

The dominant political form in the third phase of neoliberalism is ***authoritarian neoliberalism***, that is, the reproduction of a heavily financialised neoliberalism by means of authoritarian rule, within a formal (procedural) democratic shell.[2] This is a form of neoliberalism that partially breaks out of its democratic framework and foregrounds, instead, the despotic tendencies inherent to capitalism. The policies pursued by those authoritarian administrations have converged around (more or less overtly) repressive and racist forms of neoliberalism, justified by unwieldy combinations of 'national' values, the imperative of austerity and the whims of the 'leader'.

Authoritarian neoliberalism is neither an alternative to, nor a deviation from, neoliberal democracy, and it did not emerge through the forceful displacement of an older generation of respectable neoliberal-democratic politicians by a horde of authoritarians who happen to be neoliberal. Despite the anti-systemic discourse of its supporters, the post-GFC authoritarian form of the system of accumulation is an offshoot of neoliberal democracy: that is, authoritarian neoliberalism derives from the contradictions in the *successful* restructuring of production, social reproduction and the structures of representation under neoliberalism. Its purpose is to stabilise those neoliberal economies, societies and political systems through coercive and repressive forms of rule, given the inability of neoliberalism to deliver broad-based economic prosperity (Boffo et al., 2019; Bruff, 2014; Davidson, 2017; Tansel, 2017).

The repressive features of authoritarian neoliberalism are evident in the heavy-handed repression of dissent in most AEs and DEs, widespread infringements of personal freedom, privacy and the right to speech, and the relentless expansion of the prison-industrial-military complex, with the USA at the forefront, accompanied by pervasive and often paramilitarised policing, intrusive surveillance systems, aggressive crowd control, heavy policing of ethnic minority communities and working-class youth, specious wars on drugs and 'terrorism', and de facto war on immigrants and refugees through border-keeping and in other ways. These developments have been aptly characterised by Robinson (2019) as 'militarised accumulation' or 'accumulation by repression'. Yet, those authoritarian regimes generally remain attached to formally democratic practices, keeping in place regular elections and a semblance of political pluralism that both reflects their limited powers and that helps to validate their rule and the inequitable policies bolstering neoliberal accumulation (Ayers & Saad-Filho, 2020).

Authoritarian neoliberalism is, then, an original phenomenon. It has not emerged to shield capitalism against the insurgency of the left or in a period of low international integration of production, as fascism did in the 1930s; instead, this is the typical political form of post-GFC neoliberalism. It expresses the co-option of the disorganised fury of the 'losers' in evacuated neoliberal democracies, and the deployment of a politics of resentment that divides society while, simultaneously, fostering forms of collectivity grounded on nationalist, racial and religious discourses defined by wide-ranging exclusion and discrimination. These regressive forms of mobilisation are posited within and against a state that has lost legitimacy as the potential bearer of social cohesion or economic improvements. Invariably, authoritarian neoliberalism builds its legitimacy by attacking the weak: immigrants, refugees, the 'undeserving poor', the civil service, women, gays, and so on, under the guise of addressing corruption or undue privilege.

## 'Spectacular' Leaders

The 'spectacular' leaders typical of authoritarian neoliberalism are almost always male. They invariably present themselves as being strong; they appear to talk 'honestly' and appeal to common sense while, in fact, they are often rude, arrogant, selfish, self-promoting and patronising. They lie brazenly and compulsively, claim undeserved merits, deny evident truths, proclaim the non-existent 'facts' and pour abuse on doubters, fact-checkers, holders of different views, scientists and women. They are invariably short on humility, impervious to remorse and quick to claim that whatever they do is 'best in the world', even when it has failed miserably or even backfired. They pick calculated fights with the media, which brings visibility even if under an unflattering light, which, paradoxically, tends to consolidate the allegiance of their fans. These leaders often display symptoms of histrionic personality disorder if not psychopathy, and bear authoritarian ambitions to break and remake the state and the Constitution (even if, in most cases, it had eased their path to power and guarantees their privileges even as they methodically undermine social order).

Spectacular leaders cultivate a politics of resentment through demagoguery. They claim a unique ability to 'get things done' by force of will and, often, unmatched business acumen, and declare that they stand with 'the people' against unresponsive 'elites' which they pretend to reject despite their own typically privileged background, easy path towards power and prominence, and the political allegiance of those elites. Spectacular leaders also promise to deploy their strength of character and status as political outsiders to confront a never-ending array of enemies: the alien state, finance, globalisation, the elites, experts, entrenched interests, corrupt politicians, self-interested civil servants, captured institutions, foreigners and so on, who allegedly attack 'our' nation and hurt 'our' hard-working, morally pure and long-suffering people. In reality, however, they invariably operate in concert with the far right to attack the weak. While doing this, they push nationalist slogans and culture wars to confuse the field and secure the support of the 'losers', while deflecting attention from their inability to deliver material gains to them. Favourite targets include immigrants (USA, UK), Muslims (India), the left (Brazil), foreign countries (in Donald Trump's USA, China, Mexico, Canada and Germany; in the UK, the European Union) and refugees (EU, UK, and USA under Trump). Despite their anti-systemic discourse, when they reach power, the authoritarian leaders invariably implement programmes intensifying neoliberalism and financialisation (including regressive policies on taxation, trade, employment, finance, social security, housing and civil and political liberties), promoting their own personal power, and rendering ever more privileges to the neoliberal elite, while attacking all forms of opposition.

Authoritarian neoliberalism is deceptive by nature. The 'spectacular' leaders are not championing transformative economic, social or political agendas aiming to break with the ancient order, struggling to free the nation from its oppressors, or promoting a more advanced form of capitalism; nor do they derive their power from an equilibrium of forces or the convergence of interests of antagonistic classes. Instead, they make their way into political power by means of clever ploys, expensive advertising, often based on social media (a set of overtly decentralised channels that did not even exist a couple of decades ago), planned agitation and brute force, invariably aiming to enforce a radical neoliberal programme grounded on Conservative politics, while using the state and the law to steamroll the opposition. This is not populism, Bonapartism or fascism under neoliberal conditions. This is, instead, the politics of demagogues, conmen and illusionists who have achieved power through the opportunistic exploitation of country-specific fractures in the neoliberal order. To their right, however, stand even more dangerous movements claiming to represent the 'losers' in more consistent and aggressive ways.

Three planks are key to the political logic of authoritarian neoliberalism. First, the permanent reproduction of insecurity, tension and turmoil. The social disorientation associated with wave after wave of economic restructuring, social fragmentation and negation of traditional values, ways of life and forms of belonging has created fertile ground for the rise of belligerent self-assertions—whether national, racial, ethnic and/or religious, routinely inflected by hyper-masculinity, misogyny and homophobia. These self-assertions can function as a 'form of consolation … whose affirmations (the more negative forms of identity politics) are a balm for social despair' (Vanaik, 2009, p. 141). The far right has always been adept at mobilising on the grounds of insecurity, despair and alienation: in times of crisis, when the present is experienced as unsatisfactory and the future looks bleak, an idealised past can provide a sense of security and a beacon of hope. As was shown above, appeals to 'blood and nation' can become the only form of collectivity, particularly when the systemic alternatives to capitalism have apparently collapsed (Ayers & Saad-Filho, 2020; Davidson & Saull, 2017, p. 711).

Second, a Schmittian focus on political community, centred on the people's identity, determined through the distinction between 'us and them', or between 'friends and enemies'. This worldview directly implies the dehumanisation of 'the other', construed either as 'external', such as migrants, asylum seekers, radical Islam, China, or the EU, or 'internal', in the case of ethnic minorities, the poor, single parents, people with disabilities, 'antifa' and the Black Lives Matter (BLM) movement in the USA, lower castes in India, the darker-skinned and disproportionately impoverished population in Brazil, and so on. In all cases, this 'violently toxic mix of reactionary nationalism and racism' (Robinson, 2019, p. 169) pivots on the psychosocial mechanism of attributing to 'the other' responsibility for the systemic crisis, and displacing onto them the fears and anxieties imposed by capitalism in general, and neoliberalism specifically.

Third, the rise of 'spectacular' leaders is intrinsically associated with a politics of deceit, since they must promise something that they not only cannot deliver—they actually intend to implement exactly the opposite of what they had promised. In doing this while reaffirming the innate virtues of 'their people', the 'leaders' feed into a mysticism that supports their personality cult. The intellectual dregs of neoliberal society flock around these authoritarian 'leaders': cranks, conspiracy theorists, flat earthers, religious fanatics, ultra-libertarians, and all manner of racists and Nazis.

These converging pressures have mainstreamed the far right. The response from the centre-right and the centre-left has been to insist on the virtues of 'triangulation', that is, their own passive accommodation to the wider trends: they have incorporated racially-coded themes into their discourse, speak of 'getting tough' on immigration, crime and welfare dependence, and collaborate in the rollback of the non-market protections that had been secured by the left and the workers' movement in previous phases of capitalism. In doing this, they have delegitimised themselves as alternative forces, and validated the 'real thing'—the overt undermining of democracy by authoritarianism, rather than its weakening by stealth; at the same time, the centrists have reaffirmed in practice their disbelief in alternatives to neoliberalism.

In summary, the economic and political crises in neoliberalism have fostered the personalisation of politics and the emergence of 'spectacular' leaders untethered by stabilising institutions such as political party structures, constitutional checks and balances, trade unions, social movements and the law. In this context, the transformation of authoritarian neoliberalism into a material force is, on the one hand, a by-product of the failure of financialisation, the decay of neoliberal democracy and the delegitimation of dominant ideologies and modes of representation of reality. On the other hand, it is a reflex of the increasingly desperate search by the losers for ways to short-circuit a political system that is unquestionably jammed, and to secure gains for people who have grown tired of feeling unfairly disadvantaged and losing out to undeserving 'others'.

## The Paradox of Authoritarianism

The rising tide of authoritarian neoliberalism today is symptomatic of three processes. First, the prolonged slowdown, crisis and stumbling recovery of 'restructured' neoliberal economies, that would eventually slide into an unprecedented depression with the COVID-19 pandemic. Second, the decomposition of the institutions of representation under mature neoliberalism and the crisis of formally democratic political systems. They followed the GFC and were, in turn, followed by 'fiscal austerity' in several countries. Third, the hijacking of mass discontent by the far right, fronted by a new breed of 'spectacular' politicians committed both to their own self-referential power and to the intensified reproduction of neoliberalism.

Given these structural roots, authoritarian neoliberalism cannot be viewed as a transitory blip which, after its inevitable failure and as voters come to terms with their mistakes, must lead to the restoration of 'normal' (centrist, 'third-wayist', evacuated) neoliberal politics under the traditional elites (see above), nor is authoritarianism a marker of the 'end of neoliberalism' (e.g., West, 2016), despite the heated affirmations of the 'spectacular leaders' and their supporters. Instead, the rise of Abdel Fatah el-Sisi, Boris Johnson, Donald Trump, Emmanuel Macron, Jair Bolsonaro, Narendra Modi, Recep Tayyip Erdoğan, Rodrigo Duterte, Viktor Orbán and other 'leaders' signals both a *political crisis in neoliberalism*, and the emergence of a *new political normal* after the GFC.

It was shown above that, under authoritarian neoliberalism, mass frustration is not channelled primarily through the traditional institutions of representation, from trade unions to political parties, a diverse mainstream media or the judiciary. Instead, it has tended to be captured by, and expressed through, an oligarchic, vitriolic and increasingly right-wing media, various social media outlets, and far-right political organisations, movements and leaders. They have induced the 'losers' to blame 'the other' for the damages inflicted by neoliberalism, with the alleged 'victims' and the suggested 'perpetrators' being defined, more or less explicitly, through cultural and religious hierarchies and pre-existing 'racial' categories grounded in history.

The *paradox of authoritarianism* is that the economic and political crises of neoliberalism foster the personalisation of politics and the rise of 'spectacular' leaders committed to a radical version of neoliberalism and to their own personal power. They promote globalisation and financialisation while appearing to build 'national' alternatives to them, attack all forms of opposition, and relentlessly transfer power and resources to the fractions of the elite that already support them.

These policy agendas inevitably harm their political base, making the authoritarian neoliberal regimes fundamentally unstable. Society is increasingly divided, wages tend to decline, taxes become more and more regressive, social protections are eroded, economies become more unbalanced, and poverty grows. Mass frustration intensifies, feeding an unfocused discontent which the 'leaders' navigate by promoting a bitter politics of resentment and triggering new conflicts that may or may not be contained by the weakened institutions of (what remains of) neoliberal democracy. But since the 'leaders' cannot resolve actual problems, and given their attachment to neoliberalism, they cannot escape from a dynamics of escalation or their popularity suffers. They find refuge in performance, division and bombastic statements. As the political environment becomes toxic, more and more spaces are opened for the far right.[3] This suggests that the best way to confront authoritarianism and fascism is by transcending neoliberalism in a progressive direction.

## Notes

1. For a similar approach, see Chamayou (2018), Kiely (2018), and Slobodian (2018).
2. For similar approaches, see Bruff (2014, 2016), Bruff and Tansel (2020), Hendrikse (2018) and Tansel (2017).
3. For Davidson and Saull (2017, pp. 715–716), '[n]eoliberalism ... has helped create the conditions for the re-emergence of the far-right whilst, at the same time, the far-right has focused on attacking what it sees as the symptoms of neoliberalism through racializing its social, political and economic effects ... It is not then that neoliberalism *causes* racism ... in the sense that racism is an organic dimension of it, but rather that neoliberalism is grounded on a *collective socio-economic insecurity* that helps facilitate a revival of pre-existing racialized imaginaries of solidarity'.

## References


Achcar, G. (2021). *How can we revive herd immunity to fascism*. https://www.thenation.com/article/world/fascism-trump-neoliberalism-capitalism/

Ayers, A., & Saad-Filho, A. (2020). The twilight of formal democracy: Contradictions of accumulation and the political crisis of neoliberalism. *Journal of Australian Political Economy, 86*, 230–255.

Boffo, M., Saad-Filho, A., & Fine, B. (2019). Neoliberal capitalism: The authoritarian turn. In L. Panitch & G. Albo (Eds.), *Socialist register* (pp. 247–270).

Bonefeld, W. (2017). *The strong state and the free economy*. Rowman & Littlefield.

Bruff, I. (2014). The rise of authoritarian neoliberalism. *Rethinking Marxism, 26*(1), 113–129.

Bruff, I. (2016). Neoliberalism and authoritarianism. In S. Springer, K. Birch, & J. MacLeavy (Eds.), *Handbook of neoliberalism*. Routledge.

Bruff, I., & Tansel, C. B. (Eds.). (2020). *Authoritarian neoliberalism: Philosophies, practices, contestations*. Routledge.

Chamayou, G. (2018). *La société ingouvernable: Une généalogie du libéralisme autoritaire*. La fabrique.

Davidson, N. (2017). Crisis neoliberalism and regimes of permanent exception. *Critical Sociology, 43*(4–5), 615–634.

Davidson, N., & Saull, R. (2017). Neoliberalism and the far-right: A contradictory embrace. *Critical Sociology, 43*(4–5), 707–724.

Hausermann, S., Kitschelt, H., Abou-Chadi, T., Ares, M., Bischof, D., Kurer, T., van Ditmars, M., & Wagner, M. (2021). *Transformation of the left: The myth of voter losses to the radical right*. http://www.fes.de/cgi-bin/gbv.cgi?id=17385&ty=pdf

Hendrikse, R. (2018). Neo-illiberalism. *Geoforum, 95*, 169–172.

Kiely, R. (2018). *The neoliberal paradox*. Edward Elgar.

Levenson, Z. (2020). *An organic crisis is upon us*. https://spectrejournal.com/an-organic-crisis-is-upon-us/

Nedergaard, P., & Snaith, H. (2015). "As I drifted on a river I could not control": The unintended ordoliberal consequences of the Eurozone crisis. *Journal of Common Market Studies, 53*(5), 1094–1109.

Robinson, W. I. (2019). Global capitalist crisis and twenty-first century fascism: Beyond the trump hype. *Science and Society, 83*(2), 481–509.

Ryner, M. (2015). Europe's ordoliberal iron cage: Critical political economy, the Euro area crisis and its management. *Journal of European Public Policy, 22*(2), 275–294.

Slobodian, Q. (2018). *Globalists: The end of empire and the birth of neoliberalism*. Harvard University Press.

Tansel, C. B. (Ed.). (2017). *States of discipline: Authoritarian neoliberalism and the contested reproduction of capitalist order*. Rowman & Littlefield.

Vanaik, A. (2009). India's paradigmatic communal violence. *Socialist Register, 45*, 141–162.

West, C. (2016). *Goodbye, American neoliberalism. A new era is here*. https://www.theguardian.com/commentisfree/2016/nov/17/american-neoliberalism-cornel-west-2016-election

Winlow, S., Hall, S., & Treadwell, J. (2017). *The rise of the right: English nationalism and the transformation of working-class politics*. Policy Press.

PART III

# A Pandemic with Neoliberal Characteristics

CHAPTER 5

# A Neoliberal Health Crisis

Pandemics are socially and historically specific. They impact upon individuals through the collectivities in which they live, travel, work and find entertainment; correspondingly, pandemics must be tackled by societies at specific places and moments in time. The analysis of their course and the appropriate lessons must be similarly contextualised.

In the case of COVID-19, the health crisis did not simply stem from the chance arrival of a novel pathogen among humans not previously exposed to it: there is no such thing as a 'general' pandemic hitting an abstract population. Instead, the course of the pandemic derived from the features of the virus *in conjunction with* the social, economic and political circumstances in which it spread and mutated. These circumstances include the prevailing system of accumulation and the ensuing inequalities, divisions, stresses and crises; the dominant political systems and the economic, industrial, scientific, technological and institutional capacities available; the policy responses of different levels of government, from local administrations to international organisations; national(ist) myths and ideologies, and other variables. This chapter examines the relationship between neoliberalism and the pandemic, in order to review the impact of COVID-19 on the economy, politics, ideology and social life. It examines the spread of the pandemic, its implications for distinct groups and communities, and the policies adopted to address it. In view of



A. Saad-Filho, *The Age of Crisis*,
https://doi.org/10.1007/978-3-030-81608-7_5

these relationships, it is argued that this is *a pandemic with neoliberal characteristics*.

## Neoliberalism and the Pandemic

In every pandemic, some privileged individuals may seek shelter by subtracting themselves from social intercourse, perhaps following the fortunate characters in Giovanni Boccaccio's *Decameron*, or the young Isaac Newton (Levenson, 2020). This type of response cannot be generalised: human societies are integrated wholes rather than casual aggregations of individuals; they cannot be disassembled for safekeeping and put back together again once the danger has passed. It follows that pandemics can be more insightfully understood from the point of view of their impact on the collective; by the same token, pandemics are best addressed by organised collectivities, especially through the deployment of state power to control the circulation of people, goods, services and ideas; regulate economic, social and cultural production, and provide health and other public services (Snowden, 2020).

This chapter makes four claims. First, the coronavirus came at a perilous juncture for global neoliberalism, as the world economy was already sliding into a storm of economic, financial, political, social, environmental, water and food crises. The virus arrived after four decades of neoliberalism had depleted state capacities, including in healthcare, in pursuit of the 'superior efficiency' of the market,[1] fostered deindustrialisation through the 'globalised' restructuring of production, and built fragile financial structures secured by magical thinking and state guarantees, all in pursuit of short-term profitability. In the short term, the global economy was under severe stress because of persistent exchange rate misalignments between large economies, the US trade war against China, US-led aggression against Iran, catastrophic instability in the Middle East and North Africa, economic disasters across Latin America, and so on. COVID-19 exposed these faultlines, and countries buckled on impact in very different ways.

Second, the pandemic had a hothousing effect: it accelerated and intensified developments and crisis tendencies that were already unfolding. In particular, the world economy had been decelerating, and may even have become trapped in a 'Great Stagnation' after the GFC (see Chapter 2). With the pandemic, it was overwhelmed by the sharpest contraction in the history of capitalism (Elliott, 2020; Romei & Giles, 2021).

Further: neoliberal economies had witnessed an unprecedented accumulation of debt since 2008 (Dobbs et al., 2015); under the stresses of the pandemic, governments engaged in the largest debt accumulation since World War II, making the 2008 frenzy pale into insignificance. Authoritarian governments were already encroaching upon degenerating neoliberal democracies; now these governments seized unprecedented powers to control their populations, capture personal data, monitor communications, restrict movements and subsidise selected enterprises under the pretext of public safety (as opposed to, say, building a spectrum of state capacities to protect public health). Labour 'flexibility' had been increasing since the transitions to neoliberalism; with the pandemic, organised labour markets were badly weakened and even more protections were removed, especially for workers who were already precarious. There is no indication that these losses will be reversed spontaneously once the pandemic has passed.

Third, the sudden disintegration of the global economy showed that the largest, wealthiest, most globalised and uncompromising neoliberal AEs—the USA and the UK—were unable to produce enough face masks, PPE and ventilators. These insufficiencies were caused not only by misfortune, lack of productive capacity, changing technologies or China's trade and industrial policies: they were outcomes of the neoliberal policies implemented over many years. From universities to medical labs to manufacturing capacity to speculative financial systems, to disarticulated labour markets, to adverse distributional outcomes, neoliberal states systematically fragmented and dismantled a wide range of systems of provision, as individual firms scrambled for short-term profits however they could be found. The ensuing shortcomings were exacerbated by the destruction of state capacities and, during the pandemic, by the disinclination of neoliberal governments to mobilise industry, labour and private capital for a common purpose. This debacle culminated in unseemly commotions and punch-ups as the neoliberal worship of consumption dissolved into empty supermarket shelves, scrambles for hand sanitiser, pasta and sardines, and fistfights for toilet paper in some of the richest countries on Earth. This was followed by turmoil as (state-led) Chinese antivirals, PPE and ventilators were disputed all over the world.

Fourth, the trajectory of the pandemic can be largely explained by the structures and processes of accumulation under global neoliberalism. The illness was first detected in the fast-growing manufacturing hub of the world, in South-Central China, and it tended to spread along two pathways: the commercial routes laid out by globalised production, that produced early flashpoints in East Asia, Iran and Northern Italy,[2] and the international circulation of high-income individuals, especially holiday-makers meeting at ski resorts in Austria and Northern Italy, who spread COVID-19 to many countries.[3]

Many of the vulnerabilities, routes of transmission and consequences outlined above derive directly from capitalism as a mode of production; others were either created or exacerbated by neoliberalism as a system of accumulation; in turn, the consequences of the pandemic highlighted potential pathways to overcome neoliberalism.[4]

## Denialism and 'Herd Immunity'

Considerable time was spent in early 2020, especially in those countries with authoritarian neoliberal administrations—the USA, the UK, India and Brazil, as well as in Sweden, a wealthy, militarised and highly individualistic society—with government attempts to impose a pandemic strategy based on 'herd immunity'. This is the idea that, since the COVID-19 fatality rate was presumably low and concentrated among the non-workers, the coronavirus should be allowed to spread largely unimpeded, like the flu does every year. It was hoped that this light-touch strategy would give the young, healthy and productive members of society immunity at the lowest cost and with minimal economic disruption.[5]

The notion of herd immunity was transplanted from the management of farm animals into debates about the coronavirus in the expectation that it would provide an alternative to lockdowns. Although it was recognised that lockdowns would minimise the loss of life (depending on their timing as well as severity), they would hurt profits as well as, perhaps more alarmingly for diehard neoliberals, demonstrating that states can play a constructive role in social life (Conn & Lewis, 2020; Frey, 2020). In a matter of days, a panicky West was gripped by debates about the presumed trade-off between 'health' and 'the economy', fronted by the logorrheic quad of US President Donald Trump, UK Prime Minister Boris Johnson, India's Prime Minister Narendra Modi and Brazil's President Jair Bolsonaro, each backed up by their supporters in the media, business, the middle class, fringe libertarian groups, militias and religious leaders, whose revenues depend heavily on the presence of the faithful (see Chapters 8–11). The proponents of herd immunity tried to justify the dereliction of the paramount duty of the state, the protection of life, by appealing to the prohibitive costs of doing anything, their (highly selective) commitment to personal freedom, and the argument that, since democratic societies could not possibly impose rigorous lockdowns, they might as well not do anything much and, one day, the pandemic would go away 'like a miracle'.[6]

The pressure for herd immunity was evidently driven by avarice, wishful thinking, political misjudgement, irrational attachment to neoliberal ideology and a callous disregard for the lives of the old and those with fragile health or special needs who, from the point of view of the neoliberals in charge, were merely a dead weight on the fiscus (Cole, 2020; Tilley, 2020). The polemic also served as a smokescreen to cover up administrative delays and earlier policy failures. Those exchanges also brought to light a mass of supporters of herd immunity, who had considered the odds and decided to accept that brutal policy. Their views can be explained, in part, by naked greed and short-termism (Brooks, 2020) but, also, by the degradation of the welfare state and the widening social and economic inequalities under neoliberalism. They made it impossible for many workers and small businesspeople to stop earning an income even for short periods of time, regardless of the risks to their own lives and the lives of their loved ones. Many concluded that a lockdown would be economically disastrous and, in this light, accepted the hazard of COVID-19, and demanded their 'right' to work, in a tactical alliance with businesspeople who wanted their employees to risk *their* lives for the privilege of enriching them.

In other words, arguments for herd immunity did not merely reflect the short-term interests of capital, that understandably wanted workers to carry on producing profits regardless of cost in terms of lives lost. Herd immunity also reflected the economic imperatives weighing upon working people, especially the poorest, most marginalised and most precariously employed, and all those who live 'one paycheck away from poverty' (Wilpert, 2019), even in the AEs. Analysis of these material imperatives suggests that the need to choose between 'lockdowns' or 'herd immunity' was not imposed by the pandemic itself; instead, this dilemma was due to earlier political decisions. Specifically, once states dismantle safety nets and choose other priorities at the expense of protecting the public, they create an otherwise avoidable dilemma between health and the economy, with desperate masses of people lining up to support both positions and neither of them being entirely 'right' or 'wrong'.

The debates about herd immunity wasted time that could have been spent suppressing the coronavirus. Eventually, the evidence of success in China, New Zealand, Singapore, Vietnam and elsewhere, and mass pressures, especially from the middle classes and urban professionals with regular service sector jobs (that were, paradoxically, among the least vulnerable groups to the economic and health implications of the pandemic; al-Gharbi, 2020), forced even the most reluctant governments to impose movement restrictions, social distancing, mask use and, in many cases, lockdowns. However, the 'reluctant' governments generally did so as late as possible and only grudgingly and partially, while also undermining their own policies with mixed messages, convoluted rules riddled with nonsensical exceptions, topped up with incompetent implementation and premature reversals to 'normality'.[7] This would ensure that the coronavirus would spread in wave after wave of death, that would be interrupted only by mass vaccination.

In some cases, health protection duties were devolved to lower levels of administration which, nevertheless, remained under-resourced, ensuring that little could be done. In the 'reluctant' countries, testing and tracing for COVID-19 also tended to be haphazard, and health service staff were often left to cope with unmanageable workloads without adequate PPE: daily brushes with death gallantly accepted in the name of professionalism (Assa & Calderon, 2020; Barrera-Algarín et al., 2020). Dramatic pictures circulated showing nurses and doctors in wealthy countries treating desperately ill patients while wearing improvised masks and aprons made of refuse bags, because of the irresponsibility of politicians and the built-in limitations of neoliberal states (Glasser, 2020). This approach to the pandemic would lead to thousands of deaths, proving that those neoliberal governments had never really abandoned their preference for 'herd immunity'; they had merely shifted to its implementation by stealth.[8]

It is unquestionable that social distancing, masks and lockdowns saved millions of lives around the world. Given the lack of immunity of the population, the severity of the illness, the high rate of spread of the virus, the limited capacity of the world's health systems, and the absence of effective treatments or vaccines until 2021, it was always obvious that mask use and different forms of social distancing, including lockdowns, were the best health policy measures available. Since their effectiveness could not be denied through logical argument, the case for herd immunity tended to be hijacked by rowdy politicians, selfish businesspeople, science denialists, conspiracy theorists,[9] ultra-individualists, flat Earthers,

Nazi militias and religious madmen. Sometimes, they would appeal to God's will, sometimes to 'tradition' or to 'our cherished freedoms' and, while denying the severity of the pandemic, many also pushed quack cures, regardless of contradiction. The neoliberal governments wheeled their chosen medical experts into these debates; they were tasked with praising their masters' covenant with freedom, hailing the resilience of the country's health system, reminding the audience of the inevitability of death, and solemnly swearing that freedom-loving societies could not possibly contemplate a lockdown. Those scientists surrendered their integrity to plead for the protection of profits at the expense of life (Grey & Macaskill, 2020).

By mid-March 2020 the virus had already spread so widely that a global calamity was inevitable, even though masks and lockdowns could still limit contagion and protect health systems from collapse (Wearmouth, 2020). This had negative implications for the countries that had adopted a suppression strategy since the never-ending risk of contamination seeping in from abroad forced the 'successful' countries to keep their borders closed indefinitely. Conversely, as Brazil, France, Germany, Israel, Italy, the UK, the USA and other countries would discover, once the virus has taken root, any relaxation of the health measures in order to restart economic activity brought a spiralling number of cases and mounting casualties, creating the need further standstills.

Several governments found themselves paralysed by this dilemma and were unable to implement neither successful economic policies nor effective health policies (Saad-Filho, 2020a, 2020b, 2021). If, instead, the virus suppression policies enforced by several Asian countries had been followed more widely, the pandemic could have been avoided, millions of lives would have been saved, and the world economy would have been spared incalculable costs. To put it differently: the assumption of a trade-off between 'economic costs' and 'number of deaths' delayed decision-making and led to worse outcomes on both counts. The alternative of acting early and decisively against the virus could have addressed both challenges at the same time, with better outcomes and lower costs for all countries (Wren-Lewis, 2020). However, the approach to the pandemic in several authoritarian neoliberal countries led them to the worst of both worlds: countless unnecessary deaths as well as staggering economic losses, since the economy would *not* function 'normally' during the pandemic (Sinclair & Reed, 2020). It was abundantly proven that aggressive policies of elimination of the virus work best, while 'herd immunity' was worse than unworkable: it was criminal (Oliu-Barton et al., 2021).

## Inequalities and the Pandemic

The social consequences of the pandemic were jointly determined by the human vulnerability to the virus, public policies and the prevailing patterns of difference and inequality. It was soon found that COVID-19 tended to hit distinct social groups in distinct ways, which invariably penalised the weak disproportionately. Even in the same country, region or city, outcomes tended to vary depending not only on age (which became the best-known marker of vulnerability to COVID-19), but also income, wealth, employment, ancestry, ethnicity, gender, refugee status, co-morbidities, special needs and vulnerabilities, exposure to pollution and other triggers of ill-health, and ability to protect oneself from health-related hazards. These social fractures and differences offered gaps through which the coronavirus pushed its way into society.

Remarkably, as soon as the pandemic hit many of the super rich folklorically moved into their yachts and sailed away for a sublime experience of isolation (crew included; see Freeman, 2020). The merely rich tended to flee to their second homes at the beach, the countryside or the mountains. The middle classes found themselves working from home in the company of over-excited children, while the poor, already having worse health, on average, than the privileged, either lost their earnings entirely or had to risk their lives daily to perform much praised but invariably low-paid 'essential work' as nurses, care workers, porters, bus drivers, shopkeepers, builders, supermarket workers, sanitation officers, delivery workers and so on, while their families were locked up in cramped accommodation. Since they were, effectively, treated as being expendable, it is not surprising that the poor, disabled, ethnic minorities and other disadvantaged groups were dramatically over-represented in the death statistics.[10]

The class and racial impact of the pandemic overlapped with its gender implications, as women tend to crowd the lower and more precarious rungs of the labour market, cluster in the caring professions, take primary responsibility for their households and the wellbeing of elderly parents and children, and suffer more heavily from loneliness and the burdens of housework.[11] They also became more vulnerable to violence, abuse and neglect at home, as they were often trapped with the perpetrators during the lockdowns (Agüero, 2021). Adding insult to injury, some governments, especially in Eastern Europe, used emergency COVID-19 legislation to impose new restrictions to contraception and abortion services.[12] In these and other ways the pandemic worsened the inequalities that already existed under neoliberalism, with detrimental implications for democracy (Jolley, 2020).

## Notes

1. In the case of health: 'Investment in public health decreased in many countries. In the US, there was a brief infusion of cash into preparedness for perceived bioterror threats after the anthrax mailings of 2001. But funding for the Public Health Emergency Preparedness agreement among state and federal agencies fell from nearly a billion dollars in 2002 to $675 million in 2019. The minimal importance accorded public health was reflected in widespread cuts after the financial crisis of 2008. There has been a surge in hepatitis, Legionnaires', and diseases transmitted by sex or drinking water across the US, which public health experts attribute to health departments losing a fifth of their employees during that time ... In Europe, too, investment in public health plummeted after 2008. In 2019, a British think tank calculated that public health spending in England had fallen by £870 million just since 2014 and that this may have caused 130,000 deaths and a rise in chronic conditions, like diabetes, that incidentally also make you more likely to die from Covid-19' (MacKenzie, 2020, p. 41).
2. See Davis (2020a, 2020b), Egger and Zhu (2021), Lin et al. (2021), MacKenzie (2020, chs. 2–4), Ming Wang et al. (2006), Moody (2020), Vidal (2020), Wade (2021), Wallace (2016, 2020), Wallace et al. (2020), and Zahoor (2020).
3. See Oltermann (2020), Rudan (2020), Slattery et al. (2020), and Walker and Smith (2020).
4. For a detailed, country-by-country chronology of the early impact of the pandemic, see The Independent Panel (2021a, 2021b).
5. It was reported that Dominic Cummings, the British Prime Minister's Chief Adviser (apparently a title created by himself) argued for 'herd immunity, protect the economy, and if that means some pensioners die, too bad' (Sheridan 2020). This statement was denied later; see Chapter 8. For the similarly scandalous case of the USA, see Chapter 9.
6. Irish Times (2020). For an argument for 'herd immunity' drawing upon neoclassical economics, see Gourinchas (2020).
7. For an early and especially callous example of the cost of protecting profits at the expense of people, see Sidera (2020).

8. See Cockburn (2020) and Frey (2020). For the emblematic case of Sweden, see BBC News (2020), Bowman and Serodio (2020), Claeson and Hanson (2021), and I-SAGE (2020).
9. This category can include befuddled ultra-leftists, dazed hippies and the paranoid; see Bialasiewicz and Eckes (2021).
10. For an overview of the vast literature, see Hattenstone (2020), Kendi (2020), Mackey et al. (2021), Maltur et al. (2021), Marmot et al. (2020), Morales and Ali (2021), ONS (2021), PHE (2020), Qureshi et al. (2020), Romei (2020), Rosa (2020), Scheiber et al. (2020), Stevano et al. (2020), TUC (2021), and Younge (2020).
11. See, for example, Dang and Nguyen (2020), Pereznieto and Oehler (2021), Summers (2021), Tejani and Fukuda-Parr (2021), and Valentino-DeVries et al. (2020).
12. See Bijl (2020). For the wider abuse of the pandemic in order to perpetuate authoritarian governments in power, see Bueno de Mesquita et al. (2021), Gisselquist and Solanki (2020), and Johnson (2021).

## References

Agüero, J. M. (2021). COVID-19 and the rise of intimate partner violence. *World Development*, 137. https://doi.org/10.1016/j.worlddev.2020.105217

Al-Gharbi, M. (2020). *Disposable people*. https://thebaffler.com/latest/disposable-people-algharbi

Assa, J., & Calderon, C. (2020). *Privatization and pandemic: A cross-country analysis of COVID-19 rates and health-care financing structures*. https://ideas.repec.org/p/new/wpaper/2008.html

Barrera-Algarín, E. et al. (2020). COVID-19 neoliberalismo y sistemas sanitarios en 30 países de europa: Repercusiones en el número de fallecidos. *Revista Española de Salud Pública*, 94. https://recyt.fecyt.es/index.php/RESP/article/view/85707

BBC News. (2020). *Coronavirus: Sweden's Tegnell admits too many died*. https://www.bbc.co.uk/news/world-europe-52903717

Bialasiewicz, L., & Eckes, C. (2021). "Individual sovereignty" in pandemic times—A contradiction in terms? *Political Geography*, 85. https://doi.org/10.1016/j.polgeo.2020.102277

Bijl, M. (2020). *The Covid-19 crisis is exacerbating gender inequalities—But who cares?*. https://www.socialeurope.eu/the-covid-19-crisis-is-exacerbating-gender-inequalities-but-who-cares

Bowman, S., & Serodio, P. (2020). *Live free and die: Sweden's coronavirus experience*. https://thecritic.co.uk/live-free-and-die-swedens-coronavirus-experience/

Brooks, C. (2020). *Follow the money: Employers are behind the rush to reopen.* https://www.labornotes.org/2020/05/follow-money-employers-are-behind-rush-reopen

Bueno de Mesquita, J., Kapilashrami, A., & Meier, B. M. (2021). *Human rights dimensions of the COVID-19 pandemic*, Paper commissioned by The Independent Panel for Pandemic Preparedness and Response, https://theindependentpanel.org/documents/

Claeson, M., & Hanson, S. (2021). The Swedish COVID-19 strategy revisited. *The Lancet.* https://doi.org/10.1016/S0140-6736(21)00885-0-1

Cockburn, P. (2020). *Britain will seek coronavirus 'herd immunity' covertly or by default—Thanks to the failure of lockdown.* https://www.independent.co.uk/voices/boris-johnson-coronavirus-testing-nhs-covid-app-herd-immunity-b599887.html

Cole, B. (2020). *Brazil Government Aide Says COVID-19's toll on elderly will reduce pension deficit as country's outbreak escalates.* https://www.newsweek.com/brazil-government-aide-says-covid-19s-toll-elderly-will-reduce-pension-deficit-countrys-1506830

Conn, D., & Lewis, P. (2020). *Documents contradict UK government stance on covid-19 "Herd Immunity".* https://www.theguardian.com/world/2020/apr/12/documents-contradict-uk-government-stance-on-covid-19-herd-immunity

Dang, H.-A., & Nguyen, C. V. (2020). Gender inequality during the COVID-19 pandemic: Income, expenditure.

Davis, M. (2020a). *The monster is finally at the door.*ss https://mronline.org/2020/03/19/mike-davis-on-covid-19-the-monster-is-finally-at-the-door/

Davis, M. (2020b).*The monster enters: COVID-19, Avian flu, and the plagues of capitalism.* OR Books.

Dobbs, R., Lund, S., Woetzel, J., & Mutafchieva, M. (2015). *Debt and (not much) deleveraging* (McKinsey Global Institute Report). https://www.mckinsey.com/featured-insights/employment-and-growth/debt-and-not-much-deleveraging

Egger, P., & Zhu, J. (2021). How Covid-19 travels in- and outside of value chains and then affects the stock market: Evidence from China. *The World Economy.* https://doi.org/10.1111/TWEC.13134

Elliott, L. (2020). *Dozens of poorer nations seek IMF help amid coronavirus crisis.* https://www.theguardian.com/world/2020/mar/27/dozens-poorer-nations-seek-imf-help-coronavirus-crisis

Freeman, H. (2020). *Billionaires, please back off—We can't all self-isolate on a giant yacht.* https://www.theguardian.com/fashion/2020/mar/30/self-isolate-giant-yacht-david-geffen-social-media

Frey, I. (2020). *"Herd immunity" is epidemiological neoliberalism.* https://thequarantimes.wordpress.com/2020/03/19/herd-immunity-is-epidemiologi

cal-neoliberalism/?fbclid=IwAR1S6GyMrklnntU7c54CEEMceZOI92Ipf0rlWPCbY2nCKIEu3MCcARoGbOgThe
Gisselquist, R. M., & Solanki, D. (2020). *Coronavirus: Five ways some states have used the pandemic to curtail human rights and democracy*. https://theconversation.com/coronavirus-five-ways-some-states-have-used-the-pandemic-to-curtail-human-rights-and-democracy-151618
Glasser, S. B. (2020). *How did the U.S. end up with nurses wearing garbage bags?*. https://www.newyorker.com/news/letter-from-trumps-washington/the-coronavirus-and-how-the-united-states-ended-up-with-nurses-wearing-garbage-bags
Gourinchas, P.-O. (2020). *Flattening the pandemic and recession curves*. https://clausen.berkeley.edu/flattening-the-pandemic-and-recession-curves/
Grey, S., & MacAskill, A. (2020). *Johnson listened to his scientists about coronavirus—But they were slow to sound the alarm*. https://www.reuters.com/article/us-health-coronavirus-britain-path-speci-idUSKBN21P1VF
Hattenstone, S. (2020). *"The virus piggybacked on racism": Why did Covid-19 hit BAME families so hard?* https://www.theguardian.com/world/2020/aug/08/the-virus-piggybacked-on-racism-why-did-covid-19-hit-bame-families-so-hard
Irish Times. (2020). *'One day, it's like a miracle, it will disappear': Trump on Covid-19*. https://www.irishtimes.com/news/world/us/one-day-it-s-like-a-miracle-it-will-disappear-trump-on-covid-19-1.4370294
I-SAGE. (2020). *A closer look at Sweden's response to COVID-19: Independent SAGE Report 15*. https://www.independentsage.org/wp-content/uploads/2020/09/Sweden_case-study-v2.pdf
Johnson, S. (2021). *Cambodia accused of using Covid to edge towards 'totalitarian dictatorship'*. https://www.theguardian.com/global-development/2021/apr/19/cambodia-accused-of-using-covid-to-edge-towards-totalitarian-dictatorship
Jolley, R. (2020). *The regimes using coronavirus as an excuse to attack press freedom*. https://www.newstatesman.com/world/africa/2020/03/regimes-using-coronavirus-excuse-attack-press-freedom
Kendi, I. X. (2020). *What the racial data show*. https://www.theatlantic.com/ideas/archive/2020/04/coronavirus-exposing-our-racial-divides/609526/
Levenson, T. (2020). *The truth about Isaac Newton's productive plague*. https://www.newyorker.com/culture/cultural-comment/the-truth-about-isaac-newtons-productive-plague
Lin, F., Wang, X., & Zhou, M. (2021). How trade affects pandemics? Evidence from severe acute respiratory syndromes in 2003. *The World Economy*. https://doi.org/10.1111/twec.13127
MacKenzie, D. (2020). *COVID-19: The pandemic that never should have happened, and how to stop the next one*. The Bridge Street Press.

Mackey, C., et al. (2021). Racial and ethnic disparities in COVID-19-related infections, hospitalizations, and deaths: A systematic review. *Annals of Internal Medicine, 174*(3), 362–386.

Maltur, R., et al. (2021). Ethnic differences in SARS-CoV-2 infection and COVID-19-related hospitalisation, intensive care unit admission, and death in 17 million adults in England: An observational cohort study using the OpenSAFELY platform. *The Lancet, 397*(10286), 1711–1724.

Marmot et al. (2020). *Build back fairer: The COVID-19 Marmot Review*. https://www.health.org.uk/publications/build-back-fairer-the-covid-19-marmot-review

Ming Wang, et al. (2006). Food markets with live birds as source of avian influenza. *Emerging Infectious Diseases, 12*(11), 1773–1775.

Moody, K. (2020). *How "just in time" capitalism spread COVID-19*. https://spectrejournal.com/how-just-in-time-capitalism-spread-covid-19/

Morales, D. R., & Ali, S. N. (2021). COVID-19 and disparities affecting ethnic minorities. *The Lancet, 397*(10286), 1684–1685.

Oliu-Barton, M. et al. (2021). *SARS-CoV-2 elimination, not mitigation, creates best outcomes for health, the economy, and civil liberties*. https://www.thelancet.com/journals/lancet/article/PIIS0140-6736(21)00978-8/fulltext

Oltermann, P. (2020). *"Everyone was drenched in the virus": Was this Austrian Ski Resort a COVID-19 ground zero?*. https://www.theguardian.com/world/2020/sep/05/everyone-was-drenched-in-the-virus-was-this-austrian-ski-resort-a-covid-19-ground-zero

ONS [Office for National Statistics]. (2021). *Coronavirus (COVID-19) related deaths by occupation, England and Wales: Deaths registered between 9 March and 28 December 2020*. https://www.gov.uk/government/statistics/coronavirus-covid-19-related-deaths-by-occupation-england-and-wales-deaths-registered-between-9-march-and-28-december-2020

Pereznieto, P., & Oehler, I. (2021). *Social costs of the COVID-19 pandemic*, paper commissioned by The Independent Panel for Pandemic Preparedness and Response. https://theindependentpanel.org/documents/

PHE [Public Health England]. (2020). *Disparities in the risk and outcomes of COVID-19*. https://www.gov.uk/government/publications/covid-19-review-of-disparities-in-risks-and-outcomes

Qureshi, K., Kasstan, B., Meer, N., & Hill, S. (2020). *Submission of evidence on the disproportionate impact of COVID-19, and the UK government response, on ethnic minorities in the UK*. https://ghpu.sps.ed.ac.uk/ethnic-minorities-covid-19-uk/

Romei, V. (2020). *How the pandemic is worsening inequality*. https://www.ft.com/content/cd075d91-fafa-47c8-a295-85bbd7a36b50

Romei, V., & Giles, C. (2021). *UK suffers biggest drop in economic output in 300 years*. https://www.ft.com/content/96e19afd-88b3-4e8d-bc3e-a72bd1f60d3c

Rosa, S. K. (2020). *Two-thirds of coronavirus deaths are of people with disabilities*. https://novaramedia.com/2020/07/24/two-thirds-of-coronavirus-deaths-are-people-with-a-disability/

Rudan, I. (2020). A cascade of causes that led to the COVID-19 tragedy in Italy and in other European Union Countries. *Journal of Global Health*. https://www.ncbi.nlm.nih.gov/pmc/articles/PMC7125421/

Saad-Filho, A. (2020a). *Coronavirus, crisis, and the end of Neoliberalism*. https://socialistproject.ca/2020/04/coronavirus-crisis-and-the-end-of-neoliberalism/#more

Saad-Filho, A. (2020b). From COVID-19 to the end of neoliberalism. *Critical Sociology, 46*(4–5), 477–485.

Saad-Filho, A. (2021). Endgame: From crisis in neoliberalism to crises of neoliberalism. *Human Geography, 14*(1), 133–137.

Scheiber, N., Schwartz, N. D., & Hsu, T. (2020). *"White collar quarantine" over virus spotlights class divide*. https://www.nytimes.com/2020/03/27/business/economy/coronavirus-inequality.html

Sheridan, D. (2020). *No 10 forced to deny claims Dominic Cummings said 'if some pensioners die, too bad'*. https://www.telegraph.co.uk/politics/2020/03/22/no-10-forced-deny-claims-dominic-cummings-said-pensioners-die/

Sidera, A. (2020). *Bérgamo, la Masacre que la Patronal No Quiso Evitar*. https://ctxt.es/es/20200401/Politica/31884/Alba-Sidera-Italia-coronavirus-lombardia-patronal-economia-muertes.htm

Sinclair, I., & Read, R. (2020). *"A national scandal": A timeline of the UK government's woeful response to the coronavirus crisis*. https://bylinetimes.com/2020/04/11/a-national-scandal-a-timeline-of-the-uk-governments-woeful-response-to-the-coronavirus-crisis/

Slattery, G., Eisenhammer, S., & Perobelli, A. (2020). *Imported by the rich, coronavirus now devastating Brazil's poor*. https://www.reuters.com/article/us-health-coronavirus-brazil-poor/imported-by-the-rich-coronavirus-now-devastating-brazils-poor-idUSKBN22D549

Snowden, F. M. (2020). *Epidemics and society: From the Black death to the present*. Yale University Press.

Stevano, S., Ali, R., & Jamieson, M. (2020). Essential for what? A global social reproduction view on the re-organisation of work during the COVID-19 pandemic. *Canadian Journal of Development Studies*. https://doi.org/10.1080/02255189.2020.1834362

Summers, H. (2021). *UK government 'failed to consider gender' in its response to Covid pandemic'*. https://www.theguardian.com/world/2021/may/08/uk-government-failed-to-consider-gender-in-its-response-to-covid-pandemic

Tejani, S., & Fukuda-Parr, S. (2021). *Gender and Covid-19: Workers in global value chains*. https://ideas.repec.org/p/new/wpaper/2104.html

The Independent Panel. (2021a). *COVID-19: Make it the last pandemic*, paper commissioned by The Independent Panel for Pandemic Preparedness and Response, https://theindependentpanel.org/documents/

The Independent Panel. (2021b). *COVID-19: The authoritative chronology, December 2019-March 2020*, paper commissioned by The Independent Panel for Pandemic Preparedness and Response. https://theindependentpanel.org/documents/

Tilley, L. (2020). *Saying the quiet part out loud: Eugenics and the 'aging population' in conservative pandemic governance*. https://archive.discoversociety.org/2020/04/06/saying-the-quiet-part-out-loud-eugenics-and-the-aging-population-in-conservative-pandemic-governance/

TUC. (2021). *COVID-19 and insecure work*. https://www.tuc.org.uk/sites/default/files/2021-04/Covid-19%20and%20Insecure%20Work%20TUC%20template%20report%20130421.pdf

Valentino-DeVries, J., Lu, D., & Dance, G. (2020). *Location data says it all: Staying at home during coronavirus is a luxury*. https://www.nytimes.com/interactive/2020/04/03/us/coronavirus-stay-home-rich-poor.html

Vidal, J. (2020). *Human impact on wildlife to blame for spread of viruses, says study*. https://www.theguardian.com/environment/2020/apr/08/human-impact-on-wildlife-to-blame-for-spread-of-viruses-says-study-aoe

Wade, N. (2021). *The origin of COVID: Did people or nature open Pandora's box at Wuhan?*. https://thebulletin.org/2021/05/the-origin-of-covid-did-people-or-nature-open-pandoras-box-at-wuhan/

Walker, S., & Smith, H. (2020). *Why has Eastern Europe suffered less from the coronavirus that the west?* https://www.theguardian.com/world/2020/may/05/why-has-eastern-europe-suffered-less-from-coronavirus-than-the-west

Wallace, R. (2016). *Big farms make big flu: Dispatches on infectious disease, agribusiness, and the nature of science*. Monthly Review Press.

Wallace, R. (2020). *Dead epidemiologists: On the origins of COVID-19*. Monthly Review Press.

Wallace, R., Liebman, A., Chaves, L .F., & Wallace, R. (2020). *COVID-19 and the circuits of capital*. https://monthlyreview.org/2020/05/01/covid-19-and-circuits-of-capital/

Wearmouth, R. (2020). *Lockdown a week earlier would have halved UK coronavirus death toll, says Neil Ferguson*. https://www.huffingtonpost.co.uk/entry/lockdown-week-earlier-coronavirus-death-neil-ferguson_uk_5ee0f82ec5b66552b9a6e912

Wilpert, G. (2019). *Over 40% of US households are one paycheck away from poverty*. https://therealnews.com/over-40-of-us-households-are-one-paycheck-away-from-poverty

Wren-Lewis, S. (2020). *Who still thinks austerity was a good idea?* https://mainlymacro.blogspot.com/2020/04/who-still-thinks-austerity-was-good-idea.html?m=1

Younge, G. (2020). *We can't breathe*. https://www.newstatesman.com/politics/uk/2020/06/we-cant-breathe

Zahoor, B. (2020). *Health: Why new viruses continue to spread*. https://www.dawn.com/news/1546447

CHAPTER 6

# Post-pandemic Realities

This chapter reviews the impact of COVID-19 across the economy, politics and the dominant ideologies. The economic contraction caused by the pandemic was the most severe since the dawn of capitalism. The speed of the collapse was stunning, and it led most governments to draw up emergency plans that, at least initially, were based on the experience with the GFC. However, it rapidly became clear that this was much bigger and it had wider implications. The economic policy measures adapted accordingly and, in different ways, all countries managed to contain the disaster. The pandemic had more subtle but equally corrosive implications for the political systems and ideologies of neoliberalism, for example, strengthening some leaders and weakening others. Just as interestingly, examination of the ideological implications of the pandemic shows important faultlines in neoliberal thought and practices.

## Economic Policies After the Shock

The degenerating economic and political dynamics examined in previous chapters was overwhelmed by COVID-19. The arrival of the pandemic triggered a major economic contraction (Roubini, 2020; Saad-Filho, 2020; Wolf, 2020). To paraphrase *The Communist Manifesto*, all that was solid suddenly melted into air: production tumbled as workers became



A. Saad-Filho, *The Age of Crisis*,
https://doi.org/10.1007/978-3-030-81608-7_6

sick or were frightened of getting sick, or because cities, regions or countries went into lockdown; 'globalisation' went into reverse in a disorderly manner as transnational supply chains faltered and hard borders returned, at least for people, whose movements became almost impossible. Trade was also affected as some nations imposed export controls on health equipment, PPE and vaccines, while finance was not directly constrained at all (both trade and finance suffered aftershocks either because the workers became unable to perform their duties, or because production was thrown into confusion). The impact of countless disruptions would undermine centrally important systems of provision, e.g., those centred in the auto, aerospace and electronics industries.

As the world's largest economies imploded, a long line of companies rushed to their respective governments to beg for a bailout, starting with the banks—always fastest at everything that matters—followed by the railways, airlines, airports, the tourism sector, charities, food and entertainment, education, retail, construction, and so on, with the precise sectoral composition and speed of collapse depending on country and circumstances. They were successful only unevenly; for example, large capital and finance were immediately sheltered, while many small capitals would be crushed by their running costs, lack of demand and the loss of credit. Tens of millions of jobs vanished in a matter of days, while millions of businesses lost their employees, customers, suppliers and credit lines and countless precarious and (nominally) 'self-employed' workers—a typical form of employment under neoliberalism—lost everything in an instant. In contrast, logistics, deliveries, communications, social media and other sectors boomed, mostly to the benefit of large capitals. This structural readjustment of the economy led stock markets to nosedive and, subsequently, shoot up, pulled by the rescued industries and the new leading sectors (Ghosh, 2020; Toussaint, 2020).

The economic depression was accompanied by spiralling fiscal deficits that far exceeded the legal limits wherever they had been imposed in the previous phase of neoliberalism, demonstrating that those limits were purely arbitrary. At the same time, neoliberal discourses about the imperative of 'fiscal austerity' and the limitations of public policy suddenly vanished as neoliberal governments, intransigent Austrians and hardcore ideologues, shorn of principle or shame, scrambled into the lifeboat of a *faux* Keynesianism, as they invariably do when economies tank, and begged governments to do whatever was necessary to save private enterprise. Their screeching turnaround was impressed on the TV screens and splashed all over the mainstream media, with everyone that matters claiming that state intervention was imperative and that governments should be reproached only for what they had not yet done. It turns out that saving capitalism required the deployment of the state capacities that the ideologues of neoliberalism and their hired economists had, until recently, either denied on principle or rejected as being inefficient or unaffordable.

It was admitted that, in an emergency (and, consequently, at all other times) the state *can* create money from nothing and that it *can* save selected sectors, as long as they are deemed to be 'essential'—which, by implication, was not the case for housing, health, social care, employment, and so on in better economic times. No doubt the traditional discourses will return when circumstances change and memories fade. At that point, the state will become 'bad' again, and public services will be deemed ready for another round of culling.

The fact that every policy rule could be suspended to address the pandemic suggests that those rules were never meant to be unconditional (which is surely a good thing), but, if so, it remains unclear why they should be required in 'normal' times, and who gets to decide what rules should be lifted, when, by what criteria, by how much, and for how long. So much for the neoliberal fetish about 'policy rules'. The outcome was that, in many countries, the fiscal deficits in 2020 vastly exceeded anything ever recorded in peacetime, since the breakdown in economic activity led to a precipitous decline in tax revenues just as governments had to engage in massive fiscal stimulus and extraordinarily expansive monetary policies in order to salvage finance (once again), compensate selected sectors for their lost incomes and revenues, and stabilise aggregate demand.[1]

At first, many governments, especially the USA, UK and the Eurozone, simply dusted off the economic policies implemented after the GFC, and restarted their programme of subsidies to capital in general, and finance in particular, through additional public spending and quantitative easing. However, these programmes proved to be insufficient almost immediately: the economic disaster in 2020 was much more comprehensive than in 2008, the crisis was much bigger, and the bailouts would be much more costly and complex (Sandbu, 2020). In response, the main Central Banks escalated their response and started providing finance directly to large companies (Amaro, 2020; Brenner, 2020): essentially the state started handing money to selected capitalists unconditionally (in several cases, those businesses promptly passed these resources to their shareholders as dividends, in a scandalous example of corruption in the private sector, if corruption is defined as the misappropriation of public funds) (Guida, 2020; Wood, 2020). In order to disguise the unseemly spectacle of billionaires, often tax exiles, begging for subsidies from the same exchequer that they had previously evaded, several governments promised to support small businesses and the incomes of the workers as well. However, this was generally done as an afterthought, hesitantly, miserly, through their employers rather than directly and, often, for the instrumental reason of avoiding the implosion of businesses and aggregate demand, rather than to support everyone in an hour of need.

These policies contradicted even the appearance of 'free markets'; implicitly, they also recognised the dysfunctions of financialisation. At a deeper level, the privatisation of 'helicopter money' revealed the enmeshing of the state into individual circuits of capital, as Central Banks arbitrarily closed these circuits and created private profits directly. In the meantime, finance was allowed to focus on the enrichment of itself.[2]

Aside from the size of the shock and the channels of policy, there are two striking differences between the GFC and the pandemic-induced crisis in 2020. First is their origin; while the former derived from financial speculation attached to US subprime mortgages (see Chapter 2), the latter was bound to trade flows and the circulation of goods and people (see Chapter 5). In this sense, while the GFC showed the limits of neoliberal financialisation, the corona-crisis highlighted the limits of globalisation. Second is that the GFC led to immediate losses to finance; in contrast, given its origins in the 'real' economy and the adoption of finance-friendly policies in response, the pandemic triggered a stock market boom that boosted the wealth of the rich: a shocking process of state-sponsored financial engorgement, free from windfall taxes or any form of shared sacrifice.

The pandemic shattered the residual coherence of the economic policy framework in most neoliberal countries. Experience since the transitions to neoliberalism and, even more clearly, since the GFC had already shown that neoliberalism limits policy space and is incompatible with democracy. In turn, the pandemic tore the connection between neoliberal policies and fiscal austerity, that was both a symbol and a key tool of enforcement of neoliberalism itself. Like Wile E. Coyote, neoliberalism was shown to be running on air, especially in the AEs, in the fervent hope that the unprecedented fiscal impulse would allow the economy to cross the chasm of the pandemic and find solid ground on the other side. Once there, with the economy safely recovering, a new round of 'austerity' would become possible, overtly seeking to return to the pre-COVID-19 (if not pre-2007) fiscal position, even though there is no reason to do this (Atkinson, 2020). Instead, fiscal austerity would serve, once again, to give credibility to neoliberalism and as a disciplinary device enforcing social order through the pain of deprivation and scarcity, aiming to push the poor to keep producing riches for the wealthy without complaint.

This is unlikely to work as intended. First, even a decade of post-GFC 'fiscal austerity' had not managed to return most economies to the *status quo ante*. Second, after decades of neoliberalism the Western economies had already reaped all the low-hanging fruit, and further welfare cuts would likely require brutal repression, potentially rupturing the social fabric, exhausting the institutions of democracy, and fatally undermining the legitimacy of the government. Third, while many economies accumulated large debts during World War II, those debts were paid off in the following decades because of rapid economic growth and moderate inflation. These conditions no longer apply, and it is difficult to see how mountainous amounts of public debt can decline in stagnant economies operating with zero inflation. Finally, the ideology of 'austerity' has been demoralised, and the obvious fact that the billionaires have gained hugely during the pandemic makes it difficult to explain why the 'losers' should sacrifice themselves again for the betterment of the privileged (Rothwell, 2020; Sharma, 2021). This points to the possibility of a long period of crisis politics with unpredictable implications. These grave circumstances, and the bubbling political instability in the background, can help to explain the expansionary policy choices of US President Joe Biden, even if similar choices may not be either viable or acceptable elsewhere.

In the meantime, it is likely that capitalism will continue to experience severe finance-driven crises without much hope of prosperity between them. Even in the short term, the descent into the corona-crisis was accompanied by promises of a rapid V-shaped recovery, in which the economy would bottom out because of the pandemic and the lockdowns but it would just as surely bounce back since the workers, capital stock, markets, financial structures, know-how and so on were readily available. This was always unlikely: the crisis disorganised global supply chains, destroyed markets, ruptured credit lines, undermined expectations and investments and destabilised the labour markets, with severe implications for consumption and savings. Capitalist economies would recover from the shock, but neither easily nor rapidly.

The myth of a V-shaped recovery was soon replaced by the suggestion of a U-shaped trajectory, in which the economy bounces back fully, but only after a lag. This was also incredible, because of the destruction of capital stock in the bottom part of the cycle, and the need for a significant uplift in expectations in order to unleash a new cycle of (hopefully 'green') investment and growth. The next wave of optimism centred on the notion of a W-shaped trajectory, in which the economy would be gripped by a second downturn, for example, because of successive pandemic waves (which, in Israel, Iran, Italy, South Africa, the UK and elsewhere, turned out to be three or even four waves). This approach simply assumes that the economy must recover fully in a reasonable time, but there is no reason for this to happen given the collapse in demand, the structural economic changes following from the pandemic, and the likely pressures to stabilise the fiscal and monetary policy variables as soon as possible. In the end, there was no bounce-back between the pandemic waves. Two possibilities emerged subsequently: a pessimistic L-shaped trajectory, in which the economy bottoms out and becomes stuck in stagnation for many years (a scenario rendered plausible by the downward trajectory of most AEs in previous decades), and a K-shaped recovery by which, after the pandemic, some sectors prosper (especially, in the real world, the rich and the tech firms), while others continue to descend (e.g., small retail capitals, travel, tourism, transport, entertainment, and so on) (Edgecliffe-Johnson, 2020). These increasingly pessimistic scenarios suggested that capitalism was running out of ideas and energy to implement even the old ones. The most significant policy innovation in this context is the 'Biden plan' in the USA which, if taken forward fully, could offer a temporary escape route (see Chapter 9). At the time of writing, though, this remains unclear.

Finally, the pandemic is likely to bring about three long-term economic changes. First, the 'flexible' labour markets typical of neoliberalism tend to become even more flexible, for example with workers, without alternatives, being dismissed and (re)hired with worse contracts than they had before. Second, many industries, especially in the service sector, had to shift towards online work in a matter of days, rather than the years that this transition would normally have taken. This will inevitably lead to another round of restructuring involving severe devaluations of capital tied up in offices in (previously highly expensive) city centres, as workers move to satellite locations or are pushed to work from home. In turn, new forms of tech-based discipline will be needed to control the homeworkers

(Walker, 2021). Third, and closely related, collective spaces will tend to empty out, not only for reasons related to production, but also because of changes in consumption. In particular, as more work is performed from home, consumption will also tend to be dislocated to the domestic sphere, restructuring social reproduction and home life.

These dislocations of capital accumulation towards the home sphere are unlikely to expand the autonomy of the workers. The tendency is, instead, for capital to colonise the last space under the control of the working class. First, the workers lost their workplace to capital as a consequence of the enclosures and their concentration in factories and offices in the wake of the industrial revolution (Marx, 1976, part VII). Subsequently, the workers lost the high streets to commercial capital as large-scale commodity production led to the reorganisation of trade into large supermarkets and department stores. Then the workers lost the virtual space of the internet, that was originally open, to gigantic monopolies: Microsoft, Google, Apple, Facebook and the like. After the pandemic, those forces have taken over homes, work and leisure time, moving to dominate the entire day rather than merely its working part, and taking over all spaces of social reproduction.[3]

## Politics and Ideology

It was shown in previous sections that the economic implications of COVID-19 are bound to be both severe and long-running. The pandemic will also have subtle but potentially dramatic implications for democracy and the ideologies and political legitimacy of neoliberalism. In the context of the crises examined in Parts I and II, these developments could have calamitous implications for the system of accumulation.

Even before COVID-19, many democracies were already operating under stress and, in some cases, open political systems had been bent out of shape by the onslaught of different forms of authoritarian neoliberalism. It emerged that those nations were also highly vulnerable to the pandemic, and several governments found themselves enveloped by a cataclysm that they were unable to address (see Part IV). In these countries, poor preparation, self-imposed weaknesses and vulnerabilities, policy incoherence, lack of institutional capacity, political reluctance, incompetence and failures of the imagination blended into an extraordinary organisational and health chaos. The Quartet of Calamity (UK, USA,

Brazil and India) offer especially vivid examples of devastation driven by authoritarian neoliberalism.

It was shown above that, early on, some of the governments closely attached to authoritarian neoliberalism looked for excuses to avoid taking measures against the coronavirus, in line with their preference for 'herd immunity'. The US and UK governments, in particular, made a case for passivity by referring to the impossibility of democracies suppressing the virus as effectively as authoritarian regimes could, because of their wide-ranging controls over the citizenry which were presumably more abhorrent to Western 'democrats' than death itself (Kavanagh and Singh, 2020; Stasavage, 2020). The political right also tended to decry lockdowns because they allegedly violated the right to free movement (see, for example, Olson, 2020), although their concerns could be attributed to the wish to protect private profits at the expense of the health of strangers.

While the vast majority of the left pushed for strong measures to protect life regardless of economic cost, some groupuscules and academic mavericks denounced lockdowns as being both repressive and iniquitous (e.g., Agamben, 2020a, 2020b, 2020c, 2020d; Sotiris, 2020; for a critique, see Dale, 2020). These approaches are indefensible from the point of view of the preservation of life. In particular, public health policies inevitably infringe upon civil liberties, but policies can be time-limited, tempered, focused tightly and subjected to democratic control, invalidating general claims about the encroachment of the state.

In reality, however, authoritarian neoliberals were already in power. From the depths of tragedy, with deaths needlessly piling up, some governments spotted an opportunity to hoard additional powers, consolidate their rule by authoritarian means, and secure the country for neoliberalism. To do this, they blamed the health outcomes on the lack of public compliance, and claimed emergency powers to monitor the population, control movements and the provision of vital goods and services, suppress protests, intercept private communications with the excuse of cross-checking contacts and health status, and sought to impose assorted limitations on personal freedoms, sometimes deploying the military to secure these outcomes (Csernatoni, 2020). In practice, the use of these powers and their rollback after the pandemic will depend on the strength of each interest group, with capital in general, and finance in particular, enjoying an in-built advantage given their unquestionable hegemony over the neoliberal state.

The shameless power grab by authoritarian neoliberal administrations regardless of their own failure to deliver healthcare and protect the population damaged their credibility, especially in the UK and USA—precisely the epicentres of the loss of legitimacy of finance in the wake of the GFC. Bereft of plausible claims to administrative competence and leaking mass support, those authoritarian governments clung to power by the fingertips of ideology, lies and an increasingly strident discourse which, it turned out, was insufficient to save Donald Trump. In the meantime, the horror unfolded outside, since the coronavirus remained impervious to bluster and posturing. The intensity of the tragedy and the policy fog allowed some governments to get away, at least temporarily, with promises of miracle cures, improvisations and endless policy reversals.

As constitutional democracies suffered under the strain, the ideological anchors of neoliberalism were damaged at four levels. First, the pandemic showed that the neoliberal ideology of individualism, by which all social problems can be dissolved into individual responsibilities and personal calculations of pain and pleasure, was a fraud.[4] To the astonishment of staunch conservatives of many hues, it turns out that there is, after all, such a thing as society (Saunders, 2020). It became evident that a pandemic is a social phenomenon that cannot be addressed by individuals (see Chapter 5), and that social problems must be tackled by a capable public sector—surely an unwelcome development after decades of carping, undermining and dismantling the state by successive neoliberal administrations. Just as lone individuals cannot make their country safe from an epidemic or nurse themselves when they fall sick, only the state can contain the economic meltdown, save entire economic sectors, secure income flows when the economy seizes up, enforce lockdowns, resource the health service, fund the development of vaccines, and manage universal inoculations. Finally, the inhumanity of capitalism's profit imperative was unmasked through the overwhelming rejection of 'herd immunity', that would inevitably bring about millions of fatalities.

Second, neoliberal untruths about the imperative of 'fiscal austerity', drawing upon false analogies between household budgets and government deficits, were proven to be wrong. The economic policies deployed after the GFC and, with much greater force, after the pandemic, showed that the state can create money from nothing; that is, in certain circumstances there *is* a magic money tree, and its fruits can save households, selected businesses and entire sectors.

Third, the pandemic showed that capitalist myths about profits being the reward for 'abstinence' and 'risk-taking' were wholly misleading. In the pandemic, profits were determined by the luck of the draw and the economic channels kept open by the state, and they tended to benefit those who were already operating in growth fields: telecoms, tech, logistics, delivery, online platforms, and similar fields, with grave losses for retail, entertainment, transport, travel and tourism, and so on. The billionaires profited from the state-sponsored boost to the stock market, while small capitals and precarious workers tended to lose heavily (Collins et al., 2020; Rushe, 2020).

Fourth, the stresses of the pandemic facilitated the spread of anti-scientific worldviews associated with the politics of strife that are typical of 'spectacular' authoritarian leaders. For several years, mainstream politicians, excited academics, hired pundits and self-interested market operators used their privileged access to the media to praise neoliberalism and its institutions, proclaim that this is the best of all possible worlds, and insist that 'there is no alternative' regardless of actual outcomes, while belittling alternative views and the experiences of the 'losers'. They also repeated the ideologies of individualism and 'choice' that served to validate neoliberalism, and called them 'scientific truths'. Those mantras, myths and falsehoods gradually bled into a destructive mass scepticism of settled knowledge and a profound aversion to politics, academic research and even the mainstream media itself.

Eventually, the neoliberal cult of individual sovereignty fostered the *individualisation of the truth*, as audiences felt disconnected from the 'experts' and thought themselves entitled to believe in 'alternative facts' (in the immortal words of US Presidential Counsellor Kellyanne Conway, drawing upon an earlier generation of neocons) in all spheres of life, however implausible, unreasonable or conspiratorial they may be. In other words, since I can choose my favourite brand of cornflakes without regard for the opinion of others, I can also believe that the Earth is flat, that the coronavirus is a hoax, that vaccines do not work, and that the US government is run by paedophile lizards. Similarly, no one can impose masks, social distancing or lockdowns on me, and so on, in a bonfire of certainties that, if unchecked, would consume geostationary satellites, long-distance transport, the internet, statistical medicine, water treatment plants and much else. In the meantime, a demented fringe of anti-vaxxers, flat Earthers and religious fanatics uttered hilarious denials of the pandemic at great personal risk,[5] peddled miracle cures based on unproven remedies, or prayed and fasted together with Brazil's President Jair Bolsonaro (Phillips and Phillips, 2020).[6]

## Notes

1. Fiscal support during the pandemic reached almost US$16 trillion (15% of global GDP) in 2020 alone (Levy Yeyati & Filippini, 2021, p. 3). For an overview of the economic policy debates and responses during the pandemic, see Brodeur et al. (2021).
2. The timeline of the Fed's response to the crisis is reviewed in Saphir and Dunsmuir (2020).
3. For a discussion, see Collinson (2021), Harris (2021), ILO (2020), O'Brien (2020), and Usborne (2020).
4. For an overview of neoliberal ideology, see Kiely (2018) and Mirowski and Plehwe (2009).
5. This did not always end well; see, for example, 247 (2020), France24 (2020), Maqbool (2020), Risess (2020), and Torres (2020).
6. The Argentine actor and director Ricardo Darín succinctly put it, 'it is very difficult to struggle against the pandemic of imbecility' (Conti, 2020).

## References

247. (2020). *Prefeito bolsonarista, para quem a cura da Covid-19 viria de igrejas, é internado em hospital de luxo com a doença*. https://www.brasil247.com/regionais/sudeste/prefeito-bolsonarista-para-quem-a-cura-da-covid-19-viria-de-igrejas-e-internado-em-hospital-de-luxo-com-a-doenca

Agamben, G. (2020a). *The invention of an epidemic*. http://www.journal-psychoanalysis.eu/coronavirus-and-philosophers/

Agamben, G. (2020b). *Clarifications*. https://itself.blog/2020/03/17/giorgio-agamben-clarifications/

Agamben, G. (2020c). *Biosecurity and politics*. https://medium.com/@ddean3000/biosecurity-and-politics-giorgio-agamben-396f9ab3b6f4

Agamben, G. (2020d). *Requiem for the students*. https://medium.com/@ddean3000/requiem-for-the-students-giorgio-agamben-866670c11642

Amaro, S. (2020). *European Central Bank takes its pandemic bond buying to 1.35 trillion euros to try to prop up economy*. https://www.cnbc.com/2020/06/04/european-central-bank-ramps-up-its-pandemic-bond-buying-to-1point35-trillion-euros.html

Atkinson, A. (2020). *George Osborne, architect of U.K. Austerity, says new cuts needed post-crisis*. https://www.bloomberg.com/news/articles/2020-04-20/architect-of-u-k-austerity-says-retrenchment-needed-post-crisis

Brenner, R. (2020). Escalating plunder. *New Left Review, 123*, 5–22.

Brodeur, A., Gray, D., Islam, A., & Bhuiyan, S. (2021). A literature review of the economics of COVID-19. *Journal of Economic Surveys*. https://doi.org/10.1111/joes.12423

Collins, C., Ocampo, O., & Paslaski, S. (2020). *Billionaire Bonanza*. https://ips-dc.org/wp-content/uploads/2020/04/Billionaire-Bonanza-2020.pdf

Collinson, A. (2021). *The new class divide—How Covid-19 exposed and exacerbated workplace inequality in the UK*. https://www.tuc.org.uk/blogs/new-class-divide-how-covid-19-exposed-and-exacerbated-workplace-inequality-uk

Conti, J. (2020). *Ricardo Darín em entrevista disse: "É muito difícil lutar contra a pandemia de imbecis"*. https://www.contioutra.com/ricardo-darin-em-entrevista-disse-e-muito-dificil-lutar-contra-a-pandemia-de-imbecis/

Csernatoni, R. (2020). New states of emergency: Normalizing techno-surveillance in the time of COVID-19. *Global Affairs, 6*(3), 301–310.

Dale, G. (2020). *Lockdown politics: A response to panagiotis sotiris*. https://www.historicalmaterialism.org/blog/lockdown-politics-response-to-panagiotis-sotiris

Edgecliffe-Johnson, A. (2020). *Corporate America experiences 'K-shaped' recovery*. https://www.ft.com/content/258b74d8-6bac-47e5-a675-8f091b25db3e

France24. (2020). *Israel health minister under fire over ultra-Orthodox COVID-19 crisis*. https://www.france24.com/en/20200408-israel-health-minister-under-fire-over-ultra-orthodox-covid-19-crisis

Ghosh, J. (2020a). *The pandemic and the global economy*. https://www.dissentmagazine.org/online_articles/the-pandemic-and-the-global-economy

Guida, V. (2020). *Companies shed workers, paid dividends after getting Fed aid, panel finds*. https://www.politico.com/news/2020/09/23/companies-shed-workers-paid-dividends-after-getting-fed-aid-panel-finds-420537

Harris, J. (2021). *Homeworking sounds good—Until your job takes over your life*. https://www.theguardian.com/commentisfree/2021/mar/07/homeworking-job-takes-over-life-office-grind-remote-working.

ILO. (2020). Covid-19 and the world of work: Impact and policy responses. *ILO Monitor*. https://www.ilo.org/wcmsp5/groups/public/---dgreports/---dcomm/documents/briefingnote/wcms_738753.pdf

Kavanagh, M. M., & Singh, R. (2020). Democracy, capacity, and coercion in pandemic response: COVID-19 in comparative political perspective. *Journal of Health Politics, Policy and Law, 45*(6), 997–1012.

Kiely, R. (2018). *The neoliberal paradox*. Edward Elgar.

Levy Yeyati, E., & Filippini, F. (2021). *Social and economic impact of COVID-19*, paper commissioned by The Independent Panel for Pandemic Preparedness and Response, https://theindependentpanel.org/documents/

Maqbool, A. (2020). *Coronavirus: Pastor who decried 'hysteria' dies after attending Mardi Gras*. https://www.bbc.co.uk/news/world-us-canada-52157824

Marx, K. (1976). *Capital* (Vol. 1). Penguin.

Mirowski, P., & Plehwe, D. (Eds.). (2009). *The road from Mont Pèlerin: The making of the neoliberal thought collective*. Harvard University Press.

O'Brien, H. (2020). *What's behind the headlines demanding a return to the office?*. https://www.theguardian.com/commentisfree/2020/sep/01/office-workers

Olson, W. (2020). *Are the lockdown orders constitutional?* https://www.cato.org/publications/commentary/are-lockdown-orders-constitutional

Phillips, T., & Phillips, D. (2020). *Bolsonaro dragging Brazil towards Coronavirus calamity, experts fear*. https://www.theguardian.com/world/2020/apr/12/bolsonaro-dragging-brazil-towards-coronavirus-calamity-experts-fear

Rothwell, J. (2020). *The unequal distribution of economic damage from COVID-19*. https://news.gallup.com/opinion/gallup/311714/unequal-distribution-economic-damage-covid.aspx

Roubini, N. (2020). *Coronavirus pandemic has delivered the fastest, deepest economic shock in history*. https://www.theguardian.com/business/2020/mar/25/coronavirus-pandemic-has-delivered-the-fastest-deepest-economic-shock-in-history

Rushe, D. (2020). *Making billions v making ends meet: How the pandemic has split the US economy in two*. https://www.theguardian.com/us-news/2020/aug/16/us-inequality-coronavirus-pandemic-unemployment

Saad-Filho, A. (2020). From COVID-19 to the end of neoliberalism. *Critical Sociology, 46*(4–5), 477–485.

Sandbu, M. (2020). *Huge fiscal spending is needed to fight the Coronavirus downturn*. https://www.ft.com/content/9963f71e-67b2-11ea-800d-da70cff6e4d3

Saphir, A., & Dunsmuir, L. (2020). *Timeline: Fed's response—Pandemic downturn vs financial crisis*. https://www.reuters.com/article/us-health-coronavirus-fed-timeline/timeline-feds-response-pandemic-downturn-vs-financial-crisis-idUSKCN21R2BC

Saunders, R. (2020). *"There is such a thing as society": Has Boris Johnson repudiated thatcherism?*. https://www.newstatesman.com/politics/uk/2020/03/boris-johnson-thatcher-society-no-such-thing-policies

Sharma, R. (2021). *The billionaire boom: How the super-rich soaked up Covid cash*. https://www.ft.com/content/747a76dd-f018-4d0d-a9f3-4069bf2f5a93

Sotiris, P. (2020). Thinking beyond the lockdown: On the possibility of a democratic biopolitics. *Historical Materialism, 28*(3), 3–38.

Stasavage, D. (2020). Democracy, autocracy, and emergency threats: Lessons for COVID-19 from the last thousand years. *International Organization, 74*, 1–17.

Torres, E. (2020). *30-year-old dies after attending 'COVID party' thinking virus was a 'hoax'*. https://www.abc15.com/news/coronavirus/30-year-old-dies-after-attending-covid-party-thinking-virus-was-a-hoax

Toussaint, E. (2020). *The capitalist pandemic, coronavirus and the economic crisis*. http://internationalviewpoint.org/spip.php?article6458

Usborne, S. (2020). *End of the office: The quiet, grinding loneliness of working from home*. https://www.theguardian.com/money/2020/jul/14/end-of-the-office-the-quiet-grinding-loneliness-of-working-from-home.

Walker, P. (2021). *Call centre staff to be monitored via webcam for home-working "infractions"*. https://www.theguardian.com/business/2021/mar/26/teleperformance-call-centre-staff-monitored-via-webcam-home-working-infractions

Wolf, M. (2020). *The world economy is now collapsing*. https://www.ft.com/content/d5f05b5c-7db8-11ea-8fdb-7ec06edeef84

Wood, Z. (2020). *Tesco defends £635m dividend payout after coronavirus tax break*. https://www.theguardian.com/business/2020/apr/08/tesco-sales-up-30-per-cent-because-of-pre-lockdown-stockpiling-coronavirus

PART IV

# Case Studies in Disaster

CHAPTER 7

# A Very Neoliberal Tragedy

The COVID-19 pandemic was immersed in a neoliberal context, but it also developed in national circumstances and within given political conditions. Those circumstances shaped government responses, both structurally (the impact of COVID-19 and the possibilities of treatment were very different in the Global North and the Global South), and circumstantially (an election months earlier could have empowered leaders capable of confronting the pandemic, or utterly committed to denialism). This chapter examines those constraints and sets the scene for a more detailed examination of country cases in the following chapters.

## COVID-19 in the North and the South

The pandemic triggered an unprecedented economic collapse in the Global North. Output, trade and employment imploded, with devastating consequences for tens of millions of people. Production and finance were paralysed in several countries, and debts could no longer be serviced. Stock markets crashed, and tens of millions of workers either lost their jobs entirely, or were placed in limbo. In the meantime, several Western governments fumbled their response to the crisis. They wasted time, and demonstrated abundantly their disregard for the main task of governance: protecting the population and their livelihoods. The Quartet of Calamity were at the forefront of the disaster.



A. Saad-Filho, *The Age of Crisis*,
https://doi.org/10.1007/978-3-030-81608-7_7

Excruciatingly slowly, and through different combinations of QE, fiscal spending, regulatory changes, transfers, movement controls, social distancing, lockdowns, mass testing, hospital care and, eventually, mass vaccination, most Western and East Asian countries managed to contain the pandemic: social cohesion, state institutions and health systems survived their biggest challenge since World War II, despite huge disparities in performance. Outcomes depended on health systems, welfare provision, state capacity, fiscal resources, the power of the Central Bank and other variables. They allowed governments in the Global North to provide reasonably good healthcare even if, in some cases, systems only barely avoided collapse (e.g., in parts of Italy, Spain, the USA and the UK). Those states also had to manage unprecedented lockdowns.

Countries in the Global South had similar challenges, but they also had to face complex social crises in addition to the crises of health and the economy that afflicted the Global North. The DEs tend to have lower productive capacity and lower productivity than the AEs, less fiscal and financial resources and more limited institutional and managerial capacity to address the pandemic. They also tend to have larger current account deficits, heavy debt service commitments and tight balance of payments constraints, and depend on volatile commodity exports, external aid and workers' remittances, regardless of the availability of IMF lending facilities (Elliott, 2020a; Stubbs et al., 2020). These limitations implied that most DEs could not guarantee jobsor support output and demand through subsidies, tax rebates or large-scale transfers to households like the AEs could, and their Central Banks could not purchase large quantities of public and private papers in the secondarymarkets.

The impact of the pandemic in the Global South was compounded by the limited supply of public services and amenities, including clean water, food, electricity and sanitation, as well as poor housing and the prevalence of severe co-morbidities among the population, ranging from malnutrition to tuberculosis, malaria and HIV/AIDS. In turn, the economic impact of COVID-19 could be especially disruptive if the pandemic reduced import capacity or the ability to service external debt, or if it threatened inflationary spikes. In turn, the limitations in their health systems left many DEs severely exposed to the coronavirus and with limited scope to confront a surge in infections (Nordling 2020; UNECA 2020; WHO 2020).

Health systems across the Global South are often precarious in terms of capacity, staff, resilience and access. For example, 34 sub-Saharan African countries (out of 45) spend less than US$200 per capita annually on healthcare and five spend less than US$50 per capita (Saad-Filho &Ayers 2020). At the start of the pandemic, Malawi had 25 ICU beds for a population of 17 million, South Sudan had 24 ICU beds and 4 ventilators for 11 million people and Sierra Leone had 13 ventilators for 8 million people (Burke &Okiror, 2020; Cliffe, 2020). Across South Asia, there were less than 2.8 critical care beds per 100,000 people, and Bangladesh had 1100 ICU beds for 157 million people (Hanieh, 2020). Countries in the South were generally unable to send aircraft to procure PPE abroad, depended heavily on imports to keep their health systems running, and their vaccination programmes frequently had to rely on COVAX.

These vulnerabilities are partly due to poverty, and partly the outcome of recurrent rounds of structural adjustment imposed on the DEs since the early 1980s. These regressive policies systematically dismantled state capacities, ground down institutional resilience, ruined public services (including health provision), undermined job stability and economic security, reduced incomes and destroyed manufacturing industry, leaving these countries highly vulnerable to disruptions in global trade, production and finance (Ghosh, 2020; Gonzalez, 2020). These weaknesses tended to increase poverty, material deprivation, hunger and malnutrition and to create adverse patterns of employment, leading to simmering public health crises.

Even worse, around 70% of workers in the South are in the informal sector. It is nearly impossible to secure their employment or the economic survival of their employers, making it hard to enforce lockdowns or to impose other measures to contain the pandemic. Poor families also tend to live in precarious dwellings, often lacking clean water and sewerage, not to speak of reliable electricity supply or internet access. For example, the average Indian family has five members and 40% of homes have only one room (Pandey, 2020). One-sixth of India's urban population (74 million people) are slum-dwellers, for whom social distancing is largely impossible (Sur & Mitra, 2020). Reportedly, some Indians self-isolated at the top of trees to protect themselves and their family (Stubley, 2020). Large cities in the Global South pose a dilemma to people who must commute to work, since it is impossible to maintain social distancing in overcrowded public transport, which contributed to the spread of the coronavirus(Noko, 2020).

It was predicted that the combined economic and health impacts of the pandemic could increase global poverty by hundreds of millions of people, and push tens of millions to the brink of starvation (for estimates, see Decerf et al., 2020;Sumner et al., 2020; Sumner & Ortiz-Juarez, 2021). It was always possible that 'deaths from secondary impacts – poverty, hunger, diseases, and violence exacerbated by the pandemic – may dwarf the number of those who die of the novel coronavirus itself' (Turse, 2020). Because of these indirect implications of the pandemic and the systematic undercounting of the victims, the impact of COVID-19 in the Global South will never be known. The performance of the poor and middle-income economies could also suffer in the medium-term if the pandemic is followed by the residual circulation of the coronavirus, deepening poverty and deprivation and, potentially, triggering a politics of despair feeding on those economic and health insecurities (ICG, 2020). It is possible, then, that COVID-19 may contribute to the centralisation of power, militarisation of society and further curtailments of civil rights and controls of information and movements, without necessarily improving health provision or outcomes (see, for example, Ellis-Petersen, 2020; Mugabi, 2020).

At the same time, three counteracting factors have helped to moderate the impact of the pandemic in the Global South. First, many countries have experience confronting infectious diseases and epidemics, for example, Chikungunya, Ebola, H1N1, Nipah, SARS and Zika. These health emergencies have boosted the physical infrastructure for pandemic control and created a deep bank of technical know-how as well as social norms of behaviour facilitating the management of health crises (Andersen, 2020; Cliffe, 2020; Milan & Treré, 2020;Mormina &Nsofor, 2020). Second, the younger age profile of the population in the Global South and the lower proportion of people in urban areas may have helped to moderate the impact of COVID-19, since younger people are less vulnerable to the coronavirus, and people in rural zones tend to be more socially isolated. Third, it was shown in Chapter 5 that the pandemic moved along the trade channels built by the neoliberal global economy, which tend to bypass the poorer countries. This gave them additional time to prepare, which some countries used well, especially Cuba, Ghana, Laos, Senegal and Vietnam, as well as the Indian State of Kerala.

These successful experiences contrast sharply with the staggering failures in vastly wealthier countries. This performance contrast shows that, although high-income levels give greater scope to buy ventilators, support wages and businesses and subsidise economic activity, planning and decisions about the best use of funds depend on state capacity, experience and preparation, that are only weakly correlated with income per capita. In other words, although the challenge is harder, good outcomes are possible in the South as well as the North, and they depend more on policy choices than on wealth as such.

## Tales of Success and Failure

Countries had sharply distinct experiences in the pandemic; for an illustration see Table 7.1.

Despite differences in definition and in the quality of the data, Table 7.1 suggests that case rates and death rates could vary enormously between countries (similar differences are likely to exist within countries).

Relatively 'successful' (low case rates and low death rates) examples, not all included in Table 7.1, include China, Cuba, Ethiopia, Finland, Ghana, Iceland, Kerala state in India, Laos, New Zealand, Senegal, Singapore, South Korea, Taiwan, Uruguay and Vietnam. 'Unsuccessful' cases include Bosnia and Herzegovina, Brazil, Colombia, Ecuador, Hungary, India (except Kerala), Iran, Italy, Russia, Spain, Sweden, Turkey, the UK and the USA. It is important to note that performance changed over time; for example, Argentina, Germany, Greece, Kerala, Portugal and South Africa did remarkably well until mid- to late 2020, but suffered heavily later. All experiences offer lessons about the epidemiology and political economyof pandemics and, more generally, about the interaction between pathogens and the system of accumulation in which they are spreading. From a political economy perspective, three lessons are especially significant (Gentilini et al., 2020; Saad-Filho, 2020).

First, China gave the world several weeks to prepare for the pandemic while it struggled alone in early 2020; its achievements offered important lessons about how to confront COVID-19. In sequence, other East Asian governments came up with more or less intrusive or resource-intensive policies to eradicate the coronavirus. These governments tended to have successful experiences of industrial policy and a strong manufacturing base (hence their concentration in East Asia, and the irrelevance of political regime or degree of authoritarianism for the policy outcomes), strong, integrated and policy-capable governments, and centralised universal health systems with significant capillarity and experience addressing pandemics, especially after SARS, that hit East Asia in 2003 (MacKenzie, 2020, ch.1). These governments also tended to implement well-coordinated pandemic policies including, in different measures,

**Table 7.1** The impact of the pandemic (selected countries, in order of deaths per million of population)

| | *UK* | *Brazil* | *USA* | *Sweden* | *Germany* | *Turkey* | *India* | *Senegal* | *Cuba* | *South Korea* | *Singapore* | *New Zealand* | *China* | *Taiwan* | *Vietnam* | *Laos* |
|---|---|---|---|---|---|---|---|---|---|---|---|---|---|---|---|---|
| Total cases | 4,420,443 | 14,340,787 | 32,077,075 | 973,604 | 3,306,692 | 4,629,969 | 16,960,172 | 40,433 | 101,503 | 119,387 | 61,218 | 2,601 | 102,384 | 1,100 | 2,843 | 323 |
| Cases per million | 65,116 | 67,467 | 96,909 | 96,403 | 39,467 | 54,897 | 12,546 | 2,415 | 8,961 | 2,329 | 10,464 | 539 | 71 | 46 | 29 | 44 |
| Total deaths | 127,681 | 390,797 | 572,200 | 14,048 | 81,671 | 38,358 | 192,311 | 1,110 | 591 | 1,817 | 31 | 26 | 4,845 | 12 | 35 | 0 |
| Deaths per million | 1,881 | 1,839 | 1,729 | 1,391 | 975 | 455 | 141 | 66 | 52 | 35 | 5 | 5 | 3 | 1 | 0 | 0 |
| GDP per capita (2019)* | 42,329 | 8,717 | 65,298 | 51,648 | 46,468 | 9,127 | 2,100 | 1,447 | 8,822 | 31,846 | 65,233 | 41,558 | 10,217 | 25,941 | 2,715 | 2,535 |
| GDP growth in 2020 (estimate) | − 9.9 | − 4.1 | − 3.5 | − 2.8 | − 4.9 | 1.8 | − 8.0 | 0.8 | − 11.0 | − 1.0 | − 5.4 | −3.0 | 2.3 | 3.1 | 2.9 | -0.4 |

*: Cuba: GDP per capita for 2018

*Sources* World Bank Understanding the COVID-19 pandemic through data, Our World in Data, and Financial Times, IMF World Economic Outlook April 2021, Granma.cu strong border controls; early and harsh lockdowns; aggressive testing, tracing and isolation; protection of incomes, revenues and consumption levels and intrusive technologies to control contacts and population movements. These experiences could have been emulated by the 'failed states' in the West, but they refused to do so, or even to acknowledge their dismal performance. Their choices were culpable; in addition, experience shows that it was possible to eliminate COVID-19 even in low-income countries. It follows that the chaos and the worldwide tragedy were almost entirely avoidable, and that every death in the pandemic must be accounted for (Abbasi, 2021).

The second lesson is that the governments that failed most miserably tended to be authoritarian, to have advanced further along the neoliberal path of depredation of the economy and the state itself, and to have built economies grounded on individualism, exploitation, plunder and the protection of the interests of the rich to the detriment of the poor. These governments also tended to be unprepared to address systemic non-military challenges, especially in the domain of public health. Under mature neoliberalism, state capacities had been eroded almost everywhere and health systems had been hollowed out, fragmented and part-privatised even when they appeared to be publicly owned.[1] These limitations derive from the imposition of tight fiscal constraints for many years, the disorderly decentralisation of responsibilities, ideologically driven privatisations and the vulnerability of governments and regulators to predatory lobbies. At the same time, the neoliberal reforms also created a precarious and impoverished working class that was highly vulnerable to health scares and to disruptions in their earning capacity because of their low savings, poor housing, inadequate nutrition and work patterns incompatible with healthy lives (see Chapters 1 and 5 and Solty, 2020).

When they were confronted by the pandemic, the 'failed' governments—especially the Quartet of Calamity—were prone to hesitate, fumble, stumble and delay, choose contradictory policies, implement them poorly and protect rampant corruption instead of focusing on the preservation of life. In the meantime, their populations were denied knowledge of how several countries had eliminated the coronavirus. Those policy failures were symptomatic of the disarticulation of the state and public policy under neoliberalism. These dysfunctions were not merely due to the staggering incompetence of the 'spectacular' leaders in charge, the obtuseness and corruption of top politicians and civil servants or the selfishness of the economic elites. Although these factors were influential, the experiences of failure reveal a systemic political malaise in neoliberal countries, especially the authoritarian ones. There, the political system was often geared to the consolidation of the power of the 'leader' through the cultivation of divisions and the stoking of conflicts, rather than the protection of the population.

Despite their telegenic prowess, the 'leaders' found it difficult to feign sympathy for the Other or express pity, shame or remorse, and came out callous; often they could not debate the complexities of the pandemic,[2] and looked ignorant; and they could not lead the response, and looked clueless. Donald Trump, Jair Bolsonaro and Narendra Modi systematically undermined their own health expertsin order to promote quack cures, while Boris Johnson's chosen experts vanished from the official briefings whenever they went off-message (Lewis & Conn, 2020; Lintern, 2020; Merrick, 2020; Mikhailova et al., 2020; Syal, 2020). Public health responseswere delayed because the machinery of the state stalled when it was confronted by a challenge unrelated to the promotion of the leader. Accustomed to politics as war (Remain vs Leave; Tories vs Corbyn; gun owners vs gun controls; White supremacists vs BLM; Obamagate vs Russiagate; Lava Jato vs Lula; traditional media vs evangelical start-ups, Hindus vs Muslims and so on), and enmeshed in battles against the 'deep state', those leaders were ill-equipped to address COVID-19, an adversary that did not respond to the politics of division or resentment.

Instead of building national unity to attack the coronavirus, the tendency of authoritarian political systems was to shield the government, initially by denying the pandemic through bluster, lies and accusations against the 'doom-mongers'. This strategy fostered social divisions and wasted time that should have been spent learning lessons from abroad, addressing strategic shortcomings and preparing the country to confront the pandemic. In sequence, authoritarian neoliberal administrations often argued for 'herd immunity', which would be met with revulsion and would be abandoned under strong pressure from health specialists and the majority of the population. By then, however, it was already too late.

In summary, the pandemic showed that the wages of arrogance are death; it also showed that mass deaths were the avoidable consequence of a degenerating modality of neoliberalism in the 'failed' countries. The differential outcomes of the pandemic show that neoliberal states can be efficient at protecting finance, but they find it difficult to recognise their primary duty to protect public health, or to deploy resources, expertise and operational competence to respond to emergencies. It turns out that the more the state had been reconstructed along neoliberal lines in the name of the 'superior efficiency' of the market, and the greater the marketisation of social reproduction, the lower was public policy capacity, the less expertise was available to respond to emergencies, the more disarticulated were the state institutions, the greater was the extent of deindustrialisation through the 'globalisation' of production and the higher tended to be the prevalence of COVID-19 and the associated death rate.[3] The consequence was not only that several rich countries found themselves unable to produce PPE and ventilators (see Chapter 5) but, also, that their public sectors could not co-ordinate even the available policy tools to respond to the tragedy. Those economies had spent the previous decades building unsustainable financial structures in pursuit of short-term profitability (Tooze, 2018), while their health systems were unable to perform their statutory functions at a time of need.

The third lesson is that it is perfectly possible to combat pandemics in a democratic framework (Berengaut, 2020; Caduff, 2020). Nevertheless, several successful as well as unsuccessful governments used the pandemic as a pretext to move towards 'states of exception' with heavier forms of social control, regardless of the implications for controlling the virus. These states sought to centralise power in the executive, limit constitutional rights, militarise public spaces, control information flows and the social media, monitor movements and so on. In some cases, these heavy-handed measures reached their stated goals; for example, Australia, China, New Zealand and South Africa imposed harsh regulations on population movements that may have infringed civil rights, but they achieved successes driving down COVID-19 to the point where it could be managed by rigorous systems of testing, tracing and isolation (except in South Africa) (Michie, 2021). In other cases, authoritarian policies merely fed corruption and reinforced the power of the ruling groups, without any significant gains in terms of public health (e.g., Hungary, India, Paraguay and the UK).

The examples of success and failure offer valuable lessons of what must never happen again in a pandemic: fail to plan; deny or wish away the virus; promote quack treatments for short-term political gain; impose decentralised or market-driven health systems with partial coverage and minimal spare capacity because of 'fiscal austerity' or in the name of 'efficiency'; hesitate to impose lockdowns, movement controls, border closures, social distancing and compulsory use of facemasks, and allow crowds and large events in confined spaces. The successful examples also illustrate what must happen. Countries and international organisations ought to act fast (Maxmen, 2021; Sebenius & Sebenius, 2020); spend enough money to keep society together and the economy moving; have contingency plans for manufacturing industry; build centralised and resilient public health systems with sufficient intensive care beds and stocks of PPE; and prepare robust plans for testing, tracing and isolation of the sick. At a further (global) level, generic vaccines can be tried and tested in advance to prepare for the most likely pandemics, which would allow the most appropriate ones to be rolled out rapidly; and an international agreement can be reached to suspend patents on vaccines whenever a pandemic is declared by the WHO.[4] There is no doubt that these policies will be costly, but the required expenditures would be only a fraction of the losses imposed by the pandemic, not to speak of the thousands of lives sacrificed because of the limitations of neoliberalism.

The above lessons from the pandemic also illustrate two red herrings that temporarily clouded the policy debates. First, the contrast between female and male policymakers, that seemed to suggest that countries led by women were more likely to do well (with the examples of Denmark, Finland, Iceland, New Zealand and Taiwan being deployed and, for a time, also Germany).[5] In contrast, the Quartet of Calamity had phallocentric polities and were led by boisterous men who often behaved like rowdy, stubborn and inept teenagers. However, even to contemplate this debate concedes too much (after all, Margaret Thatcher was a woman, and many successful countries during the pandemic were led by men). The relevant point is not the 'essential' qualities of female versus male politicians. Instead, the relevant lesson is that more egalitarian societies tend to have more democratic states, and these are *also* countries where women tend to be more valued at home, respected on the job and, partly as a consequence, more successful in politics. The issue, then, is not simply to push more women into positions of power regardless of their views; it is about systems, values, policies and citizenship, and the construction of open, egalitarian and democratic societies. These countries will tend to have more women politicians, but also more progressive taxation and more integrated and comprehensive health systems, and they will be better able to protect everyone in a pandemic.

Second was the assumption that the pandemic would mark a transfer of global hegemony from West to East, since the latter obviously did so much better while the former was wallowing in disaster, losing prestige and, inevitably, would have a delayed economic recovery. The point, however, is that there is not an undifferentiated 'West' versus 'East': the story of the pandemic is not about geography but about systems of accumulation, state capacities and public policy; in particular, the pandemic is a story about the crises in neoliberalism and how they impacted public health. This ought to be the focus, and lessons must be learned from wherever they may come.

## Notes

1. For the emblematic case of the UK, see Leys (2020), Siddique (2020) and Wren-Lewis (2020).
2. The counter-example is Angela Merkel's precise explanation of the pandemic; see Oltermann (2020).
3. For an overview of the implications, see Bueno de Mesquita et al. (2021).
4. For a wider discussion, see Hoen et al. (2021) and Wallace-Wells (2020).
5. See, for example, Henley (2020); for a rebuttal, see Randall (2021).

## References

Abbasi, K. (2021). Covid-19: Social murder, they wrote—Elected, unaccountable, and unrepentant. *British Medical Journal, 372*(314). https://doi.org/10.1136/bmj.n314.

Andersen, H. (2020). *Unlike the UK, many African nations have an effective test and trace system—This is why*. https://www.independent.co.uk/voices/africa-test-and-trace-covid-b1774982.html.

Berengaut A. A. (2020). *Democracies are better at fighting outbreaks*. https://www.theatlantic.com/ideas/archive/2020/02/why-democracies-are-better-fighting-outbreaks/606976/.

Bueno de Mesquita, J., Kapilashrami, A., & Meier, B. M. (2021). *Human rights dimensions of the COVID-19 pandemic*. Paper commissioned by The Independent Panel for Pandemic Preparedness and Response, https://theindependentpanel.org/documents/.

Burke, J., & Okiror, S. (2020). *Africa's fragile health systems rush to contain coronavirus*. https://www.theguardian.com/world/2020/mar/20/africas-fragile-health-systems-rush-to-contain-coronavirus.

Caduff, C. (2020). What went wrong: Corona and the world after the full stop. *Medical Anthropology Quarterly, 34*(4), 467–487.

Cliffe, J. (2020). *Coronavirus hits the global south*. https://www.newstatesman.com/world/south-america/2020/04/coronavirus-hits-global-south.

Decerf, B., Ferreira, F. H. G., Mahler, D. G., & Sterck, O. (2020). *Lives and livelihoods: Estimates of the global mortality and poverty effects of the Covid-19 pandemic*. http://eprints.lse.ac.uk/105825/.

Elliott, L. (2020a). *Dozens of poorer nations seek IMF help amid coronavirus crisis*. https://www.theguardian.com/world/2020/mar/27/dozens-poorer-nations-seek-imf-help-coronavirus-crisis.

Elliott, L. (2020b). *IMF estimates global Covid cost at $28tn in lost output*. https://www.theguardian.com/business/2020/oct/13/imf-covid-cost-world-economic-outlook.

Ellis-Petersen, H. (2020). *India's Covid-19 app fuels worries over authoritarianism and surveillance*. https://www.theguardian.com/world/2020/may/04/how-safe-is-it-really-privacy-fears-over-india-coronavirus-app.

Gentilini, U. et al. (2020). *Social protection and jobs responses to COVID-19: A real-time Review of Country Measures*. https://openknowledge.worldbank.org/handle/10986/33635.

Ghosh, J. (2020). *The pandemic and the global economy*. https://www.dissentmagazine.org/online_articles/the-pandemic-and-the-global-economy.

Gonzalez, M. (2020). *Coronavirus in Latin America*. https://www.rs21.org.uk/2020/05/02/coronavirus-in-latin-america/.

Hanieh, A. (2020). *This is a global pandemic—Let's treat it as such*. https://www.versobooks.com/blogs/4623-this-is-a-global-pandemic-let-s-treat-it-as-such.

Henley, J. (2020). *Female-led countries handled coronavirus better, study suggests*. https://www.theguardian.com/world/2020/aug/18/female-led-countries-handled-coronavirus-better-study-jacinda-ardern-angela-merkel.

Hoen, E. et al. (2021). *Scaling-up vaccine production capacity: Legal challenges and recommendations*, Paper commissioned by The Independent Panel for Pandemic Preparedness and Response, https://theindependentpanel.org/documents/.

ICG. (2020). COVID-19 and conflict: Seven trends to watch. *Crisis Group Special Briefing No.4*. https://d2071andvip0wj.cloudfront.net/B004-covid-19-seven-trends.pdf.

Lewis, P., & Conn, D. (2020). *UK scientists condemn 'stalinist' attempt to censor Covid-19 advice*. https://www.theguardian.com/world/2020/may/08/revealed-uk-scientists-fury-over-attempt-to-censor-covid-19-advice.

Leys, C. (2020). *How market reforms made the NHS vulnerable to pandemics*. https://socialistproject.ca/2020/03/how-market-reforms-made-the-nhs-vulnerable-to-pandemics.

Lintern, S. (2020). Chief nurse dropped from downing street coronavirus briefing 'after refusing to back Dominic Cummings. https://www.independent.co.uk/news/uk/politics/coronavirus-chief-nurse-dominic-cummings-ruth-may-daily-briefing-downing-street-a9562741.html.

MacKenzie, D. (2020). *COVID-19: The pandemic that never should have happened, and how to stop the next one*. The Bridge Street Press.

Maxmen, A. (2021). *How the world failed to curb COVID-19*. https://www.nature.com/articles/d41586-021-01284-5.

Merrick, J. (2020). Health experts 'banished' from Downing Street briefing after failing to toe government line. https://inews.co.uk/news/politics/coronavirus-latest-health-experts-banished-downing-street-briefings-explained-dominic-cummings-445004.

Michie, S. (2021). *This UK lockdown must be the last. Here's how we can achieve that*. https://www.theguardian.com/commentisfree/2021/feb/21/uk-lockdown-health-livelihoods-2021-sage-committee.

Mikhailova, A., Hope, C., Gillard, M., & Wells, L. (2020). *Government scientist Neil Ferguson resigns after breaking lockdown rules to meet his married lover*. https://www.telegraph.co.uk/news/2020/05/05/exclusive-government-scientist-neil-ferguson-resigns-breaking/.

Milan, S., & Treré, E. (2020). *A widening data divide: COVID-19 and the global south*. https://www.opendemocracy.net/en/openmovements/widening-data-divide-covid-19-and-global-south/.

Mormina, M., & Nsofor, I. M. (2020). *What developing countries can teach rich countries about how to respond to a pandemic*. https://theconversation.com/what-developing-countries-can-teach-rich-countries-about-how-to-respond-to-a-pandemic-146784?.

Mugabi, I. (2020). *COVID-19: Security forces in Africa brutalizing civilians under lockdown*. https://www.dw.com/en/covid-19-security-forces-in-africa-brutalizing-civilians-under-lockdown/a-53192163.

Noko, K. (2020). *In Africa, social distancing is a privilege few can afford*. https://www.aljazeera.com/indepth/opinion/africa-social-distancing-privilege-afford-200318151958670.html.

Nordling, L. (2020). *A ticking time bomb: Scientists worry about coronavirus spread in Africa*. https://www.sciencemag.org/news/2020/03/ticking-time-bomb-scientists-worry-about-coronavirus-spread-africa.

Oltermann, P. (2020). *Angela Merkel draws on science background in Covid-19 explainer*. https://www.theguardian.com/world/2020/apr/16/angela-merkel-draws-on-science-background-in-covid-19-explainer-lockdown-exit.

Pandey, G. (2020). *Coronavirus: Is social distancing an oxymoron in India?* https://www.bbc.co.uk/news/world-asia-india-52393382.

Randall, I. (2021). *Countries led by women have NOT fared significantly better in the COVID-19 pandemic than those led by men, study finds*. https://www.dailymail.co.uk/sciencetech/article-9102585/COVID-19-Countries-led-women-NOT-fared-significantly-better-pandemic.html.

Saad-Filho, A. (2020). From COVID-19 to the end of neoliberalism. *Critical Sociology, 46*(4–5), 477–485.

Saad-Filho, A., & Ayers, A. (2020). A ticking time bomb: The global south in a time of coronavirus. *Journal of Australian Political Economy, 85*, 84–93.
Sebenius, I., & Sebenius, J. K. (2020). *How many needless Covid-19 deaths were caused by delays in responding? Most of them*. https://www.statnews.com/2020/06/19/faster-response-prevented-most-us-covid-19-deaths/.
Siddique, H. (2020). *Despite PM's praise of nurses, it's Tory policies that made them suffer*. https://www.theguardian.com/society/2020/apr/13/despite-pms-praise-of-nurses-its-tory-policies-that-made-them-suffer.
Solty, I. (2020). *The bio-economic pandemic and the western working Classes*. https://socialistproject.ca/2020/03/bioeconomic-pandemic-and-western-working-classes/.
Stubbs, T. et al. (2020). *Whatever it takes? The global financial safety net, Covid-19*.
Stubley, P. (2020). *Coronavirus: Indians self-isolate in trees to protect relatives*. https://www.independent.co.uk/news/world/asia/coronavirus-india-trees-quarantine-lockdown-vangidi-purulia-bengal-modi-a9434966.html.
Sumner, A., & Ortiz-Juarez, E. (2021). *Global monetary poverty, 1981–2030*. Paper prepared for the United Nations Virtual Inter-Agency Expert Group Meeting on the Implementation of the Third United Nations Decade for the Eradication of Poverty, May, UNDESA, New York.
Sumner, A. Ortiz-Juarez, E., & Hoy, C. (2020). *Estimates of the impact of COVID-19 on global poverty* (WIDER Working Paper 2020/43). https://www.wider.unu.edu/sites/default/files/Publications/Working-paper/PDF/wp2020-43.pdf.
Sur, P., & Mitra, E. (2020). *Social distancing is a privilege of the middle class: For India's Slum Dwellers it will be impossible*. https://edition.cnn.com/2020/03/30/india/india-coronavirus-social-distancing-intl-hnk/index.html.
Syal, R. (2020). *Chief nurse was dropped from briefings after refusing to back Cummings*. https://www.theguardian.com/politics/2020/jul/20/englands-chief-nurse-dropped-from-covid-19-briefing-after-refusing-to-back-cummings-ruth-may.
Tooze, A. (2018). *Crashed: How a decade of financial crises changed the world*. Viking.
Turse, N. (2020). *"Exceptionally dire": Secondary impacts of Covid-19 could increase Global poverty and hunger*. https://theintercept.com/2020/05/03/exceptionally-dire-secondary-impacts-of-covid-19-could-increase-global-poverty-and-hunger/.
UNECA. (2020). *COVID-19 in Africa: Protecting lives and economies*. https://www.uneca.org/sites/default/files/PublicationFiles/eca_covid_report_en_24apr_web1.pdf.
Wallace-Wells, D. (2020). *We had the vaccine the whole time*. https://nymag.com/intelligencer/2020/12/moderna-covid-19-vaccine-design.html.

WHO. (2020). *New WHO estimates: Up to 190,000 could die of COVID-19 in Africa if not controlled*. https://www.afro.who.int/news/new-who-estimates-190-000-people-could-die-covid-19-africa-if-not-controlled.

Wren-Lewis, S. (2020). *Who still thinks Austerity was a good idea?* https://mainlymacro.blogspot.com/2020/04/who-still-thinks-austerity-was-good-idea.html?m=1.

CHAPTER 8

# The UK: A Convergence of Disasters

In early 2020, UK public life became dominated by the convergence of a calamitous Brexit with a catastrophic pandemic. The clash culminated in one of the highest death totals in the world, around 130,000 at the time of writing (May 2020), and one of the highest rates of deaths per capita, almost 2,000 per million. Poignantly, the tragedy penalised disproportionately the poor, minorities, the elderly and those with special needs.

## The Conservative Party and the Pandemic

Although the pandemic was imposed by exogenous events, the policy response was in the gift of the British government. Instead of emulating the successful examples elsewhere, especially in Asia (including New Zealand and Taiwan, also islands), the Conservative administration led by the ever-unreliable Prime Minister Boris Johnson engaged in a shocking sequence of blunders driven by their fanatical devotion to the ideologies of neoliberalism and private money-grabbing.

It did not have to be this way. The likelihood of a flu-type pandemic figured highly in the government's risk register, and the UK was evidently vulnerable because of its deep international connections, major airports, large tourism sector and the British habit of holidaying abroad.[1] It would, then, be relatively easy for a new virus to enter the UK. Viruses would



A. Saad-Filho, *The Age of Crisis*,
https://doi.org/10.1007/978-3-030-81608-7_8

also find there a favourable terrain to spread, because of the country's severe inequalities of income and wealth,[2] poor housing and chronic overcrowding at homes and in public transport, especially in London, the Midlands and the North—precisely the areas that would be hit most severely by COVID-19. These vulnerabilities had been enhanced by forty years of neoliberalism and ten years of 'austerity', that had had severe implications for public health (Marmot et al., 2020; Michell, 2020). For example, the repeated culling of National Health Service (NHS) hospital beds in the name of 'efficiency savings' led to 90% bed occupancy being seeing as 'normal', with 100% occupation in winter becoming a regular occurrence. Symptomatic of the degradation of the NHS is that staffing levels had been cut to the point where the emergency 'Nightingale' hospitals built in a matter of days to look after victims of the pandemic could never be used as intended due to the lack of nurses and specialist equipment.

When it arrived, the pandemic rapidly unmasked the Conservative Party (and, at a further remove, the ill-fated Coalition government [2010–2015] and its predecessor, New Labour [1997–2010]), for having attacked social resilience and systematically ground down the NHS. Even when money was spent in the health service, as was the case during New Labour, the primary goal was to slice up and hollow out the system, privatise whatever could be sold off, introduce competition or pseudo-market forms of management regardless of cost or implications for efficiency and expand the health system's reliance on the profit motive (Hall et al., 2020; Lawrence et al., 2020; Leys & Player, 2011; Marmot et al., 2010). Finally, the UK's strategic stockpileof PPE was privatised, centralised at an unsuitable location, cut down, left to rot, and disregarded almost entirely, as the state lost capacity to plan and manage health emergencies (Davies, 2020; Foster & Neville, 2020; Syal, 2020). These shortcomings were starkly revealed by Operation Cygnus, a flu pandemic simulation exercise carried out in 2016. Cygnus revealed severe gaps in readiness, lack of equipment and inability to co-ordinate public responses—but nothing was done about it, partly because of the fragmentation of responsibilities between the government and the NHS and, partly, because of the lack of resources(Hopkins, 2020; Wenham, 2020).

There was a chance to adopt an elimination strategy against the coronavirus at the start of the pandemic, in early 2020, but a political choice was made to accommodate it instead, in order to 'protect the economy'. In contrast with China, New Zealand and Taiwan, that adopted a strategy of elimination (Bissett, 2020; Klein, 2020; Fitzpatrick, 2021), the British government's choice implied that COVID-19 would root itself and become a permanent plague, inevitably with global implications. This blunder was compounded by a staggering level of incompetence of the Brexiteers (i.e., devotees of the UK's withdrawal from the European Union) who had seized power under Boris Johnson, and their complete inability to do what had become essential: implement a consistent strategy of social distancing, including an early lockdown; supply the NHS with equipment and trained staff; protect the vulnerable; shield the elderly, the disabled, minorities and key workers; and keep the UK safe from the repeated importation of new strands of the coronavirus. In reality, public health was never the government's priority. Their attention was always focused elsewhere; on the one hand on Brexit and, on the other hand, on capturing as much public money as possible for private enterprise, regardless of the consequences for public health.

It is, then, unsurprising that in the first weeks in 2020 the government chose 'herd immunity' as their preferred approach to tackling the virus. The UK government's Chief Medical Adviser, Sir Patrick Vallance, stated in March 2020 that 'Our aim [is to] try and reduce the peak – not suppress [the virus] completely, also because most people get a mild illness, to build up some degree of herd immunity whilst protecting the most vulnerable'. In Vallance's view, approximately 60% of the British population would have to get infected to achieve that goal (Kermani, 2020).

Despite later denials, the words and actions of several UK public officials were consistent with a strategy of herd immunity (Bourgeron, 2021). Even though Prime Minister Johnson did not speak about it publicly, the Italian health minister reported that Johnson told him in a private call that his goal was herd immunity (Payne, 2020). The strategy was again considered in September 2020, as the Prime Minister had a meeting with three well-known advocates of herd immunity, including the designer of the fateful Swedish approach (McNally, 2020). This insistence was due to the decision that profits to oneself and close friends (what became known as the 'chumocracy' around Johnson) matter more than other people's lives (Geoghegan, 2020; Newton, 2021). After a certain point, this became a *fait accompli*, since the UK would become unable to do much else. The life-and-death implications of these policy choices were compounded by the mendacity, corruption and staggering dysfunctionality of the British government(Coburg, 2020; Kinder & Plimmer, 2020; Whyte, 2015).

The government's studied dereliction of duty was confronted by a growing mass revolt, including an open letter demanding action signed by 200 scientists (van Wagtendonk, 2020). On 17th March, Patrick Vallance stated that 20,000 deaths from COVID-19 would be 'a good outcome' for the UK (Heffer, 2020). This statement was met with cries of disbelief since that number was perceived to be unacceptably high. Soon after, the Imperial College team led by a member of the government's Scientific Advisory Group for Emergencies (SAGE) committee, Neil Ferguson, estimated that the ongoing (if only implicitly, through inaction) policy of 'herd immunity' would lead to 250,000 deaths—in retrospect, likely to be a massive underestimate but, at the time, that number seemed unimaginably high (Cookson, 2020). Their leaked paper turned the rumblings of dissatisfaction with the government's inaction into a frenzy. Ferguson's revelation infuriated the administration, and its officials may or may not have leaked rumours about Ferguson personal life to the right-wing media, forcing him to resign from SAGE in May 2020.

Running out of arguments and facing an increasingly angry public opinion, Prime Minister Johnson turned around dramatically, and announced a national lockdown from 23 March 2020—but, by then, it was far too late. The coronavirus was everywhere, almost 13,000 cases had already been recorded and 365 people had died of COVID-19 in the UK. In the meantime, massive events had taken place without any form of control. This included 250,000 people at the Cheltenham Festival (a horseracing competition) between 10 and 13 March, and the 11 March football match between Liverpool and Atlético de Madrid, attended by 50,000 people, including 3,000 visitors from Spain, already a COVID-19 hotspot (Cunningham, 2020). The number of deaths started climbing rapidly, but the government remained firmly behind the curve. In early May, the UK became the European country with the highest number of COVID-19 deaths, a questionable distinction that would be retained (Kontopantelis et al., 2020). Finally, throughout the pandemic, the callousness with which the British government treated those with special needs and in care homes, previously already at the rough end of neoliberalism, must rank as one of the gravest scandals in post-war Western Europe (Giles, 2020; Pegget al., 2020; Walsh & Krever, 2020).

Because of the government's early decision to turn a blind eye to the pandemic, minimise the problem and delay action as much as possible (Booth, 2021; Merrick & Woodcock, 2021; Sridhar, 2021), their astonishing ineptitude when trying to do something, and the incompetence of the private sector, that received billions from the government in exchange for very little, the UK ended up in the worst of both worlds: countless dead (literally countless, since for several months there was a deliberate effort to under-report the loss of life), and economic lossesin the hundreds of billions of pounds: UK national income fell 9.9% in 2020, compared with 3.5% in the US and 4.9% in Germany, while China's national income actually grew (IMF, 2021). Even worse, the decision to let the virus spread in the UK, USA, Brazil, India and elsewhere guaranteed that it would become impossible to eliminate it anywhere, and that new variants would keep emerging. The inevitable consequence is that Big Pharma will laugh all the way to the bank for years to come, producing streams of vaccines for guaranteed markets at public expense, while the chronically and historically underserved, the poor and the unlucky will continue to suffer and die (Kollewe, 2021; Sell, 2020).

It became clear in a matter of weeks that the government's pandemic strategy—centred around pumping public resources into private pockets as rapidly as possible—was a colossal failure. Nothing could be more emblematic of this disaster than the privatisation of (so-called) NHS Test and Trace, responsible for nationwide COVID-19 tests, and for tracing and isolating those who tested positive and their contacts. This effort received £22 billion in 2020–2021, but it was so poorly managed that the National Audit Office concluded that it made no measurable difference to outcomes; among other things, it failed completely to contain the second and third waves of the pandemic in the autumn and winter of 2020, even though they had been predicted for several months (NAO, 2021; Pollock, 2021). In summary:

> [The Test and Trace] project was … fundamentally misconceived, having no component for monitoring or enforcing the isolation of Covid-positive people and their contacts, and making no realistic provision for maintaining their incomes while not working. So on top of the late delivery of test results and the limitations of the 'call-centre' approach to tracing and providing contacts (only some 60% of the contacts of people who tested positive were reached in time to prevent them transmitting the virus if they had got it), compliance with isolation was minimal: in August 2020, five months after NHS Test and Trace was set up, fewer than a fifth of people who tested positive, and only 11 per cent of their identified contacts, were self-isolating. In short, the whole purpose of mass testing was defeated, yet nothing has been done to change this. Two weeks of isolation is unpleasant: two weeks without income is impossible for breadwinners on

> low incomes, many of whom decline to be tested for fear of being told to self-isolate and risk losing their income or even their jobs ... [T]he cost of providing full income support for two weeks to people in isolation would be much less than the estimated cost of keeping several million people on furlough (about £5.5 billion a month down to December 2020); and it would have a major impact on suppressing the virus, eventually making income support for everyone else unnecessary. (Leys, 2021)

There can be little doubt that a transfer of £22 billion directly to households would have made a greater contribution to social welfare, but that would not have brought gains to the friends of the UK Cabinet. Needless to say, this option was never considered seriously by the government (FitzRoy & Spencer, 2020).

## The Magical Realism of Brexit

Brexit was a poison injected entirely unnecessarily into the nation's body, with toxic consequences for the poor, ethnic minorities, immigrants and the young, and possibly lethal implications for the UK itself—all for the benefit of a predatory financialised elite wedded to a radical version of neoliberalism. As a class project, Brexit expressed an exhausted, end-of-Empire choice against any form of long-term economic strategy or democratisation of the country, disguised as a rebellion of the 'losers' against the metropolitan elite. In reality, Brexit sought to open new spaces for predatory and financialised accumulation, with Britain specialising, increasingly, in global plunder and the intermediation of flows of surplus value, rather than the making of things. In other words, the real project behind Brexit is to chain the nation ever more closely to global finance, so the UK can live off commissions from the traffic of the fruits of exploitation anywhere in the world. The consequences will haunt the UK nations for decades.

At the margins of this debate, the Lexiteers, or (mostly) ultra-left Brexiteers, advanced the notion that the EU was a neoliberal club which the UK should leave, because the EU's malignant bureaucracy would prevent a progressive UK government from implementing its chosen policies. This must be one of the most misguided contributions to UK political debates in recent times, for three reasons. First, some of the EU's most restrictive rules were originally designed and tested in Britain, while successive UK governments refused to implement other EU rules because they were not neoliberal enough (a typical example being the working time directive). Second, in recent years EU rules had protected more than hindered labour rights and civic freedoms in the UK (for example, around human rights, freedom of information and the protection of privacy). Third, the 'Lexiteer' position implied that the workers, minorities and the poor stood to gain from a project driven by the Murdoch press, the far-right elite, transnational hedge funds, a handful of buccaneer capitalists (who, once the Brexit referendum had been won, sorted out their foreign passports and relocated abroad) and a cabal of corrupt lumpen-bourgeois operators fronted by Boris Johnson, Michael Gove, Arron Banks, Nigel Farage and Dominic Cummings. They are not exactly the vanguard of the proletariat. Wealthy Brexiteers expect to laugh all the way to the Cayman Islands, until they manage to turn the City of London into a tax haven with better restaurants.

In contrast with the Lexiteer politics of dreams, Brexit was firmly grounded in material realities. However, given its reactionary implications, this project could win a referendum only through the careful curation of lies and strife to divide the working class (see Chapter 4). Just like the Christian Holy Trinity, Brexit was always clouded in mystery and marked by the impossibility of knowledge of what was being decided in 2016. The Brexiteers pretended to be certain when they had no idea; peddled lies that the 'respectable' media repeated either thoughtlessly or shamelessly; spoke loudly when they had doubts; turned complex debates into screaming matches, and split the country to avoid having to explain themselves, since there was no possibility of an agreement about which falsehood, illusion or mirage would be most effective at each point in time.

The avaricious adventurism and political irresponsibility of the Brexiteers shed new light onto former Prime Minister Theresa May's tautology that 'Brexit means Brexit': that nonsense implied that Brexit would be whatever the gang of thieves leading the project could get away with. And so the UK ended up impoverished and in an unholy political mess, with an unavoidable but also unenforceable treaty with the EU, a confused bourgeoisie and a working class even more bereft of rights and protections than before. It was all going to plan, and abundant opportunities for plunder were certain to come by. Given this epochal background, the arrival of the pandemic seemed to be a matter of detail, and it was treated as such for several weeks by the Conservative Party and their friends in business and the media.

## The Opposition Vanishes

In nominal opposition to the Conservative Party-led double-pronged chaos of Brexit and the pandemic, stands the Labour Party, led by Sir Keir Starmer KCB QC MP. Sadly for a dashing chisel-chinned charmer who took off magnificently, Starmer soon became a political embarrassment and a repository of disappointments and squandered hopes.

Starmer's first interventions in the House of Commons were greeted with adoration by the ageing remnants of Tony Blair's fan club, and their approval grew into a frenzy when Starmer took up his real job, not of opposing the Tory government in the middle of a muddled Brexit and a tragic pandemic, but the seemingly more important task of purging the left of his own Party. On the other issues, Starmer mostly approved government policies, regardless of the death rate, while trying to present a more 'responsible' image than Boris Johnson's. This cannot be a difficult task. However, Starmer's drab passivity made him tedious, and boredom does not sell newspapers or win elections.

The fall from grace was both rapid and humiliating. Cries of approval were replaced by the drum of fingers on tables, awaiting Labour's next surrender to the most mediocre government in British history, at least since the previous one, led by Theresa May and, before that, the one led by David Cameron, suggesting that Britain is experiencing a relentless political decline. Facing the lazy, lying and larcenous nonentities under Johnson, Starmer positioned himself as the spare wheel of the state, ready to serve if Johnson became excessively dysfunctional. In the meantime, to Starmer's surprise, the English establishment decided to keep Boris Johnson in place, since he can at least entertain the masses. Life can be unfair.

Having made itself useless in the face of the greatest challenge to this country since 1940, despite the dysfunctionality of the Tory government, the Labour Party was abandoned as irrelevant by the political elite, tens of thousands of members, and millions of voters. This death drive is not unique to the British Labour Party: the party may be feeling the pressures of neoliberalism that destroyed Social Democracy in France, Germany, Greece, Italy and elsewhere. In recent times, the Labour Party was protected from those deadly winds by, first, the movement around Jeremy Corbyn, that made Labour stand for something other than 'triangulation' with the political right since, faced with a pale copy, the voters tend to embrace the real thing. Second, the First Past the Post electoral system, that limits the space for alternatives. Today, only First Past the Post remains, but history shows that this system can lead to the sudden collapse of major parties. This happened in recent times in Canada and Italy, and years ago in the UK, when the Liberal Party imploded; it might happen again.

In these dire circumstances, the Labour Party finds itself at the margins of politics, contemplating the success of the vaccination programme led by the NHS, on the back of massive government support for AstraZeneca (Jones, 2021; Safi, 2021), clever purchasing of hundreds of millions of doses of multiple vaccines, and a massive transfer of resources to the chumocracy. Yet, there is no doubt that the NHS and other public services will be sliced up and part-privatised as soon as the nightmare is over. At the same time, the UK is witnessing an escalating authoritari-anismand the rapid conversion of the state into a corrupt machine driven by liars, jesters and fascists.

## Lessons from Disaster

While the consequences of Brexit cannot be addressed here—they range across the unity of the UK and the viability of its nations, the structure of employment, the prospects for economic growth and much more—the pandemic has shown that health policy must be centralised, integrated and kept in public hands. The NHS has gained huge respect from the vast majority, but the system remains underfunded, fragmented and hampered by the lack of staff and equipment. The relationship between the NHS and (privatised, fragmented and deprived of funding) social care ought to be rebuilt into a new, integrated system with no room for private profits(I-SAGE 2020).

The costs of the pandemic, in terms of lives lost and damages to the economy, have shown that the protection of public health is cheap. What is expensive is the institutionalised robbery under the private health system, especially when it is sponsored by the most powerful politicians in the land.

## Notes

1. UK airports received 7–11 million passengers per month in 2019, see UK Home Office (2020) and Leys (2021), which is an important source for what follows.
2. https://data.oecd.org/inequality/income-inequality.htm.

## References


Bissett, A. N. (2020). *Elimination policy, business funds, and total transparency: Jacinda Ardern is showing how to lead a country through crisis*. https://www.independent.co.uk/news/world/australasia/jacinda-ardern-new-zealand-coronavirus-world-leaders-mental-health-cases-a9470531.html.

Booth, R. (2021). *Delaying England's winter lockdown "caused up to 27,000 extra Covid deaths"*. https://www.theguardian.com/uk-news/2021/mar/18/delaying-englands-winter-lockdown-caused-up-to-27000-extra-covid-deaths.

Bourgeron, T. (2021). 'Let the virus spread'. A doctrine of pandemic management for the libertarian-authoritarian capital accumulation regime. *Organization*. https://journals.sagepub.com/doi/https://doi.org/10.1177/1350508421995741.

Coburg, T. (2020). *The £5.5bn PPE scandal that goes to the core of government incompetence—And that's just for starters*. https://www.thecanary.co/uk/analysis/2020/07/11/the-5-5bn-ppe-scandal-that-goes-to-the-core-of-government-incompetence-and-thats-just-for-starters/.

Cookson, C. (2020). *UK's original coronavirus plan risked 'hundreds of thousands' dead*. https://www.ft.com/content/249daf9a-67c3-11ea-800d-da70cff6e4d3.

Cunningham, S. (2020). *Liverpool vs Atletico Madrid: The champions league match that should never have happened*. https://inews.co.uk/sport/football/champions-league/liverpool-atletico-madrid-coronavirus-merseyside-spain-champions-league-fixture-march-2020-420585.

Davies, H. (2020). *Private firm running UK PPE stockpile was sold in middle of pandemic*. https://www.theguardian.com/world/2020/apr/22/revealed-private-firm-running-uk-ppe-stockpile-was-sold-in-middle-of-pandemic.

Fitzpatrick, P. (2021). *How Taiwan beat COVID-19—New study reveals clues to its success*. https://theconversation.com/how-taiwan-beat-covid-19-new-study-reveals-clues-to-its-success-158900.

FitzRoy, F., & Spencer, D. (2020). *Economic policy response to the pandemic: From COVID-19 emergency to economic democracy*. https://www.iza.org/publications/pp/160/economic-policy-response-to-the-pandemic-from-covid-19-emergency-to-economic-democracy.

Foster, P., & Neville, S. (2020). *How poor planning left the UK without enough PPE*. https://www.ft.com/content/9680c20f-7b71-4f65-9bec-0e9554a8e0a7.

Geoghegan, P. (2020). *Cronyism and clientelism*. https://www.lrb.co.uk/the-paper/v42/n21/peter-geoghegan/cronyism-and-clientelism.

Giles, G. (2020). *Deaths from coronavirus far higher in England than first reported*. https://www.ft.com/content/c07e267b-7bca-418f-ad9e-8631a29854cb.

Hall, D. et al. (2020). *Privatised and unprepared: The NHS supply chain*. https://gala.gre.ac.uk/28230.

Heffer, G. (2020). *Coronavirus: Experts once said 20,000 deaths was a 'good outcome'—So where is the UK headed now?* https://news.sky.com/story/coronavirus-experts-once-said-20-000-deaths-was-a-good-outcome-so-where-is-the-uk-headed-now-11978609.

Hopkins, N. (2020*). Revealed: UK ministers were warned last year of risks of coronavirus pandemic*. https://www.theguardian.com/world/2020/apr/24/revealed-uk-ministers-were-warned-last-year-of-risks-of-coronavirus-pandemic.

IMF. (2021). *January)*. World economic outlook.

I-SAGE. (2020). *COVID-19 and health inequality: Independent SAGE Report 21*. https://www.independentsage.org/covid-19-and-health-inequality/.

Jones, O. (2021). *It's not 'greed' behind the Covid vaccine success. It's state finance and the NHS*. https://www.theguardian.com/commentisfree/2021/mar/24/greed-covid-vaccine-success-state-finance-nhs.

Kermani, S. (2020*). Coronavirus: Whitty and Vallance faced 'herd immunity' backlash, emails show*. https://www.bbc.co.uk/news/uk-politics-54252272.

Kinder, T., & Plimmer, G. (2020). *UK government paid £1.7bn to private groups for coronavirus contracts*. https://www.ft.com/content/7fe7c2d5-24df-431b-9149-50417fa0236a.

Klein, A. (2020). *Why New Zealand decided to go for full elimination of the coronavirus*. https://www.newscientist.com/article/2246858-why-new-zealand-decided-to-go-for-full-elimination-of-the-coronavirus.

Kollewe, J. (2021). *Pfizer forecasts $26bn from annual sales of Covid-19 vaccine*. https://www.theguardian.com/business/2021/may/04/pfizer-forecasts-26bn-annual-sales-covid-vaccine.

Kontopantelis, E., et al. (2020). Excess mortality in England and Wales during the first wave of the COVID-19 pandemic. *Journal of Epidemiology and Community Health*. https://doi.org/10.1136/jech-2020-214764

Lawrence, F. et al (2020*). How a decade of privatisation and cuts exposed England to coronavirus*. https://www.theguardian.com/world/2020/may/31/how-a-decade-of-privatisation-and-cuts-exposed-england-to-coronavirus.

Leys, C. (2021). *100,000 deaths and a White Paper: What we need instead in Britain*. https://socialistproject.ca/2021/03/100000-deaths-and-a-white-paper/.

Leys, C., & Player, S. (2011). *The plot against the NHS*. Merlin Press.

Marmot, M. et al. (2010). *Fair society, healthy Lives: The Marmot review*. https://www.parliament.uk/globalassets/documents/fair-society-healthy-lives-full-report.pdf.

Marmot, M., Allen, J., Boyce, T., Goldblatt, P., & Morrison, J. (2020). *Health equity in England: The Marmot review 10 years on*. https://www.health.org.uk/publications/reports/the-marmot-review-10-years-on.

McNally, A. (2020). *Backers of 'herd immunity' shouldn't have been allowed near Boris Johnson*. https://www.theguardian.com/commentisfree/2020/dec/14/herd-immunity-boris-johnson-coronavirus.

Merrick, R., & Woodcock, A. (2021). *Downing Street fails to deny report that Boris Johnson said UK should 'ignore' threat from Covid*. https://www.independent.co.uk/news/uk/politics/covid-boris-johnson-ignore-pandemic-b1817719.html.

Michell, J. (2020). *Coronavirus reveals the cost of austerity*. https://tribunemag.co.uk/2020/04/coronavirus-reveals-the-cost-of-austerity.

NAO. (2021). *The government's approach to test and trace in England—Interim report*. https://www.nao.org.uk/report/the-governments-approach-to-test-and-trace-in-england-interim-report/.

Newton, F. (2021). Britain's chumocracy. *Tribune*, winter, 14–15.

Payne, A. (2020). *Boris Johnson told Italy's prime minister the UK had been aiming for coronavirus herd immunity, new documentary reveals*. https://www.businessinsider.com/boris-johnson-told-italian-pm-conte-coronavirus-herd-immunity-plan-2020-6?r=US&IR=T.

Pegg, D., Booth, R., & Conn, D. (2020). Revealed: The secret report that gave ministers warning of care home coronavirus crisis. https://www.theguardian.com/world/2020/may/07/revealed-the-secret-report-that-gave-ministers-warning-of-care-home-coronavirus-crisis.

Pollock, A. (2021). *Test-and-trace workers are paying the price for the government's outsourcing zeal*. https://www.theguardian.com/commentisfree/2021/may/12/test-trace-workers-government-outsourcing.

Safi, M. (2021). *Oxford/AstraZeneca Covid vaccine research 'was 97% publicly funded'*. https://www.theguardian.com/science/2021/apr/15/oxfordastrazeneca-covid-vaccine-research-was-97-publicly-funded.A

Sell. (2020). What COVID-19 reveals about twenty-first century capitalism: Adversity and opportunity. *Development, 63*, 150–156.

Sridhar, D. (2021). *Here are five ways the government could have avoided 100,000 Covid deaths*. https://www.theguardian.com/commentisfree/2021/jan/27/five-ways-the-government-could-have-avoided-100000-covid-deaths.

Syal, R. (2020). *Government ignored warning to stockpile PPE as Covid-19 spread*. https://www.theguardian.com/world/2020/jun/12/government-ignored-warning-to-stockpile-ppe-as-covid-19-spread.
UK Home Office. (2020). *Statistics relating to passenger arrivals since the COVID-19 outbreak, August 2020*. https://www.gov.uk/government/statistics/statistics-relating-to-passenger-arrivals-since-the-covid-19-outbreak-august-2020/statistics-relating-to-passenger-arrivals-since-the-covid-19-outbreak-august-2020.
Van Wagtendonk, A. (2020). *The UK backs away from "herd immunity" coronavirus proposal amid blowback*. https://www.vox.com/world/2020/3/15/21180414/coronavirus-uk-herd-immunity-vallance-johnson.
Walsh, N. P., & Krever, M. (2020). *The UK's "coronavirus dashboard" may be under-reporting deaths significantly*. https://edition.cnn.com/2020/04/07/uk/coronavirus-uk-deaths-intl-gbr/index.html.
Wenham, C. (2020). *The UK was a global leader in preparing for pandemics. What went wrong with coronavirus?* https://www.theguardian.com/commentisfree/2020/may/01/uk-global-leader-pandemics-coronavirus-covid-19-crisis-britain.
Whyte, D. (Ed.). (2015). *How corrupt is Britain?* Pluto Press.

CHAPTER 9

# The USA: Decentralisation and Denial

The USA had the highest number of COVID-19 cases (32.1 million) and deaths (572,200) in the world, as of 26 April 2021. These tragic outcomes were due to large-scale mismanagement, that started even before the arrival of the pandemic. It is widely known that the US healthcare system is both extensively privatised and highly decentralised, with a skeletal and chronically underfunded public system underpinning a system of provision of health services including highly profitable transnational pharmaceutical corporations, massive corporate healthcare providers and small-scale clinics operating under different rules both within and across state boundaries. This system is notoriously expensive, inefficient, and it rules out most forms of co-operation even in emergencies (Hook & Kuchler, 2020).

After several decades of restructuring, 'efficiency savings', outsourcing and deindustrialisation, by early 2020 the USA lacked emergency stocks of PPE (they had been depleted in 2009, during the H1N1 outbreak, and were never replenished), as well as capacity to manufacture PPE and hospital equipment (Levey et al., 2020). In the meantime, the country's health system became heavily dependent on imports, primarily from

This chapter was co-authored with Nicolás Águila.



A. Saad-Filho, *The Age of Crisis*,
https://doi.org/10.1007/978-3-030-81608-7_9

China. Finally, the administration led by President Donald Trump deliberately dismantled the institutions of pandemic control; for example, Timothy Ziemer, head of global health security at the National Security Council, was dismissed in April 2018, and his team was disbanded. Similarly, the Trump administration cut the budget of the Centers for Disease Control and Prevention (CDC), in order to fund the detention of immigrant children (Mars & Guimón, 2020). It is mind-boggling.

## Just like the Flu

The US response to the coronavirus was marked by denialism, a persistent underestimation of the impact of the pandemic, grave mismanagement of the federal response and almost complete disregard for science, except in the potentially profitable manufacture of vaccines (Milman, 2020). Responsibility for that mangled response and its tragic consequences lies squarely with President Donald Trump (Parton, 2020).

Trump's narcissism, crude electoral calculations and dysfunctional government fed an inconsistent discourse drawing upon both denialism and the trade-off between 'health' and 'the economy' (see Chapter 5), with most politicians giving the latter greater priority regardless of the abundance of resources in the richest country on Earth (Marcetic, 2020). In the words of the Republican Party Congressman Trey Hollingsworth, 'it is always the American government's position to say, in the choice between the loss of our way of life as Americans and the loss of life, of American lives, we have to always choose the latter' and 'It is not zero evil, but it is the lesser of these two evils and we intend to move forward that direction' (LeBlanc, 2020). Given this viewpoint, once the coronavirus arrived, instead of focusing on the health crisis Trump and his band of followers preferred to divert attention by engaging in scrapes with China, the WHO, journalists, the civil service, state governors, foreign countries and assorted politicians at home and abroad. All that Trump achieved—perhaps deliberately—was the paralysis of the public administration (Aratani, 2020).

Trump was informed about the pandemic in January 2020 and proceeded to ignore it in public almost entirely until March, when he made a statement at the CDC declaring that everything was under control and that the coronavirus posed no significant risks (Saletan, 2020). He ridiculed social distancing and facemasks, to the point of going to a medical equipment factory in Maine without protective equipment. The firm later discarded that day's output, perhaps because of the risk of contamination (Fritze & Collin, 2020). The President also insisted that hydroxychloroquine should be used against COVID-19, even though it had no proven efficacy (BBC News, 2020a), and suggested that disinfectant could be injected to rid patients of the coronavirus (it was left unclear if this should be done orally, intravenously, or in other ways). Trump would persistently undermine his public health officials, and suggested several times that he would fire Anthony Fauci (whom Steve Bannon reportedly wanted to behead; Lee, 2020), the popular epidemiologist acting as health spokesman for the White House's Coronavirus Task Force (McCarthy, 2020a). Finally, the US President launched unprecedented attacks on the media because of their unflattering coverage of the pandemic and heavy criticisms of his government (Smith, 2020).

In the international sphere, far from promoting co-operation, the US government displayed almost as much hostility against its allies as it did against its so-called strategic enemies. First, Trump attributed the virus to Chinese biological warfare and uttered coarse slurs against the Chinese people, for example by calling the coronavirus 'kung flu', 'China flu' or 'the Chinese virus' (Itkowitz, 2020). Trump's attacks triggered escalating violence against Asian Americans (BBC News, 2020b). Second, the USA left the WHO and suspended its funding in mid-April 2020, accusing the organisation of bending to Chinese influence (Luce, 2020). Yet, the policy confusion in the USA and the country's inability to produce enough PPE opened spaces that China was quick to occupy. China became the most prominent international donor in the pandemic, dislocating the USA as it increased production and started sending both money and equipment worldwide. In the meantime, the USA stumbled. As casualties increased, Trump would regularly moan and complain on television and spread lies and insults in social media, so much so that he would eventually be excluded from Facebook and Twitter. Third, released from the usual conventions and restraints, the US administration unleashed extraordinary attacks against foreign countries, hijacked stocks of foreign- (usually Chinese-) made masks and ventilators en route to their legitimate buyers and hurled insults at other countries for being too weak to do anything about it. These depredations inflicted grave damage to the legitimacy of the American Empire (Doğantekin, 2020; Jeffery, 2020; Wright, 2020).

Domestically, the absence of federal coordination forced states to compete against one another for supplies of PPE, pushing up prices and reducing the efficiency of procurement (Hook & Kuchler, 2020). In the meantime, some local authorities (e.g., the City of New York and several states) imposed lockdowns, but their governors and mayors were publicly berated by Trump, who urged his supporters to 'liberate' these areas (Shear & Mervosh, 2020).

Trump's insistence that COVID-19 was 'like the flu' (Beer, 2020) was strongly supported by right-wing militias, fanatical religious sects, conspiracy theorists and anti-vaxxers, many overtly adorned with Nazi paraphernalia. They led noisy demonstrations against the lockdowns, ritually burned facemasks and threatened state governors with kidnapping or worse, in an escalation that would culminate with the frenzied attack on the US Capitol on 6 January 2021 (Baxter, 2020; Beckett, 2020; Bessner & A'Lee Frost, 2021). Yet Trump supported them, declaring that they are 'great people' whose 'life was taken away from them' (Sevastopulo & Shubber, 2020).

The mounting crisis in the USA was not merely a problem of public health. The impact of the coronavirus was compounded by the extreme 'flexibility' of the US labour market, that shed more than 40 million jobs as soon as the pandemic arrived and the economy shut down (Aratani, 2020). This 'first wave' of unemployment was compounded by a second wave, in which mid-level posts (office managers, law clerks and so on) were culled, since they had no production to oversee and no one left to supervise. This was a textbook-case Keynesian downward spiral that could be halted only by public policy (Tooze, 2020). Symptomatically, long lines of pedestrians and automobiles soon formed at food banks across the USA, while homeless people were regimented into sleeping in improvised (but scrupulously socially distant) spaces in car parks in Las Vegas, below hotel towers that, although empty, were too lavish for them: astonishing spectacles of need and waste in a country long habituated to other people's suffering.

Several hospitals collapsed as COVID-19 spread, revealing the shortcomings of the US healthcare system (Hook & Kuchler, 2020). While health providers counted their losses, since emergency care for COVID-19 patients was far less profitable than the cosmetic surgeries and other expensive treatments dislocated by the pandemic, their workers were pushed to the limit. They had to work long hours without appropriate pay and lacking PPE, which led to a grave loss of life among frontline nurses and other workers, especially migrants and people of colour, reflecting the precarity of their working conditions (The Guardian, 2021).

Beyond hospital care, the US testing strategy was slow and limited, partly because of capacity constraints and partly because of insufficient coordination. First, not enough tests could be produced in the early months because of shortages and bottlenecks; there were no national guidelines for the distribution and management of tests, and no federal standards for reporting the results (The Independent, 2020). These limitations were made worse by Trump's decision to transfer responsibility for testing to the states, that immediately began competing for resources and raising prices for everyone (see above). Second, there never was a federal plan for contact tracing or quarantines, which facilitated the spread of the disease (Lewis, 2021; McCarthy, 2020b; Reich, 2020; Stein 2020). Even when the states attempted to cover the gap, they tended to lack resources to do so adequately (Aschwanden, 2020). Third, when federal funds were made available, most states lacked complementary services, for example, residences for people who could not isolate themselves at home and meals, healthcare, financial assistance and other support for those in quarantine. Consequently, compliance tended to be low and patchy, helping to spread the virus (Madad2020). Even though Trump invoked early on the Defense Production Act, introduced during the Korean War, allegedly to compel firms to produce PPE, this was never effective, and most executive orders actually issued were unrelated to the production of medical equipment (Jacobs, 2020).

It was just as bad at the individual level. Millions of US residents do not have health insurance, and many of those who did could not afford their COVID-19-related expenses. It was reported that individual bills because of coronavirus treatment ranged from US$100 to US$4,000 for insured people, and up to US$100,000 for the uninsured (Herman, 2020; Holpuch, 2021)— in a country where 40% of people do not have US$400 for an emergency (Youn, 2019). These costs not only left many people trapped in debt in the depths of a severe crisis; they also prevented many from seeking care or even self-isolating when they fell ill.

Despite the dramatic failings described above, Trump declared in March that he took no responsibility at all and blamed, instead, his predecessor Barack Obama and the outdated rules and health regulations he had inherited (Oprysko, 2020).

## No Responsibility at All

The pandemic hit the US economy severely, with the IMF (2021a) estimating a GDP contraction of 3.4% in 2020, the largest decline in national output since 1946. However, the most significant economic feature of the pandemic in the USA was the dramatic growth of unemployment at first contact (see above). In April 2020 alone, 20.5 million jobs disappeared, taking the unemployment rate to 14.7%, the highest level since the Great Depression.

In response, the US government adopted expansionary fiscal policies amounting to 16.7% of GDP, plus an additional 2.4% in equity, loans and guarantees, that drove the fiscal deficit to 18.7% of GDP (IMF, 2021b). The most important piece of legislation in this regard was the Coronavirus Aid, Relief, and Economic Security (CARES) Act approved on 27 March 2020, providing approximately US$3 trillion for economic recovery, including cheques of US$1,200 to households, US$600 per week in benefits and loan forgiveness to small businesses. However, it appears that most of the funds were used to bail out large companies, many of which also benefitted from soaring profits during the pandemic.

The CARES Act included funding for the so-called Operation Warp Speed, a public–private partnership to expedite the development of COVID-19 vaccines and advance-purchase output from Moderna, Pfizer, Merck, Novavax, Johnson & Johnson and other large companies. These were partnerships of unequal whereby, in essence, the US government funded private capital to produce vaccines with guaranteed demand at any price, and no downside risks in case of failure (Brenner, 2020; Sirota, 2020; Stone, 2020). This was the most successful federal initiative during the pandemic. Vaccine distribution began on 14 December 2020, and moved at a fairly quick pace; by mid-April 2021, 38% of the population had already received at least one vaccine dose, and 24% had received two doses (Carlsen et al., 2021).

Employment recovered swiftly from the catastrophe, falling to 6% by March 2021.[1] The rapid loss of jobs and the fast-paced recovery reveal a key fragility of the world's largest neoliberal economy: it is heavily dependent on unskilled, low-paid, unprotected and non-unionised jobs. This difficulty was worsened by the lack of universal healthcare, which implied that, often, as workers lost their jobs they and their families also lost their health cover: a tragedy for households, and a disaster for the collective (Conley, 2020; Healy, 2020; Herman, 2020). Their loss of income forced many people to look for a job during the pandemic, making it harder to self-isolate or take precautions against the coronavirus.

Despite the rapid recovery of the US economy, there is no prospect that government finances can stabilise any time soon. In particular, the domestic public debt will continue to rise, as President Biden rapidly passed a US$1.9 trillion COVID-19 relief plan, with an additional US$3 trillion long-term funding being considered for infrastructure (Wolf, 2021). In the meantime, the focus on the pandemic helped the Trump administration and Republican states pass unrelated legislation with minimal scrutiny, for example, reducing curbs on pollution, raising penalties for abortion and restricting the right to vote (Friedman, 2020; Glenza, 2020).

## 'I Can't Breathe'

The pandemic affected disproportionally African Americans, Latino and Native American (famously the Navajo) communities (Cheetham, 2020), where rates of infection and death were significantly above average (Cuthbertson, 2020; Fedor & Zhang, 2020; Lerner, 2020; Kendi, 2020; Oladipo, 2020; Oppel Jr. et al., 2020). For example, Latinos and African Americans were three times more likely to get infected and two times more likely to die from coronavirus than whites. At the same time, the government's distributionally skewed response to the pandemic is bound to have increased the already enormous inequalities of income and wealth in the USA (Politi et al., 2020; Rushe, 2020; Thorbecke & Mitropoulos, 2020). Tax breaks for the rich, support to finance and government guarantees pumped up financial asset prices to the benefit of speculators, while the assistance going to workers and small businesses was both drastically insufficient and time-limited (Nolan, 2020). Awareness of these inequalities was part of the background of the demonstrations following the murder by police officers of Breonna Taylor, in March 2020, and George Floyd, in May 2020. The video showing Floyd being suffocated despite pleading that he could not breathe sparked protests in 60 countries and over 2,000 cities.

Politically, the year was also marked by the presidential elections, in November, which were won by the Democratic Party challenger, Joe Biden. President Trump notoriously refused to accept the results claiming fraud (Breuninger, 2020). Trump went to the courts repeatedly attempting to overturn the results or, at least, trying to create doubts about the outcome. Although Trump eventually conceded, his campaign spurred protests by a myriad of right-wing groups, culminating with the invasion of the Capitol as Congress was certifying Biden's victory (Bessner & A'Lee Frost, 2021).

In summary, the US pandemic response suffered from the combination of extensive deindustrialisation; a fragmented, bloated and inefficient health system; high inequality of income and wealth, extreme flexibility in the labour markets and high informalisation of labour; lack of a welfare state and universal safety nets; highly fragmented and decentralised political and administrative systems fostering policy incoherence, competition rather than resource-sharing, systemic inefficiencies and, above all, the unwillingness of the federal government to recognise the problem and act accordingly.

## Notes

1. https://www.statista.com/statistics/273909/seasonally-adjusted-monthly-unemployment-rate-in-the-us/

## References

Aratani, L. (2020). US job losses pass 40m as coronavirus crisis sees claims rise 2.1m in a week. https://www.theguardian.com/business/2020/may/28/us-job-losses-unemployment-coronavirus

Aschwanden, C. (2020). Contact Tracing, a Key Way to Slow COVID-19, Is Badly Underused by the U.S. https://www.scientificamerican.com/article/contact-tracing-a-key-way-to-slow-covid-19-is-badly-underused-by-the-u-s/

Baxter, H. (2020). The Americans who think that coronavirus is a hoax. https://www.independent.co.uk/independentpremium/long-reads/coronavirus-conspiracy-theory-trump-us-hoax-a9498081.html

BBC News. (2020a). Coronavirus: Hydroxychloroquine ineffective says Fauci. https://www.bbc.co.uk/news/world-us-canada-53575964

BBC News. (2020b). Covid "hate crimes" against Asian Americans on rise. https://www.bbc.co.uk/news/world-us-canada-56218684

Beckett, L. (2020). 'All the psychoses of US history': how America is victim-blaming the coronavirus dead. https://www.theguardian.com/world/2020/may/21/all-the-psychoses-of-us-history-how-america-is-victim-blaming-the-coronavirus-dead

Beer, T. (2020). All The Times Trump Compared Covid-19 To The Flu, Even After He Knew Covid-19 Was Far More Deadly. https://www.forbes.com/

sites/tommybeer/2020/09/10/all-the-times-trump-compared-covid-19-to-the-flu-even-after-he-knew-covid-19-was-far-more-deadly/?sh=b613007f9d2f
Bessner, D., & A'Lee Frost, A. (2021). How the QAnon Cult Stormed the Capitol. https://www.jacobinmag.com/2021/01/q-anon-cult-capitol-hill-riot-trump
Brenner, R. (2020). Escalating Plunder. *New Left Review, 123*, 5–22.
Breuninger, K. (2020). Trump refuses to accept election results, says it's 'far from over'. https://www.cnbc.com/2020/11/07/trump-refuses-to-accept-election-results-says-it-is-far-from-over.html
Carlsen, A. Huang, P. Levitt, Z. and Wood, D. (2021). How Is The COVID-19 Vaccination Campaign Going In Your State? https://www.npr.org/sections/health-shots/2021/01/28/960901166/how-is-the-covid-19-vaccination-campaign-going-in-your-state?t=1618592090650
Cheetham, J. (2020). Navajo Nation: The people battling America's worst coronavirus outbreak. https://www.bbc.co.uk/news/world-us-canada-52941984
Conley, J. (2020). 'The Next Crisis': Up to 43 Million Americans Could Lose Health Insurance Due to Pandemic, Study Shows. https://www.commondreams.org/news/2020/05/10/next-crisis-43-million-americans-could-lose-health-insurance-due-pandemic-study?amp&__twitter_impression=true
Cuthbertson, A. (2020). Coronavirus tracked: How Covid-19 deaths in the US compare by race and ethnicity. https://www.independent.co.uk/news/world/americas/coronavirus-deaths-us-race-black-white-asian-latino-racism-a9544401.html
Doğantekin, V. (2020). US "steals" medical supplies amid pandemic. https://www.aa.com.tr/en/americas/us-steals-medical-supplies-amid-pandemic-expert/1800001
Fedor, L., & Zhang, C. (2020). Covid-19 pandemic hits black voters' incomes hardest, FT poll shows. https://www.ft.com/content/e22636d7-8259-4b97-bcf8-19349cee61fd?shareType=nongift
Friedman, L. (2020). E.P.A., Citing Coronavirus, Drastically Relaxes Rules for Polluters. https://www.nytimes.com/2020/03/26/climate/epa-coronavirus-pollution-rules.html
Fritze, J., & Collins, M. (2020). As Trump touts increased production, coronavirus swabs made during his Maine factory tour will be tossed in the trash. https://eu.usatoday.com/story/news/politics/2020/06/05/trump-maine-puritan-throw-away-coronavirus-swabs/3153622001/
Glenza, J. (2020). States use coronavirus to ban abortions, leaving women desperate: 'You can't pause a pregnancy'. https://www.theguardian.com/world/2020/apr/30/us-states-ban-abortions-coronavirus-leave-women-desperate

Healy, J. (2020). Workers Fearful of the Coronavirus Are Getting Fired and Losing Their Benefits. https://www.nytimes.com/2020/06/04/us/virus-unemployment-fired.html?referringSource=articleShare

Herman, B. (2020). Coronavirus likely forced 27 million off their health insurance. https://www.axios.com/coronavirus-27-million-lost-employer-health-insurance-c77fe46a-691d-49b3-9cd2-3ad6d19df159.html

Holpuch, A. (2021). 'I don't make enough': the financial cost of having Covid in the US. https://www.theguardian.com/us-news/2021/feb/12/us-financial-cost-covid-coronavirus

Hook, L., & Kuchler, H. (2020). How coronavirus broke America's health-care system. https://www.ft.com/content/3bbb4f7c-890e-11ea-a01c-a28a3e3fbd33

IMF. (2021a). World Economic Outlook, January 2021 Update.

IMF. (2021b). Fiscal Monitor April 2021: A fair shot.

Itkowitz, C. (2020). Trump again uses racially insensitive term to describe coronavirus. https://www.washingtonpost.com/politics/trump-again-uses-kung-flu-to-describe-coronavirus/2020/06/23/0ab5a8d8-b5a9-11ea-aca5-ebb63d27e1ff_story.html

Jacobs, A. (2020). Despite Claims, Trump Rarely Uses Wartime Law in Battle Against Covid. https://www.nytimes.com/2020/09/22/health/Covid-Trump-Defense-Production-Act.html

Jeffery, L. (2020). German, French Officials Accuse U.S. of Diverting Supplies. https://www.npr.org/2020/04/04/827321294/german-french-officials-accuse-u-s-of-diverting-supplies?t=1586817225869

Kendi, I. X. (2020). What the Racial Data Show. https://www.theatlantic.com/ideas/archive/2020/04/coronavirus-exposing-our-racial-divides/609526/

LeBlanc, P. (2020). GOP Congressman Says Letting More Americans Die of Coronavirus is Lesser of Two Evils Compared to Economy Tanking. https://edition.cnn.com/2020/04/14/politics/trey-hollingsworth-coronavirus/index.html

Lee, B. Y. (2020). Steve Bannon Suggests Beheading Fauci, What To Do About Threats To Health Experts. https://www.forbes.com/sites/brucelee/2020/11/06/twitter-bans-steve-bannon-account-after-talk-of-a-beheaded-anthony-fauci-wray/?sh=358ea96a4ac8

Lerner, S. (2020). Coronavirus numbers reflect New York City's deep economic divide. https://theintercept.com/2020/04/09/nyc-coronavirus-deaths-race-economic-divide/

Levey, N. N., Christensen, K., & Phillips, A. M. (2020). A disaster foretold: Shortages of ventilators and other medical supplies have long been warned about. https://www.latimes.com/politics/story/2020-03-20/disaster-foretold-shortages-ventilators-medical-supplies-warned-about

Lewis, T. (2021). How the U.S. Pandemic Response Went Wrong—and What Went Right—during a Year of COVID. https://www.scientificamerican.com/article/how-the-u-s-pandemic-response-went-wrong-and-what-went-right-during-a-year-of-covid/

Luce, E. (2020). Inside Trump's coronavirus meltdown. https://www.ft.com/content/97dc7de6-940b-11ea-abcd-371e24b679ed

Madad, S., Nuzzo, J., & Bourdeaux, M. (2020). The missing piece in America's COVID-19 isolation and quarantine strategy: Wraparound services. https://doi.org/10.1377/hblog20201207.458415/full/

Marcetic, B. (2020). Give Me Liberty — No, Wait, Give Me Death. https://jacobinmag.com/2020/05/republicans-conservatives-coronavirus-economy-terrorism

Mars, A., & Guimón, P. (2020). Los 100.000 muertos de Estados Unidos: así ha fracasado el país más poderoso del mundo. https://elpais.com/internacional/2020-05-26/los-100000-muertos-de-estados-unidos-asi-ha-fracasado-el-pais-mas-poderoso-del-mundo.html?s%E2%80%A6

McCarthy, T. (2020a). Trump claims 'total authority' and attacks media in chaotic coronavirus briefing. https://www.theguardian.com/world/2020/apr/13/trump-us-coronavirus-briefing-latest-media

McCarthy, T. (2020b). No leadership and no plan: is Trump about to fail the US on coronavirus testing? https://www.theguardian.com/us-news/2020/may/02/donald-trump-us-coronavirus-testing

Milman, O. (2020). Scientists alarmed as Trump embraces fringe views and extreme theories amid pandemic. https://www.theguardian.com/us-news/2020/jun/03/trump-coronavirus-conspiracy-theories-pandemic

Nolan, H. (2020). There Is No Plan (For You). https://inthesetimes.com/article/covid-19-coronavirus-unemployment-eviction-healthcare-united-states

Oladipo, G. (2020). 'It's like they're waiting for us to die': Why Covid-19 is battering Black Chicagoans. https://www.theguardian.com/us-news/2020/oct/23/covid-19-battering-black-chicagoans

Oppel Jr., A. Gebeloff, R. Lai, K.K.R. Wright, W., & Smith, M. (2020). The fullest look yet at the racial inequity of coronavirus. https://www.nytimes.com/interactive/2020/07/05/us/coronavirus-latinos-african-americans-cdc-data.html

Oprysko, C. (2020). 'I don't take responsibility at all': Trump deflects blame for coronavirus testing fumble. https://www.politico.com/news/2020/03/13/trump-coronavirus-testing-128971

Parton, H. D. (2020). How Trump's chaotic incompetence – and the "deconstruction" of the "deep state" – got us here. https://www.rawstory.com/2020/03/how-trumps-chaotic-incompetence-and-the-deconstruction-of-the-deep-state-got-us-here/

Politi, J., Fontanella-Khan, J., & Aliaj, O. (2020). Why the US pandemic response risks widening the economic divide. https://www.ft.com/content/d211f044-ecf9-4531-91aa-b6f7815a98e3
Reich, R. (2020). *Donald Trump rushed to reopen America—Now Covid is closing in on him.* https://www.theguardian.com/commentisfree/2020/jul/05/donald-trump-reopen-america-covid-19-coronavirus
Rushe, D. (2020). Making billions v making ends meet: How the pandemic has split the US economy in two. https://www.theguardian.com/us-news/2020/aug/16/us-inequality-coronavirus-pandemic-unemployment
Saletan, W. (2020). The Trump Pandemic. https://slate.com/news-and-politics/2020/08/trump-coronavirus-deaths-timeline.html
Sevastopulo, D., & Shubber, K. (2020). Trump cheers as anti-lockdown protests spread. https://www.ft.com/content/c8f6f413-39c4-47ce-b1ff-0e02969cb612
Shear, M. D., & Mervosh, S. (2020). Trump encourages protest against governors who have imposed virus restrictions. https://www.nytimes.com/2020/04/17/us/politics/trump-coronavirus-governors.html
Sirota, D. (2020). The US public paid to develop this COVID-19 drug. It will cost $3,000 a dose. https://www.jacobinmag.com/2020/06/gilead-remdesivir-drug-coronavirus-treatment-cost-pharma
Smith, D. (2020). Trump reverts to media-bashing and blame-casting in latest press conference. https://www.theguardian.com/us-news/2020/mar/19/trump-us-coronavirus-briefing-media
Stein, R., Wroth, C., & Hurt, A. (2020). U.S. Coronavirus Testing Still Falls Short. How's Your State Doing? https://www.npr.org/sections/health-shots/2020/05/07/851610771/u-s-coronavirus-testing-still-falls-short-hows-your-state-doing?t=1591694986359
Stone, J. (2020). The People's Vaccine—Moderna's Coronavirus Vaccine Was Largely Funded By Taxpayer Dollars. https://www.forbes.com/sites/judystone/2020/12/03/the-peoples-vaccine-modernas-coronavirus-vaccine-was-largely-funded-by-taxpayer-dollars/?sh=3ccf47146303
The Guardian. (2021a). Our key findings about US healthcare worker deaths in the pandemic's first year. https://www.theguardian.com/us-news/ng-interactive/2020/dec/22/lost-on-the-frontline-our-findings-to-date
The Independent. (2020). Will the US ever have a national COVID-19 testing strategy? https://www.independent.co.uk/news/will-the-us-ever-have-a-national-covid19-testing-strategy-donald-trump-strategy-people-joe-biden-us-b1767005.html
Thorbecke, C., & Mitropoulos, A. (2020). 'Extreme inequality was the preexisting condition': How COVID-19 widened America's wealth gap. https://abcnews.go.com/Business/extreme-inequality-preexisting-condition-covid-19-widened-americas/story?id=71401975&cid=social_twitter_abcn

Tooze, A. (2020). Shockwave. https://www.lrb.co.uk/the-paper/v42/n08/adam-tooze/shockwave

Wolf, M. (2021). Larry Summers: 'I'm concerned that what is being done is substantially excessive'. https://www.ft.com/content/380ea811-e927-4fe1-aa5b-d213816e9073

Wright, B. (2020). U.S. Accused of stealing ventilators from Barbados as coronavirus spreads in the Caribbean. https://newsone.com/3924158/barbados-accuses-us-ventilators-seized/

Youn, S. (2019). 40% of Americans don't have $400 in the bank for emergency expenses: Federal reserve. https://abcnews.go.com/US/10-americans-struggle-cover-400-emergency-expense-federal/story?id=63253846:~:text=Almost%2040%25%20of%20American%20adults,a%20Federal%20Reserve%20survey%20finds

CHAPTER 10

# Brazil: Inequality and Catastrophe

The course of COVID-19 was exceptionally tragic in Brazil, arguably the country with the worst pandemic response on Earth, the only one where the government not only neglected its basic duties but actively *undermined* measures that could have contained the pandemic and protected the population, and the greatest experiment in 'herd immunity' in modern times. The death toll in Brazil reached 1,000 on 12 April 2020, 10,000 on 11 May, 100,000 on 10 August, 200,000 on 9 January 2021 and 400,000 on 1 May.[1] Matters deteriorated considerably since the emergence of more contagious variants in the country. On 8 April 2021, daily fatalities reached 4,250, the highest number in the world.[2] The health system descended into chaos in numerous cities, where oxygen supplies had to be rationed, ICU beds were fully occupied, and both staff and equipment were lacking. Reports pointed to patients being tied up in order to be intubated, for want of anaesthetics. Hundreds died in trolleys, hospital floors or at home, even when their families could procure much-needed oxygen tubes in the parallel market (Pellegrini 2021). There is no question that these tragic outcomes were driven by far-right President Jair Bolsonaro, whose choices triggered an unparalleled tragedy in the country, potentially with tragic implications worldwide (Mattoso, 2021).


A. Saad-Filho, *The Age of Crisis*,
https://doi.org/10.1007/978-3-030-81608-7_10

## Roots of the Tragedy

Brazil's tragedy resulted from the convergence of three factors. First, it was shown in Chapters 5 and 7 that more equal societies with strong states implementing coordinated policies generally addressed the pandemic more effectively, while unequal societies with weak states, unresponsive governments and poorly coordinated policies tended to do much worse. Brazil's spectacular failure can be viewed from both angles. Although the country had enough economic resources to confront the pandemic (for example, Brazil's GDP per capita exceeds US$9,000, while Vietnam's barely reaches US$2,500), Brazil is famously one of the most unequal on Earth: one-quarter of its population lives in poverty, despite the country's large economy, sophisticated manufacturing industry and powerful extractive and agribusiness sectors. These deep and overlapping inequalities created grave vulnerabilities among the disadvantaged populations.[3]

Brazil has always had acute political and institutional limitations, but they worsened markedly with the unprecedentedly long and deep economic crisis starting in 2014, that was followed in 2016 by a judicial-parliamentary *coup d'état* that removed elected President Dilma Rousseff. The governments in power since 2016 sponsored neoliberal 'reforms' that increased labour precarity, worsened social security and left public services dramatically underfunded. These reforms were underpinned by Constitutional Amendment 55, which froze the non-financial expenditures of the federal government in real terms for 20 years. These destructive 'reforms' would culminate in the election of Jair Bolsonaro, in 2018.[4] Bolsonaro, a former Army officer, is widely known for his authoritarian impulses, fascist discourse, threats against the Constitution and, increasingly, corruption too. His whims, unbalanced personality and policy preferences would play an outsized role in the Brazilian catastrophe. In other words, entrenched inequalities, institutional dysfunctionalities, economic crisis and political disasters contributed to the pandemic onslaught, and to the public policies that would be deployed—or not—to address it.

Second, Brazil's 1988 Constitution designed a Scandinavian-style welfare state in the country, including a universal health system (*Sistema Único de Saúde*, SUS) free at the point of use, inspired by the British NHS. SUS is recognised as an exemplary health system in the Global South. However, it was clear before the pandemic that SUS was being systematically degraded and starved of funds by the post-2016 administrations. These processes were marked by the dramatic removal of thousands of Cuban doctors serving in Brazil's remotest regions, in 2018, purely for political reasons. Thousands of COVID-19 deaths can be directly attributed to the lack of trained staff, intensive care beds, ventilators, oxygen tubes and even gloves and medicines in the public hospitals (Ortega & Orsini, 2020; Ricardo, 2020; Rocha et al., 2021; Salluh & Lisboa, 2016). Partly as a consequence of the social and economic inequalities in the country, and partly because of the policy-induced limitations in the health system, Brazil has suffered recently from waves of dengue fever, Chikungunya, Zika, H1N1 and other plagues that, invariably, afflict disproportionately the most marginalised and vulnerable, especially the poor, the unemployed, and Black and Indigenous communities (De Negri et al., 2020; Garcia & Silva., 2016; Marinho et al., 2021; Neri & Soares, 2002, Oxfam Brasil, 2020).

Third, while the pandemic made its way around the world President Bolsonaro systematically downplayed the risks because precaution would look bad, suggest 'feminine' weakness, or endanger his re-election in 2022. Uniquely among the leaders of the world's largest countries, Brazil's President did not 'dither' when the country was confronted with the pandemic. Instead, Bolsonaro deliberately undermined public safety and actively sought to prevent any form of coordinated or effective response by the political and health institutions in the country. The President blamed the left for the 'hysteria', referred to the disease as 'a little flu' that would affect only the weak, and proclaimed that 'we will not get [too badly hit] ... because Brazilians ... don't catch anything; I saw a guy jump into a sewer, diving there ... nothing happened to him' (Silva & Pasti, 2020; UOL, 2020). Bolsonaro relentlessly criticised mayors and governors when they tried to impose lockdowns, social distancing rules or mask use, promoted fake cures (especially ivermectin and hydroxychloroquine, which he ordered to be purchased in deals tainted by allegations of corruption; 247 [2021b]; Gussen [2021]), sabotaged every step of the vaccination programme, held many maskless public events and neglected the health system, while using the pandemic to divert attention away from the rollout of a host of neoliberal policy changes, including the removal of protections to labour and the environment.

## The Role of the Individual in History

In the face of a mounting death toll Bolsonaro asked rhetorically 'what do you want me to do?', and claimed that he 'did not have responsibility for anything', since 'we all die in the end'. As the number of deaths surpassed 260,000, Bolsonaro complained that people were 'moaning' too much and, if they expected vaccines, 'they are idiots … go look for [vaccines] at your mother's home!' (Pereira, 2021; Ribeiro, 2021). As deaths piled up, Bolsonaro continued to pander to his core supporters among the upper middle classes, capital, the far right and pentecostal church-business conglomerates. His Ministers of Health (four, in the first year of the pandemic) invariably ran into trouble if they challenged Bolsonaro's obsession with minimising the pandemic, avoiding any form of lockdown or social distancing and, above all, if Bolsonaro suspected that they could threaten him electorally with untimely expressions of competence.[5] Only psychiatrists can explain Bolsonaro's behaviour. He never accounted for his necropolitics in detail,[6] and, when questioned, responded with insults and threats of violence. Needless to say, Bolsonaro never expressed regret for the hundreds of thousands of lives lost under his watch.

Bolsonaro's bluster, slurs and lies were similar in character to those spouted by other 'spectacular' authoritarian leaders, even if Bolsonaro's discourse tended to be more coarse, cruel and unpredictable than theirs (Donald Trump, Jarosław Kaczyński and Rodrigo Duterte are tame and polite in comparison with Jair Bolsonaro). In 'normal' times, brutal attacks had often been sufficient to extract those leaders from political trouble, especially if they were supported by a pliant Congress, a sympathetic judiciary and a tolerant commentariat ('hehe, that's naughty, isn't it, but this is him, what can we do, he really is a character, but he is genuine, and no one is perfect anyway', and so on, in an embarrassing roll of excuses for the inexcusable)—mercies that would never have been extended to left-wing political leaders.

It was symptomatic of Brazil's entrenched inequalities that the pandemic reached the country through rich tourists returning from Italian ski holidays, but the first person to die was one of their domestic workers (Nunes, 2020; Rudan, 2020; Saad-Filho, 2020; Sakamoto, 2020). The pandemic made its way from there, trickling down from the rich to kill mainly the poor, first in the periphery of the wealthy cities of São Paulo and Rio de Janeiro and, later, reaching the poor North and Northeast regions, where its impact was multiplied by the precarious housing, health, nutrition and other circumstances of the poor. In rich as well as poor regions, the coronavirus spread among the poor first, and with the greatest lethality (Marino et al., 2020).

As the virus spread, Bolsonaro refused to impose a national lockdown, followed Donald Trump in declaring that quack cures would resolve the problem and, anyway, individuals with athletic bodies 'like myself' need not worry about COVID-19 (Maia, 2020). His employees agreed, with staff from the Ministry of Finance stating that 'It's good that deaths are concentrated among the old … That will improve our economic performance as it will reduce our pension deficit' (Cole, 2020). By refusing to act Bolsonaro abandoned the matter to local mayors and state governors, but they were never resourced appropriately by the federal government, and Bolsonaro never stopped criticising the public health measures taken at any level of the administration (Bahia et al., 2021; Nicolelis, 2021; Richmond, 2020).

Denialism from Brasília clashed with local pressures, leading to a patchwork of rules that Bolsonaro used as an argument against all restrictions: shopping centres closed in some cities but remained open in neighbouring ones, different regulations on mask use and public transport applied in each city and state and rules were set according to local lobbies rather than medical evidence, often focusing more on the protection of profits than on public health. Inevitably, policies would soon make little sense even in the same city (e.g., in São Paulo, in mid-2020, the shopping centres were open but public parks were closed; Bonduki, 2020). The tug-of-war between Bolsonaro, the governors and the mayors culminated in Bolsonaro's threats, in April 2021, to deploy the armed forces *against* local lockdowns. You could not make it up.

As the public health crisis worsened, and the contrast between the emerging global consensus and the chaos in Brazil became increasingly evident, large sections of the middle class and the mainstream media broke away from Bolsonaro, and started criticising him in more and more strident terms. The President radicalised his discourse to shore up his base of support. He picked daily fights with the media, invented grievous lies about the pandemic, cursed every critic and proffered escalating threats against the political establishment, the Supreme Court, the Constitution, the media, the left, former President Lula and every source of opposition. As his popularity dipped, Bolsonaro escalated his assaults, openly threatened a *coup d'état* and increased his reliance on the military (Mercier

& Gortázar, 2020); he even tried a 'self-coup' in March 2021, but it failed because the military high command refused to support Bolsonaro's adventure. In the meantime, COVID-19 mass testing never took off, contact tracing never even started and the country only had a vaccination campaign because of pressure from the state governors and a decision by the Supreme Court—surely a unique case in the world.

The escalating disagreements about lockdowns and other preventative policies were not merely due to Bolsonaro's posturing, perversity or his possible mental health problems (Schwartsman, 2021). They had a material basis; first, in the economic vulnerability of most workers in a poor, unequal and highly deregulated economy. More than half of workers in Brazil are in the informal sector, and they would have little economic security in a lockdown; survival would depend entirely upon state transfers, which Bolsonaro and his Minister of Finance, Paulo Guedes, opposed (see below and Saad-Filho & Feil, 2021). Second, many employers were against lockdowns, social distancing and even mask use, because of the perception that they would hurt profits. In turn, a lockdown would leave millions of workers and small entrepreneurs with zero income, and many firms with zero sales and zero credit, lending plausibility to Bolsonaro's statements about a trade-off between health and the economy, and the need to protect the latter. Perversely, lockdowns would also push the poor into crowded homes lacking water, sewerage and, with rising unemployment, also food and medicines (Mercier & Gortázar, 2020). In the favelas of Rio de Janeiro, drug gangs took the initiative to impose a lockdown, in order to reduce the health risks in the community and improve their own business environment (Schipani & Harris, 2020). No pandemic policy is sustainable under these circumstances.

The early stages of the crisis were accompanied by a significant under-counting of the victims (Collucci, 2021). By mid-2020, for every ten deaths due to COVID-19 another eight were attributed to the generic category 'acute respiratory distress syndrome' (ARDS) (Rossi & Buono, 2020; Sivakumaran et al., 2020). By the end of the year, with improved reporting systems, Brazil had registered 226,528 deaths from all respiratory illnesses, of which 195,000 were attributed to COVID-19. This leaves a residue of 31,500 deaths attributed to ARDS while, in the previous six years, the average number of ARDS deaths was only 5,600.[7] These deaths do not include those due to the indirect impact of the pandemic, especially those wrongly attributed to something else because of the lack of tests, family objections to the word 'coronavirus' on the death certificate of their loved ones (Redação, 2020), or misidentification, since the coronavirus ravages not only the lungs but also the heart, kidneys, brain and other organs. In addition, there were countless premature deaths due to the inability of patients with cancer or other illnesses to obtain the care that would otherwise have been available to them (Jornal da USP, 2020).

## Bolsonaro Seizes the Initiative

The only significant measure to protect the poor was initiated by the left parties in Congress, offering emergency transfers of R$600 (US$117) per month during the pandemic to 65 million people (out of a population of 210 million): the most generous transfer programme in Brazilian history (Richmond, 2020; Saad-Filho & Feil, 2021). Bolsonaro and his Minister of Finance, the ex-Chicago Boy Paulo Guedes, rejected it on the neoliberal grounds of 'fiscal restraint'. Under growing pressure, Bolsonaro offered R$200 (US$40) per month. The left forced a vote, and the measure was approved as part of a 'War Budget' bypassing the fiscal deficit limits. For the bottom half of earners, this transfer programme raised incomes by more than the pandemic had reduced them, cutting poverty and neutralising the inequality-generating impact of the pandemic (Nassif-Pires et al., 2020).

Shockingly, given his entirely negative role in the pandemic, Bolsonaro rushed to present the income support as 'his' grant to the poor, together with other expansionary measures including credit lines for small and medium enterprises. His approval ratings rose among the poor, just as they were tumbling among the middle class (Richmond, 2020). However, the income support programme ended with the start of the new fiscal year, in January 2021, and it was replaced in April by a much smaller grant of R$250 (US$44) per month for three months, conditional on deeper reforms of the public administration and fiscal cuts elsewhere (Londres & Aguiar, 2021). The lack of federal income support has made it impossible for the states and municipalities to impose local lockdowns, virtually guaranteeing that the pandemic would get worse.

In common with other countries, the opinion polls in Brazil have shown a correlation between disregard for the pandemic and support for the 'spectacular' authoritarian leader. In these countries, the fatalities tend to be attributed to God's will, destiny, bad luck, or the victims themselves, because of their frailty or irresponsible behaviour. In addition, the rising death toll and mass exhaustion with the erratic policies being implemented in Brazil tended to increase the tolerance to risk in a society that was already wedded to inequality, crime, violence, illness, risky behaviours, deaths and disregard for the Other. Many people continued to visit their friends, shop in the high streets and congregate in bars and restaurants. Mask use was never generalised. The virus spread even more, feeding the disaster.

Finally, the pandemic offered Bolsonaro's administration an opportunity to roll out destructive policies with minimal scrutiny. In May 2020, Environment Minister Ricardo Salles was caught on video declaring, at a ministerial meeting, that: 'We need to make an effort while we are in this calm moment in terms of press coverage, because they are only talking about COVID, and push through changes in all the [environmental protection] rules and [we must] simplify norms' (Spring, 2020). This would lead, for example, to his attempt to abolish the 'permanent protection zones' around Brazil's mangroves and other fragile coastal ecosystems, which would later be blocked in Court (BBC, 2020). Similar attacks were launched against protections for Indigenous and Quilombola (descendants of escaped slaves) communities,[8] while the government accelerated its privatisation programme and intensified the repression against dissent. No less significantly, the pandemic also diverted attention from corruption scandals involving the president's family (Alves, 2021; The Guardian, 2021; Londoño et al., 2020).

To add insult to injury, on the day when the death toll reached 4,000 (and total deaths approached 350,000), in early April 2021, the Chamber of Deputies passed legislation allowing private firms to purchase coronavirus vaccines, in direct violation of the Constitution. This parallel route to vaccines would allow the rich to bypass the (halting) vaccination programme led by SUS, and reduce the political pressures to make it succeed at national level. In the meantime, the Armed Forces prevented civilians from accessing their health facilities, even when occupation reached 100% in civilian hospitals, while military facilities often had 85% spare capacity (Filgueiras, 2021).

## Moving Forward

After more than 400,000 reported deaths, the fact that Jair Bolsonaro's toxic discourse and behaviour still find resonance among large (though, fortunately, declining) segments of the population is a sad reminder that political debates can have lethal consequences. Bolsonaro bears personal responsibility for the Brazilian tragedy, but this is due not only to his incompetence, stupidity or mental health condition(s) or the perversity of his supporters, although these are undoubtedly contributing factors. The Brazilian President has actively promoted the spread of COVID-19 for his own political gain (Brum, 2021). Bolsonaro benefits from the corrosion of social bonds, delegitimation of public policies and institutions and deepening political divisions, as they prepare the ground for Bolsonaro's ultimate goal of self-perpetuation through a *coup d'état*. This danger will remain as long as he is in power; in the meantime, the population has been left exposed to the coronavirus. The outcome has been the exponential growth of deaths, the worst economic contraction in Brazilian history and creeping social and political chaos. Meanwhile, the neoliberal reforms, the dismantling of the state and the destruction of the environment remain top of the government's agenda.

## Notes

1. See https://covid19.who.int/region/amro/country/br
2. See https://susanalitico.saude.gov.br/extensions/Covid-19_html/Covid-19_html.html; https://covid19.who.int/, https://susanalitico.saude.gov.br/extensions/Covid-19_html/Covid-19_html.html; https://ourworldindata.org/coronavirus/country/brazil
3. 'Inequality makes it difficult for people to see themselves and others as equals and worthy of the same consideration. It leads to the perception that public power exists to serve the most affluent and to control the poor' (Sakamoto 2020).
4. For an overview of Brazil's political economy during this period, see Loureiro and Saad-Filho (2019), Saad-Filho and Boffo (2020), Saad-Filho and Morais (2018); for an illustration of the impact of the coup against President Dilma Rousseff on poverty and inequality, see 247 (2021a; Douglas, 2018).
5. See Harris and Schipani (2020), Lipton et al. (2020a; 2020b), Phillips and Phillips (2020), Richmond (2020), Silva and Pasti (2020). The concept of 'medical populism' can offer useful insights for the understanding of Bolsonaro's approach to the pandemic (Lasco, 2020; Speed & Mannion, 2020).
6. Mbembe's (2003) notion of necropolitics stems from the assumption that 'the ultimate expression of sovereignty resides, to a large degree, in the power and the capacity to dictate who may live and who must die'

(p. 11). This modality of politics therefore accounts 'for the various ways in which, in our contemporary world, weapons are deployed in the interest of maximum destruction of persons and the creation of *death-worlds*, new and unique forms of social existence in which vast populations are subjected to conditions of life conferring upon them the status of *living dead*' (p. 40). For a more detailed examination, see Mbembe (2019). For the case of Brazil, see Jorge (2020).

7. Data from http://info.gripe.fiocruz.br/
8. See Ribeiro Scaldaferri (2020), Rocha (2020) and https://cebrap.org.br/pesquisas/desigualdades-raciais-e-covid-19/

## References


247. (2021a). Desigualdade cresceu em todos os trimestres após o golpe contra Dilma. https://www.brasil247.com/brasil/desigualdade-cresceu-em-todos-os-trimestres-apos-o-golpe-contra-dilma-nkkpcroh

247. (2021b). A história secreta da cloroquina. https://www.brasil247.com/midia/a-historia-secreta-da-cloroquina-o-novo-documentario-da-tv-247-xnz4f6r4

Alves, R. (2021). Money-laundering scheme a Bolsonaro family business? https://brazilian.report/power/2021/03/16/money-laundering-scheme-a-bolsonaro-family-business/

Bahia, L., Chade, J., Dedecca, C. S., Domingues, J. M., Gonçalves, G. L., Herz, M., Lavinas, L., Ocké-Reis, C., Ortiz, M. E. R., & Santos, F. (2021). *A tragédia brasileira do coronavírus/covid-19: Uma análise do desgoverno do governo federal, 2020–2021.* https://www.clacso.org/en/a-tragedia-brasileira-do-coronavirus-covid-19/

BBC News. (2020). Brazil judge stymies plan to revoke mangrove protection. https://www.bbc.com/news/world-latin-america-54350180

Bonduki, N. (2020). Bruno Covas: por que os shoppings estão abertos e os parques fechados? https://www1.folha.uol.com.br/colunas/nabil-bonduki/2020/06/bruno-covas-por-que-os-shoppings-estao-abertos-e-os-parques-fechados.shtml

Brum, E. (2021). Pesquisa revela que Bolsonaro executou uma "estratégia institucional de propagação do coronavírus". https://brasil.elpais.com/brasil/2021-01-21/pesquisa-revela-que-bolsonaro-executou-uma-estrategia-institucional-de-propagacao-do-virus.html

Cole, B. (2020). Brazil government aide says COVID-19's toll on elderly will reduce pension deficit as country's outbreak escalates. https://www.newsweek.com/brazil-government-aide-says-covid-19s-toll-elderly-will-reduce-pension-deficit-countrys-1506830

Collucci, C. (2021). Subnotificação esconde ao menos 30% das mortes, diz estudo. https://www1.folha.uol.com.br/equilibrioesaude/2021/05/subnotificacao-dos-casos-de-covid-esconde-ate-30-das-mortes-mostra-estudo.shtml

De Negri, F., Galliez, R. M., Miranda, P., Koeller, P., Zucoloto, G. F., Costa, J. S. D. M., Farias, C. M. D., Travassos, G. H., & Medronho, R. D. A. (2020). Chances de óbito por COVID-19 entre os trabalhadores formais: Evidências do Estado do Rio de Janeiro. http://repositorio.ipea.gov.br/handle/11058/10301

Douglas, B. (2018). Number of Brazilians Living in Poverty Rises 2 Million in a Year. https://www.bloomberg.com/news/articles/2018-12-05/number-of-brazilians-living-in-poverty-rises-2-million-in-a-year

Filgueiras, L. (2021). Que País é Esse? https://www.bnews.com.br/artigo/1431,que-pais-e-esse.html

Garcia, L. P., & Silva, G. D. M. (2016). *Doenças Transmissíveis e Situação Socioeconômica no Brasil: Análise Espacial.* https://www.ipea.gov.br/portal/index.php?option=com_content&view=article&id=29193%3Atd-2263-doencas-transmissiveis-e-situacao-socioeconomica-no-brasil-analise-espacial&catid=390%3A2016&directory=1&Itemid=1

Gussen, A. F. (2021). O que há por trás do lobby de Bolsonaro pelo uso da cloroquina. https://www.cartacapital.com.br/politica/o-que-ha-por-tras-do-lobby-de-bolsonaro-pelo-uso-da-cloroquina/

Harris, B., & Schipani, A. (2020). Jair Bolsonaro triggers furore by firing Brazil's health minister. https://www.ft.com/content/5c362cbc-aadf-4849-94a6-ed9b19ef0a29

Jorge, M. R. (2020). Bolsonaro's Brazil in times of COVID-19: A necropolitical pharmakon. https://www.e-ir.info/2020/05/19/bolsonaros-brazil-in-times-of-covid-19-a-necropolitical-pharmakon/

Jornal da USP. (2020). Com poucos testes de covid-19, mortes por todas as causas viram dado crucial. https://jornal.usp.br/atualidades/calculo-do-pico-da-covid-19-deve-levar-em-conta-quantidade-de-mortes/

Lasco, G. (2020). Medical populism and the COVID-19 pandemic. *Global Public Health, 15*(10), 1417–1429.

Lipton, E., Sanger, D., Haberman, M., Shear, M., Mazzetti, M., & Barnes, J. (2020a). He could have seen what was coming: Behind Trump's failure on the virus. https://www.nytimes.com/2020/04/11/us/politics/coronavirus-trump-response.html#click=https://t.co/njIugzJ3bq

Lipton, E., Sanger, D., Haberman, M., Shear, M., Mazzetti, M., Barnes, J., Londoño E., & Simões, M. (2020b). Brazil president embraces unproven "cure" as pandemic surges. https://www.nytimes.com/2020/06/13/world/americas/virus-brazil-bolsonaro-chloroquine.html

Londoño, E., Andreoni, M., & Casado, L. (2020). "A family business:" Graft investigation threatens Brazil's Bolsonaro. https://www.nytimes.com/2020/08/28/world/americas/brazil-bosonaro-corruption.html
Londres, M., & Aguiar, P. (2021). Congresso Nacional aprova a PEC que recria auxílio emergencial. https://noticias.r7.com/prisma/r7-planalto/congresso-nacional-aprova-a-pec-que-recria-auxilio-emergencial-12032021
Loureiro, P. M., & Saad-Filho, A. (2019). The limits of pragmatism: The rise and fall of the Brazilian workers' party (2002–2016). *Latin American Perspectives, 46*(1), 66–84.
Maia, G. (2020). Quem tem 'bom preparo' não tem que se preocupar com Covid-19, diz Bolsonaro. https://oglobo.globo.com/sociedade/quem-tem-bom-preparo-nao-tem-que-se-preocupar-com-covid-19-diz-bolsonaro-24620080
Marinho, F., Teixeira, R., Machado, H. A., Lima, M., Venturini, A. C., Sousa, C. J., & Bertolozzi, T. B. (2021). Disparidades raciais no excesso de mortalidade em tempos de Covid-19 em São Paulo. https://cebrap.org.br/pesquisas/desigualdades-raciais-e-covid-19/
Marino, A., Klintowitz, D., Brito, G., Rolnik, R., Santoro, P., & Mendonça, P. (2020). Circulação para trabalho explica concentração de casos de Covid-19. https://www.cartamaior.com.br/?/Editoria/Sociedade-e-Cultura/Circulacao-para-trabalho-explica-concentracao-de-casos-de-Covid-19/52/48008
Mattoso, C. (2021). Vice do Amazonas diz que política de imunidade de rebanho apoiada por Bolsonaro levou Manaus ao colapso. https://www1.folha.uol.com.br/colunas/painel/2021/05/vice-do-amazonas-diz-que-politica-de-imunidade-de-rebanho-apoiada-por-bolsonaro-levou-manaus-ao-colapso.shtml
Mbembe, A. (2003). Necropolitics. *Public Culture, 15*(1), 11–40.
Mbembe, A. (2019). *Necropolitics*. Duke University Press.
Mercier, D., & Gortázar, N. G. (2020). Bolsonaro da alas al golpismo en un acto contra la cuarentena. https://elpais.com/internacional/2020-04-20/el-presidente-bolsonaro-da-alas-al-golpismo-en-un-acto-con-seguidores.html
Nassif-Pires, L., Carvalho, L., & Rawed, E. (2020). *Multidimensional inequality and COVID-19 in Brazil*, Levy Economics Institute of Bard College Public Policy Brief. http://www.levyinstitute.org/files/download.php?file=ppb_153.pdf&pubid=2690
Neri, M., & Soares, W. (2002). Desigualdade social e saúde no Brasil. Cadernos de Saúde Publica 18. https://www.scielo.br/scielo.php?script=sci_arttext&pid=S0102-311X2002000700009
Nicolelis, M. (2021). Brazil's pandemic is a 'biological fukushima' that threatens the entire planet. https://www.scientificamerican.com/article/brazils-pandemic-is-a-lsquo-biological-fukushima-rsquo-that-threatens-the-entire-planet/

Nunes, J. (2020). The COVID-19 pandemic: Securitization, neoliberal crisis, and global vulnerabilization. *Cadernos de Saúde Pública*, 36(5).

Ortega, F., & Orsini, M. (2020). Governing COVID-19 without government in Brazil: Ignorance, neoliberal authoritarianism, and the collapse of public health leadership. *Global Public Health, 15*(9), 1257–1277.

Oxfam Brasil. (2020). Pandemia de coronavírus escancara desigualdades brasileiras. https://www.oxfam.org.br/noticias/pandemia-de-coronavirus-escancara-desigualdades-brasileiras/

Pellegrini, A. (2021). O cenário trágico nos hospitais do Brasil que chega a 300 mil mortos. https://www.nexojornal.com.br/expresso/2021/03/24/O-cen%C3%A1rio-tr%C3%A1gico-nos-hospitais-do-Brasil-que-chega-a-300-mil-mortos

Pereira, F. (2021). Bolsonaro: "Tem idiota que diz 'vai comprar vacina'. Só se for na casa da tua mãe!". https://www.opovo.com.br/noticias/politica/2021/03/04/bolsonaro---tem-idiota-que-diz--vai-comprar-vacina---so-se-for-na-casa-da-tua-mae.html

Phillips, T., & Phillips, D. (2020). Bolsonaro dragging Brazil towards coronavirus calamity, experts fear. https://www.theguardian.com/world/2020/apr/12/bolsonaro-dragging-brazil-towards-coronavirus-calamity-experts-fear

Redação, (2020). Família ameaça médico que anotou suspeita de COVID-19 em óbito. https://catracalivre.com.br/cidadania/familia-ameaca-medico-que-anotou-suspeita-de-COVID-19-em-obito/

Ribeiro Scaldaferri, L. (2020). Bolsonaro promove genocídio contra os povos indígenas. https://esquerdaonline.com.br/2020/08/06/bolsonaro-promove-genocidio-contra-os-povos-indigenas/

Ribeiro, M. (2021). Brasil, 200 mil mortes por Covid: 200 frases de Bolsonaro minimizando a pandemia. https://br.noticias.yahoo.com/200-frases-de-bolsonaro-minimizando-a-pandemia-do-coronavirus-203647435.html

Ricardo, L. (2020). Sinpro condena falta de investimento do governo na saúde pública. https://www.sinprodf.org.br/sinpro-condena-falta-de-investimento-do-governo-na-saude-publica/

Richmond, M. A. (2020). "A Little Flu" Could Be Fatal for Jair Bolsonaro. https://jacobinmag.com/2020/03/jair-bolsonaro-coronavirus-covid-political-crisis

Rocha, C. (2020). Os vetos de Bolsonaro à lei de proteção de indígenas e quilombolas. https://www.nexojornal.com.br/expresso/2020/07/08/Os-vetos-de-Bolsonaro-%C3%A0-lei-de-prote%C3%A7%C3%A3o-de-ind%C3%ADgenas-e-quilombolas

Rocha, R., Atun, R., Massuda, A., Rache, B., Spinola, P., Nunes, L., Lago, M., & Castro, M. C. (2021). Effect of socioeconomic inequalities and vulnerabilities on health-system preparedness and response to COVID-19 in Brazil:

A comprehensive analysis. https://www.thelancet.com/journals/langlo/article/PIIS2214-109X(21)00081-4/fulltext
Rossi, A., & Buono, R. (2020). As mortes incógnitas da pandemia. https://piaui.folha.uol.com.br/as-mortes-incognitas-da-pandemia/
Rudan, I. (2020). A cascade of causes that led to the COVID-19 tragedy in Italy and in other European Union Countries. *Journal of Global Health*, https://www.ncbi.nlm.nih.gov/pmc/articles/PMC7125421/
Saad-Filho, A. (2020). Coronavirus: How Brazil became the second worst affected country in the world. https://theconversation.com/coronavirus-how-brazil-became-the-second-worst-affected-country-in-the-world-141102
Saad-Filho, A., & Boffo, M. (2020). The corruption of democracy: Corruption scandals, class alliances, and political authoritarianism in Brazil. *Geoforum*. https://www.sciencedirect.com/science/article/pii/S0016718520300373
Saad-Filho, A., & Feil, F. (2021). COVID-19 in Brazil: How Jair Bolsonaro created a calamity. https://theconversation.com/covid-19-in-brazil-how-jair-bolsonaro-created-a-calamity-159066
Saad-Filho, A., & Morais, L. (2018). *Brazil: Neoliberalism versus democracy*. Pluto.
Sakamoto, L. (2020). Coronavírus: Brasil mostra que é projetado para matar pobre em pandemia. https://noticias.uol.com.br/colunas/leonardo-sakamoto/2020/05/06/coronavirus-brasil-mostra-que-e-projetado-para-matar-pobre-em-pandemia.htm?cmpid=copiaecola
Salluh, J. I. F., & Lisboa, T. (2016). Critical care in Brazil. *ICU Management and Practice*. https://healthmanagement.org/c/icu/issuearticle/critical-care-in-brazil-1
Schipani, A., & Harris, B. (2020). Drug gangs in Brazil's favelas enforce coronavirus lockdown. https://www.ft.com/content/aaef1591-2fc5-4e6f-ab84-0e83b5a146ca
Schwartsman, H. (2021). Bolsonaro é louco? https://www1.folha.uol.com.br/colunas/helioschwartsman/2021/01/bolsonaro-e-louco.shtml
Silva, R., & Pasti, D. (2020). Da "gripezinha" ao "e daí?": as falas de Bolsonaro em cada fase da pandemia. https://www.agazeta.com.br/es/politica/da-gripezinha-ao-e-dai-as-falas-de-bolsonaro-em-cada-fase-da-pandemia-0520
Sivakumaran, S., Davies, G., & Al Sallakh, M. (2020). Coronavirus can cause lasting lung damage – but the effects may ease over time. https://theconversation.com/coronavirus-can-cause-lasting-lung-damage-but-the-effects-may-ease-over-time-140398
Speed, E., & Mannion, R. (2020). Populism and health policy: Three international case studies of right-wing populist policy frames. *Sociology of Health & Illness, 42*(8), 1967–1981.

Spring, J. (2020). Brazil minister calls for environmental deregulation while public distracted by COVID. https://www.reuters.com/article/us-brazil-politics-environment-idUSKBN22Y30Y

The Guardian. (2021). The Guardian view on Jair Bolsonaro: A danger to Brazil, and the world. https://www.theguardian.com/commentisfree/2021/apr/05/the-guardian-view-on-jair-bolsonaro-a-danger-to-brazil-and-the-world

UOL. (2020). Bolsonaro: Brasileiro tem que ser estudado. Pula no esgoto e nada acontece. https://noticias.uol.com.br/politica/ultimas-noticias/2020/03/26/bolsonaro-brasileiro-tem-que-ser-estudado-cai-no-esgoto-e-nada-acontece.htm

CHAPTER 11

# India: From Hubris to Disaster

In early June 2021, India had reported nearly 30 million cases and 350,000 deaths due to COVID-19, placing it near the top of the lists of worst-affected countries (these figures are likely to be significant under-estimates; Gettleman et al., 2021; *The Economist*, 2021). The spiralling death toll and the countless tragedies that it encompasses were unquestionably due to the arrogance, carelessness and opportunism of Prime Minister Narendra Modi, of the 'Hindutva nationalist' Bharatiya Janata Party (BJP) (Kaul, 2021; Purewal, 2021), one of the largest and most aggressive organisations associated with authoritarian neoliberalism in the world.

## The First Wave

On 24 March 2020, the government led by Prime Minister Modi announced, quite suddenly, a strict national lockdown which, in theory, would confine the highest number of people in the world. The lockdown was imposed with only 4 hours' notice and it lacked compensatory economic measures. Inevitably, it sparked a scarcely imaginable turmoil as

This chapter was co-authored with Nicolás Águila.



A. Saad-Filho, *The Age of Crisis*,
https://doi.org/10.1007/978-3-030-81608-7_11

several million migrants, day labourers and poor workers and their families were suddenly locked out of their jobs and found themselves deprived of employment and money and, consequently, food and housing. Many desperate and penniless people felt compelled to return to their villages in order to survive, and rushed to catch overpriced buses, trains or any other means of transportation available, where exploitation was rife and social distancing impossible. Others decided to travel hundreds of miles on foot or illegally crammed into trucks, risking death by hunger or exhaustion (Lakhani, 2020). The chaos led to the deaths of up to 1,000 people, including at least 12 victims of police brutality, often gratuitous (Chowdhury & Narayanan, 2021; Krishnan, 2020), as well as several victims of violence against Muslims, who were accused by the far right linked to the BJP of being 'spreaders of the virus' (Loh et al., 2020). The uncontrollable mass migration spread the coronavirus all over India: a thoughtless policy mistake that spawned a tragedy (Ghosh, 2020, 2021). This was not the first time that Modi's government triggered mass panic with poorly considered policy changes; the most severe earlier event was the sudden demonetisation of the INR 500 and INR 1,000 banknotes, in 2016, which achieved none of its stated goals and caused untold stress and heavy losses to many poor people (Chandrasekhar & Ghosh, 2015).

Despite the imperative to confront the coronavirus, it was always obvious that a lockdown would have limited efficacy in India, given the poverty and precarious living conditions of hundreds of millions of people, the fact that the vast majority of workers (possibly in excess of 95%) are in the informal sector and lack most forms of social protection (Ghosh, 2020), and the overcrowding, lack of water, poor sanitation and limited possibilities for isolation at home for hundreds of millions of people (Newsclick, 2020). The lockdown created not only health challenges and widespread economic hardship; it also led to a surge in gender-based violence and sexual abuse, especially against Dalit women (Loh et al., 2020).

In the meantime, the government introduced a highly limited testing strategy that assumed that there was no local transmission and focused, instead, on protecting the country's borders (Ferry et al., 2020). This strategy may have been motivated, in part, by a misperception of the prevalence of the coronavirus in India and, in part, by the lack of laboratory capacity to process a large number of tests; for example, in Uttar Pradesh, the most populous state in India, one testing lab was supposed to serve 30 million people (Rukmini, 2020; Yadav et al., 2020). Although private labs rapidly ramped up their testing capacity, their prices were invariably too high for most people. Finally, the Indian health system is notoriously fragile; the vast majority of people cannot afford private health, the public institutions routinely operate at full capacity, services are underfinanced and there are significant regional differences in terms of access, availability and quality of care (Dennis, 2021). Ventilators are limited in number and cannot be manufactured in the country, and the availability of intensive care beds is low by international standards (according to the World Bank, India had 0.53 hospital beds per 1,000 people, which is significantly below the world average of 2.9). Fatally, as would be tragically revealed later, supplies of oxygen for medical purposes were also limited.

The first wave of COVID-19 peaked in mid-September 2020, when the seven-day average of new cases hit 93,199; cases subsequently declined until mid-February 2021, when the seven-day average reached 'only' 11,145.

## Authoritarianism

The policies of the Modi administration were marked by authoritarianism and brutality. The administration imposed the lockdown invoking the Disaster Management Act of 2005, that allows the central government to take extraordinary measures and requires local authorities to comply and implement the commands from the centre (Gul, 2020). However, there was a pattern of inadequate coordination between different levels of government. For example, the national government issued more than 4,000 new rules during the two months of the lockdown (*The Economist*, 2020), frequently without consultation or adequate preparation time. The state governments were expected to abide by the rules of the moment, and were mandated to deliver a growing set of health and economic relief measures without either resources or capacity for implementation, and with severe limitations on their ability to borrow (Ghosh, 2020).

In the meantime, the national government seized the opportunity to crack down on the protests that had been brewing since the introduction of laws discriminating against Muslims, in December 2019, which centred on the reforms of the National Register of Citizens and the Citizenship Amendment Act. The government immediately attacked the dissenters, and charged organisers and journalists alike under India's severe anti-terror laws (Ellis-Petersen, 2020; Lakhani, 2020). Further waves of protest followed, culminating on what was probably the largest strike in history, on 26 November 2020, involving up to 250 million people (Crowley, 2020). Finally, the government ordered Twitter to censor tweets and deactivate accounts critical of their handling of the pandemic (BBC, 2021a).

The national government launched relatively early on a contact tracing app which institutions and individuals were ordered to install, with penalties for non-compliance. This became the fastest downloaded app on record, reaching 50 million downloads in two weeks, and 181 million users by May 2021, even if this remains a low proportion of the country's population.[1] The app requires a considerable amount of personal information, and it is designed to allow users to assess their own symptoms and calculate the risk of infection. It also has access to GPS and Bluetooth data to keep track of the user's status and location (Al Dahdah & Javed Alam, 2020). Serious concerns have been expressed about this app, because the data is sent to servers under the control of the national government, and there has been a blank refusal to explain how it will be used, who has access to it and for how long. Although the government insists that the data are anonymised, it has declined to explain how, or to release the computer codes. The terms of the app also exclude the government from any liability for its use, and the country does not have a privacy law. Violations predictably followed; they included the publication of the personal details of people on quarantine lists, as well as evidence that the police in Karnataka tracked people using their GPS data (Al Dahdah & Javed Alam, 2020; Ellis-Petersen, 2020).

## The Second Wave

In January 2021, Modi declared that: 'With made-in-India solutions, we controlled the spread of the virus and improved our health infrastructure' (*The Economist*, 2021). In February, a BJP resolution claimed that: 'It can be said with pride, India … defeated Covid-19 under the able, sensible, committed and visionary leadership of Prime Minister Modi … The party unequivocally hails its leadership for introducing India to the world as a proud and victorious nation in the fight against Covid' (Rachman, 2021). At the beginning of March, the health minister said that India was in the 'end game of the Covid-19 pandemic' (Press Trust of India, 2021). The confidence of the government can also be seen in Modi's declaration that the country was 'the world's pharmacy' (Mumbai

Mirror, 2021). India's pharmaceutical industry, comprising more than 3,000 companies and 10,000 manufacturing facilities, is the third largest in the world in volume and it supplies 20% of generic drugs and 62% of the world's vaccines (Avhad, 2020). Against COVID-19, the country has been producing Covishield, Johnson & Johnson, Covaxin, Sputnik V and ZyCoV-D (Menon, 2021).

The government and the BJP could not have been more wrong. Since mid-February 2021, there has been a staggering surge in cases (on 22 April, India had almost 333,000 cases, the highest one-day number ever recorded until then, and that record would be surpassed over several consecutive days subsequently). The real figures are likely to be far worse, given the lack of testing and the generalised practice of undercounting, sometimes by political *diktat*, with some estimates placing the real number of cases and deaths between 10 and 30 times higher than those reported by the government (Gettleman et al., 2021; *The Economist*, 2021). The predictable consequences followed. Hospitals ran out of beds, blood and oxygen and mortuaries became so full that bodies would be mass cremated or allowed to decompose at home or on the streets, and many were simply thrown into the river Ganges (*The Guardian*, 2021). The situation was so dire that black markets emerged for oxygen tubes and other health equipment (Roy, 2021).

The spike in infections was partly attributed to the so-called 'double mutant' or Delta (B.1.617) variant that seems to have emerged in the country.[2] However, it was left unclear how much more contagious or fatal this variant actually is, so at the time of writing scientists remain cautious about attributing to it the surge in cases and deaths. It may be, instead, that government policies bear most of the responsibility for the tragedy (Rao, 2021; Sample & Davis, 2021). Simply put, the administration did little to prepare for the inevitable second wave; they failed to expand hospital capacity, increase production or stockpile PPE and oxygen and did not boost testing capacity sufficiently (Taneja & Singh Bali, 2021).

The central government also miscalculated massively the transmissibility of the coronavirus, as it allowed cricket matches and religious festivals to go ahead with minimal requirements for social distancing and mask use. A staggering 25 million people attended the Kumbh Mela festival since January, and two million devotees crammed together to bathe in the River Ganges on 12 April, in the northern city of Haridwar. The government accused its critics of being 'ignorant' and 'hinduphobic'

(Ellis-Petersen & Hassan, 2021; Farrer, 2021; Safi & Dhillon, 2021). Similarly, Modi held huge maskless rallies as late as 17 April, pursuing his dream of winning the elections in West Bengal (the BJP failed miserably). By then, the number of new daily cases already exceeded 200,000 (*The Guardian*, 2021).

Despite a promising start in mid-January, India's vaccination programme lagged badly and, by the end of April, only around 10% of the population had received the first dose of a vaccine (BBC, 2021b). The government placed orders late, did not properly fund local suppliers and was slow to approve foreign vaccines for domestic use (*The Economist*, 2021). Vaccine production did not expand fast enough largely because of input shortages, in some cases because of the US export ban. Additionally, a large number of vaccines was either exported for commercial reasons, or used in exercises in 'vaccine diplomacy' (Kolhatkar, 2021), perhaps in an attempt to rival China, until an Indian export ban was imposed in late March (Findlay et al., 2021). To add insult to injury, the national government placed the responsibility for vaccination on the states, that suddenly found that they had to compete with each other for scarce doses without sufficient funding and with rising prices because of the bidding war engineered by the government in Delhi. As a result, the facilities where Indians can get free vaccines are severely limited, while rich people can easily pay large sums to be vaccinated in private facilities (Ghosh, 2021).

## The Economy

The pandemic triggered an economic disaster. GDP fell 8% in 2020, worsening the already weak position of the most vulnerable members of society. Millions of people need their daily income to survive and pay their debts, and they rely on internal migration to get jobs. Daily wage workers, including homeless and landless people, migrant workers, agricultural labourers, displaced persons, street children, persons with disabilities, older people, tribal and other remote communities, single women and others were severely hit by the pandemic and the economic crisis, and suffered significant losses of income and surges in hunger and violence (Newsclick, 2020). Around 120 million jobs were lost in April 2020, leading to a record-high unemployment rate of 23.5%,[3] but this rate fell to 6.5% in January 2021. However, a survey in October showed that only 3% of the respondents were earning their pre-pandemic income (Chowdhury & Narayanan, 2021; Vyas, 2020).

Despite these difficulties, the government's fiscal response was extremely limited, partly because of fears that it might trigger a downgrade in the country's sovereign rating (Ahmed & Kumar 2020). At the beginning, not only the government did not increase its spending sufficiently, but it even went under budget to limit the fiscal deficit due, given the sharp decline in tax collection due to the health crisis and the lockdowns (Chandrasekhar & Ghosh, 2020). After six weeks of lockdown the government finally announced a package supposedly equivalent to 10% of GDP, but only 1% was in the form of expansionary fiscal measures; the rest was through credit, which does not imply any additional fiscal outlays (Ghosh, 2020).

Eventually, the government increased spending and, given the decline in tax collection, the fiscal deficit reached 12.3% of GDP, while government debt hit 89.6% of GDP. Nevertheless, the additional spending and forgone revenues were only 3.3% of GDP, and the new loans, equity and guarantees amounted to 5.1% of GDP, lagging significantly behind the stimulus in the AEs and even in many DEs (IMF, 2021). Even worse, the fiscal budget for 2021–2022 shows a decrease in spending in health, education, food and the rural employment guarantee (Chowdhury & Narayanan, 2021). This is hardly a basis for long-term economic recovery.

## The Kerala Exception

The Southwestern state of Kerala was India's beacon of hope during the first wave of the pandemic: by early August 2020, the state had only 94 deaths in a population of 36 million (Jenkins & Ram, 2020).

Kerala's success was due not only to the immediate response of its health authorities but, also, to its continued investment in universal healthcare (every village has a health centre and medical staff) and education (its literacy rate and life expectancy are the highest in India; Varghese, 2020). The state is governed by the Left Democratic Front, a coalition of Marxist and other left-wing parties, and the local government actively involves trade unions and civil society organisations. Kerala has a relatively high human development index despite the state's low per capita income, and a successful history dealing with crises, such as the Nipah virus, in 2018, as well as frequent floods (Krishna, 2020). Economically, it has the advantage of receiving more remittances than any other Indian state, mostly from skilled workers in the Gulf. The state is also an important tourism hub (Kurian, 2020).

Kerala was among the first states in India to introduce precautionary measures, including a statewide lockdown imposed before the national one. Additionally, the government of Kerala implemented mechanisms to identify, isolate and treat those infected, including external border controls (Spinney, 2020). In part, the early response (starting on 20 January 2020) was required due to the close connection between the state and Wuhan, the original locus of the virus in China.

The government included different groups (including religious and civil society organisations) in the design and implementation of its policies, which guaranteed community support and avoided the resistance seen elsewhere, for example, against the closure of places of worship. Additionally, the government created a community force to address the crisis, to which more than 300,000 volunteers signed up. They were trained, given PPE, and paid to provide food, essentials and assistance to those under lockdown. The government also created community kitchens to feed the hungry.

The strategy consisted of promoting physical distancing and sanitary precautionary measures even before the lockdown. The state hired manual contact tracers, who used anonymised GPS data from mobile phones and CCTV footage, and posted routes online with a number to call if people had been in contact with anyone who had tested positive for COVID-19. The local government also communicated effectively in several languages, in order to educate the population about the pandemic. In addition, a mental health helpline was available for people in quarantine, and a WhatsApp helpline was set up for victims of domestic abuse (Varghese, 2020). There was also a WhatsApp group to inform about government measures related to the pandemic (Spinney, 2020). The government of Kerala transformed houseboats used for tourism into isolation wards, housed migrants in empty buildings and delivered meals to children at home. Additionally, they supported the production of hand sanitiser and masks, and Kerala was the first Indian state to provide rapid test kits: all of this while being discriminated against by the national government, and despite the severe limitations in the state's own resources (Chowdhury & Sundaram, 2020).

Despite these successes, Kerala had to face difficult challenges in the second wave of the pandemic, when it was the second-worst affected state after Maharashtra. The surge in cases in Kerala has been attributed to the early loosening of restrictions and insufficient mass compliance with the remaining regulations. The latter led to increased enforcement by the police, including fines to those not wearing masks or maintaining social distancing (Jacob, 2021). Local elections and religious festivals may also have contributed to the upsurge in cases. Still, the state continued to do well in some respects. For example, Kerala was the only state that did not suffer a shortage of oxygen during the second wave, because it increased production capacity by 60% early on, which allowed it to supply neighbour states (Dutta, 2021). Kerala also tested more people relatively early. Because of that, it can manage patients better, and it has less need for oxygen. Additionally, by mid-April 2021 Kerala had vaccinated more than 14% of its population, which is significantly above the national average (Mathrubhumi, 2021).

The case of Kerala shows, on the one hand, how even a state with limited sovereignty and strictly rationed resources can address a pandemic efficiently, as long as it enjoys legitimacy and has strong planning capacities. On the other hand, it also shows how fortunes can change under the relentless pressure of an unforgiving virus, and that will force its way into society by any gap it can find. The lesson, then, is that the best way to protect the population is through careful and comprehensive systems of control, linked to a drastic strategy of elimination of the coronavirus. Any slip could allow the virus to entrench itself, making it hugely expensive and potentially impossible to eliminate in the future—which is exactly the same lesson drawn from experiences around the world.

## Notes

1. See Upadhyay (2020), Vikram (2021) and https://www.aarogyasetu.gov.in/.
2. The name comes from the two key mutations (although it has more than a dozen) of the variant. Scientifically, the name "double mutant" is inaccurate as the virus mutates all the time and there are many other strains with two mutations. See Doucleff (2021).
3. https://tradingeconomics.com/india/unemployment-rate.

## References

Ahmed, A., & Kumar, M. (2020). *Exclusive: India set to cap stimulus package at $60 billion to protect credit rating, sources say.* https://www.reuters.com/article/us-health-coronavirus-india-economy-excl/exclusive-india-set-to-cap-sti mulus-package-at-60-billion-to-protect-credit-rating-sources-say-idINKBN22D5JX?edition-redirect=in

Al Dahdah, M., & Javed Alam, M. (2020). *Tracing apps to fight Covid-19. Are surveillance technologies effective?* https://booksandideas.net/Tracing-Apps-to-Fight-Covid-19.html

Avhad, P. (2020). *The Indian pharmaceutical industry: The 'pharmacy of the world'?* https://blogs.deloitte.co.uk/health/2020/03/the-indian-pharmaceutical-industry-the-pharmacy-of-the-world.html

BBC News. (2021a). *India Covid: Anger as twitter ordered to remove critical virus posts*. https://www.bbc.co.uk/news/world-asia-56883483

BBC News. (2021b). *India coronavirus: Over-18s vaccination drive hit by shortages*. https://www.bbc.co.uk/news/world-asia-india-56345591

Chandrasekhar, C. P., & Ghosh, J. (2015). The financialization of finance? Demonetization and the dubious push to cashlessness in India. *Development and Change, 49*(2), 420–436.

Chandrasekhar, C. P., & Ghosh, J. (2020). *Economic contraction and the fiscal stance of the Indian government*. https://www.networkideas.org/featured-articles/2020/06/economic-contraction-and-the-fiscal-stance-of-the-indian-government/

Chowdhury, A., & Sundaram, J. (2020). *Kerala Covid-19 response model for emulation*. http://www.ipsnews.net/2020/04/kerala-covid-19-response-model-emulation/

Chowdhury, S., & Narayanan, R. (2021). *A made-in-India shock doctrine, with a little help from Latin America*. https://mronline.org/2021/04/27/a-made-in-india-shock-doctrine-with-a-little-help-from-latin-america/

Crowley, T. (2020). *"This is a revolution, sir"*. https://www.jacobinmag.com/2020/12/general-strike-india-modi-bjp-cpm-bihar

Dennis, S. (2021). *How Modi's failures led to India's covid catastrophe*. https://tribunemag.co.uk/2021/05/how-modis-failures-led-to-indias-covid-catastrophe

Doucleff, M. (2021). *People are talking about a 'double mutant' variant in India. What does that mean?* https://www.npr.org/sections/goatsandsoda/2021/04/24/988744811/people-are-talking-about-a-double-mutant-variant-in-india-what-does-that-mean

Dutta, P. (2021). *Why Kerala is not facing oxygen crisis in Covid-19 second wave*. https://www.indiatoday.in/coronavirus-outbreak/story/kerala-oxygen-crisis-covid-19-second-wave-1795603-2021-04-27

Ellis-Petersen, H. (2020c). *India's Covid-19 app fuels worries over authoritarianism and surveillance*. https://www.theguardian.com/world/2020/may/04/how-safe-is-it-really-privacy-fears-over-india-coronavirus-app

Ellis-Petersen, H., & Hassan. (2021). *Kumbh Mela: How a superspreader festival seeded Covid across India*. https://www.theguardian.com/world/2021/may/30/kumbh-mela-how-a-superspreader-festival-seeded-covid-across-india
Farrer, M. (2021). *Why is India seeing such a huge surge in Covid-19 cases?* https://www.theguardian.com/world/2021/apr/21/why-is-india-seeing-such-a-huge-surge-in-covid-19-cases
Ferry, M., Venkatasubramanian, G., Guérin, I., & Al Dahdah, M. (2020). *Una tragedia humanitaria en ciernes*. https://vientosur.info/una-tragedia-humanitaria-en-ciernes/
Findlay, S., Peel, M., & Mancini, D. (2021). *India blocks vaccine exports in blow to dozens of nations*. https://www.ft.com/content/5349389c-8313-41e0-9a67-58274e24a019
Gettleman, J., Kumar, H., Raj, S., & Yasir, S. (2021). *As Covid-19 devastates India, deaths go undercounted*. https://www.nytimes.com/2021/04/24/world/asia/india-coronavirus-deaths.html?referringSource=articleShare
Ghosh, J. (2020). A critique of the Indian government's response to the COVID-19 pandemic. *Journal of Industrial and Business Economics, 47*, 519–530.
Ghosh, J. (2021). *Covid-19 in India—Profits before people*. https://www.socialeurope.eu/covid-19-in-india-profits-before-people
Gul, R. (2020). *Explained: The legal framework behind the lockdown*. https://www.nationalheraldindia.com/india/explained-the-legal-framework-behind-the-lockdown
IMF. (2021). *Fiscal monitor April 2021: A fair shot*. Washington, DC.
Jacob, J. (2021). *Why Kerala is not following Covid protocols*. https://www.indiatoday.in/india-today-insight/story/why-kerala-is-not-following-covid-protocols-1795236-2021-04-26
Jenkins, D., & Ram, L. (2020). *Kerala's pandemic response owes its success to participatory politics*. https://novaramedia.com/2020/08/07/keralas-pandemic-response-owes-its-success-to-participatory-politics/
Kaul, N. (2021). *COVID in India: A tragedy with its roots in Narendra Modi's leadership style*. https://theconversation.com/covid-in-india-a-tragedy-with-its-roots-in-narendra-modis-leadership-style-160552
Kolhatkar, S. (2021). *India's pandemic disaster: The responsibility of Modi and the BJP*. https://socialistproject.ca/2021/05/india-pandemic-disaster-modi-bjp/
Krishna, Y. (2020). *India's Kerala is combating COVID-19 through participatory governance*. https://socialistproject.ca/2020/05/india-kerala-combating-covid19-participatory-governance/
Krishnan, M. (2020). *Police excesses for lockdown violation led to 12 deaths: Study*. https://www.hindustantimes.com/india-news/police-excesses-for-lockdown-violation-led-to-12-deaths-study/story-qj5dZ68nxPBc3B0HbSBg3L.html

Kurian, O. (2020). *How the Indian state of Kerala flattened the coronavirus curve*. https://www.theguardian.com/commentisfree/2020/apr/21/kerala-indian-state-flattened-coronavirus-curve

Lakhani, S. (2020). *Shaheen Bagh sit-in protest cleared amid coronavirus lockdown*. https://indianexpress.com/article/cities/delhi/shaheen-bagh-protests-delhi-coronavirus-6328815/

Loh, J. U., Wilson, K., & Purewal, N. (2020). *Weaponising the COVID-19 crisis in India*. https://femrev.wordpress.com/2020/05/08/weaponising-the-covid-19-crisis-in-india-a-view-from-feminist-review-issue-119/

Mathrubhumi. (2021). *COVID vaccination: Kerala focuses on frontline workers in 2nd phase*. https://english.mathrubhumi.com/news/kerala/covid-vaccination-kerala-focuses-on-frontline-workers-in-2nd-phase-1.5429845

Menon, S. (2021). https://www.bbc.co.uk/news/world-asia-india-55571793. https://www.bbc.co.uk/news/world-asia-india-55571793

Mumbai Mirror. (2021). *PM Narendra Modi: Amid Covid-19 pandemic, India has become world's pharmacy*. https://mumbaimirror.indiatimes.com/news/india/pm-narendra-modi-amid-covid-19-pandemic-india-has-become-worlds-pharmacy/articleshow/81375010.cms

Newsclick. (2020). *COVID 19 lockdown has exposed major gaps in social protection systems, says report*. https://www.newsclick.in/India-Lockdown-COVID-19-Migrant-Workers-Housing-Land-Rights

Press Trust of India. (2021). *We are in the endgame of Covid-19 pandemic in India: Health minister Harsh Vardhan*. https://www.indiatoday.in/coronavirus-outbreak/story/we-are-in-the-endgame-of-covid-19-pandemic-in-india-vardhan-1776697-2021-03-07

Purewal, N. (2021). *COVID in India: How the Modi government prioritised politics over public health*. https://theconversation.com/covid-in-india-how-the-modi-government-prioritised-politics-over-public-health-160016?fbclid=IwAR23zk8dHlfhI7g5JsWrNjRAOqEsd6CLRGo51QVovodtLE-gDQH3i6pg-TM

Rachman, G. (2021). *Narendra Modi and the perils of Covid hubris*. https://www.ft.com/content/fa3096ff-4325-4a02-97fd-89095e44d5c1

Rao, A. (2021). *India is hiding its Covid crisis—and the whole world will suffer for it*. https://www.theguardian.com/commentisfree/2021/may/06/india-covid-crisis-narenda-modi-government-hiding

Roy, A. (2021). *We are witnessing a crime against humanity*. https://www.theguardian.com/news/2021/apr/28/crime-against-humanity-arundhati-roy-india-covid-catastrophe?CMP=Share_AndroidApp_Other

Rukmini, S. (2020). *India had one of the world's strictest lockdowns. Why are cases still rising?* https://www.theguardian.com/commentisfree/2020/jul/04/india-lockdowns-cases-rising_

Safi, M., & Dhillon, A. (2021). *Ganges crowds highlight distancing challenges as Covid cases soar in India.* https://www.theguardian.com/world/2021/apr/12/ganges-crowds-highlight-distancing-challenges-as-covid-cases-soar-in-india

Sample, I., & Davis, N. (2021). *What do we know about the Indian coronavirus variant?* https://www.theguardian.com/world/2021/apr/19/what-do-we-know-about-the-indian-coronavirus-variant

Spinney, L. (2020). *The coronavirus slayer! How Kerala's rock star health minister helped save it from Covid-19.* https://www.theguardian.com/world/2020/may/14/the-coronavirus-slayer-how-keralas-rock-star-health-minister-helped-save-it-from-covid-19?CMP=share_btn_tw

Taneja, P., & Singh Bali, A. (2021). *India's staggering COVID crisis could have been avoided. But the government dropped its guard too soon.* https://theconversation.com/indias-staggering-covid-crisis-could-have-been-avoided-but-the-government-dropped-its-guard-too-soon-159538

*The Economist.* (2020). India's bureaucrats are fighting covid-19 with red tape. https://www.economist.com/asia/2020/06/11/indias-bureaucrats-are-fighting-covid-19-with-red-tape?utm_campaign=coronavirus-special-edition&u%E2%80%A6

*The Economist.* (2021). India is struggling with a catastrophic second wave. https://www.economist.com/asia/2021/04/24/india-is-struggling-with-a-catastrophic-second-wave

*The Guardian.* (2021). The Guardian view on Modi's mistakes: A pandemic that is out of control. https://www.theguardian.com/world/commentisfree/2021/apr/23/the-guardian-view-on-modis-mistakes-a-pandemic-that-is-out-of-control

Upadhyay, H. (2020). *Aarogya Setu app enters 150 Mn user club in 4 months.* https://entrackr.com/2020/08/aarogya-setu-app-enters-150-mn-user-club-in-4-months/

Varghese, S. (2020). *Why has Kerala been so successful in tackling coronavirus?* https://www.newstatesman.com/world/asia/2020/05/kerala-coronavirus-cases-response-india-KK-Shailaja

Vikram, K. (2021). *Not many takers for Aarogya Setu app, Delhi and Chandigarh see highest users.* https://www.newindianexpress.com/nation/2021/mar/21/not-many-takers-for-aarogya-setu-appdelhi-and-chandigarh-see-highest-users-2279311.html

Vyas, M. (2020). *The jobs bloodbath of April 2020.* https://cmie.com/kommon/bin/sr.php?kall=warticle&dt=2020-05-05%2008:22:21&msec=776

Yadav, P., Mehndiratta, A., Chalkidou, K., Rupani, S., & Reddy, K. (2020). *India's COVID-19 testing capacity must grow by a factor of 10: Here's how that can happen.* https://www.cgdev.org/publication/indias-covid-19-testing-capacity-must-grow-factor-10-heres-how-can-happen

# Conclusion

This book is about neoliberalism and the crises in three of its dimensions: the economy, politics and health. The book reviews the meanings of neoliberalism in theory and its implications for daily life and argues that neoliberalism is best seen as the contemporary stage or mode of existence of capitalism, driven by financialisation. Neoliberalism and financialisation transformed the structures of production and social reproduction, with implications for the patterns of accumulation, employment, consumption and many other aspects of social life in most countries.

Neoliberalism has also been entangled with developments in the political sphere. It was originally established in different countries through a variety of political paths, including in longstanding democracies, in military dictatorships or conjointly with transitions to political democracy. In general, however, by the 1990s a democratic form of neoliberalism had become globally hegemonic. This was partly for national-historical reasons and, partly, for instrumental reasons since, in exchange for basic civil liberties, democratic regimes could offer (financial) capital and the US empire[1] legal security, certainty of a dominant political role and legitimacy to justify the inequitable outcomes of neoliberalism as if they expressed the general good.

Despite these strengths, democratic political forms had to contend with tensions and displacements due to the economic implications of neoliberalism, since they tend to amplify inequalities, worsen the pattern of employment and concentrate economic, political and media power.



A. Saad-Filho, *The Age of Crisis*,
https://doi.org/10.1007/978-3-030-81608-7

In doing this, neoliberalism systematically corrodes the civic equalities that must underpin a democratic polity. Ultimately, the system of accumulation found stability only by means of institutional rigidity and the narrowing of democracy. They were enforced in order to insulate the economic structures, policies and processes that define and secure neoliberalism from the vagaries of electoral accountability or any form of influence by the majority. This was done through institutional reforms embedding neoliberalism into the constitutional fabric of the nation. For example, laws enshrined deficit ceilings, independent Central Banks, inflation targets and the imperative of privatisations and 'competition', while a barrage of propaganda promoted the financialisation of daily life and glorified overconsumption as the essence of a good life. The unavoidable consequence of locking neoliberalism institutionally was the narrowing of the political debate because of the exclusion of economic matters and the related laws and institutions from legitimate consideration. This made it increasingly difficult to challenge the system of accumulation within the rules that neoliberalism itself had imposed: under neoliberalism, the superiority of 'the market' (however defined) and the imperative of inflation control could not be challenged or even debated (Saad-Filho & Boffo 2021).

The 'democratic' alternation in power of political parties committed to marginally different versions of neoliberalism helped to fine-tune the extension of the law of value across most spheres of social reproduction, the commercialisation of social provision, the diffusion of the profit imperative and growing economic inequalities. In other words, neoliberalism builds a totalising policy environment supporting its own expanded reproduction while, at the same time, it turns political democracy into a formal shell: empty of content but securing the institutional framework for neoliberalism itself. Institutional rigidity and the shrinkage of the policy space made it difficult for states and societies to find negotiated solutions to the contradictions, limitations and crises emerging under neoliberalism. Over time, and under the impact of economic and other crises, democratic politics lost both legitimacy and efficacy .

This 'mature' form of neoliberalism was shaken by the GFC, which severely undermined the ideological hegemony of finance and the notion of the optimality of 'free markets'. The crisis of legitimacy of the system of accumulation can be seen from two angles. On the one hand, it became widely accepted that there is a moral hazard problem under neoliberalism, since large financial institutions can capture growing profits but they systematically claim the right to socialise losses because they are 'too big to fail'. This allows them to keep a stranglehold on the 'real' economy and to hijack public policy and resources through endless demands for self-preservation at someone else's cost, with strongly adverse implications for distribution. This policy practice under neoliberalism contradicts the moral justification for private profits, which centres on the encouragement to invest wisely in order to reap gains and avoid punishing losses. However, if society must pick up those losses, especially when they are large, the justification for profits—at least in finance and, potentially, more widely—disappears. Increasingly, since the GFC we find that neoliberal capitalism is sustained only by the 'silent compulsion of economic relations' (Marx, 1976, p. 899) backed up by the raw power of the state, but denuded of the comforts of ideology. On the other hand, since the GFC, AE governments have been showering resources onto the banks in the hope that they will lend to businesses and households and drive economic growth. However, given the economic stagnation in the Global North, many financial institutions used those resources to build reserves and clean up their balance sheets, and then moved huge quantities of (public) funds into speculative activities both in the Global North and in the Global South, perpetuating a parasitic system of accumulation veering dangerously between deepening stagnation and destabilising speculative bubbles.

The GFC led to the introduction of policies of 'fiscal austerity' in many countries, allegedly to cover the costs of the crisis in general, and to rescue finance specifically. However, given the creation of large cohorts of economic 'losers' since the earlier transitions to neoliberalism, and the loss of legitimacy of neoliberalism and financialisation after the GFC, these policies could be sustained only by authoritarian means. Alienation inevitably followed and, given the earlier destruction of the left, a political vacuum emerged in which the potential sources of opposition were dissolved into anomie, overwhelmed by the far right or enraptured by 'spectacular' authoritarian neoliberal leaders promising to resolve the problems that the 'losers' found themselves unable to confront. The rise to prominence of authoritarian leaders was facilitated by a growing disregard for science, evidence and established truths that often degenerated into a quasi-religious attachment to individuals peddling comforting but misleading claims, and whose every trespass could be forgiven because they seemed 'genuine'.

When they were climbing the electoral ladder, those leaders would speak loudly against selected aspects of neoliberalism, even if they led political parties or mass movements associated with nationalism, imperialism, militarism or fascism. Yet, when they reached positions of power those authoritarian leaders invariably implemented policies intensifying neoliberalism and hurting their own electoral base. Despite the discomfort of mainstream commentators, the appealing personality of these leaders would often excuse their managerial incompetence and the dysfunctionality of their administrations. Shockingly, their opinion poll ratings would generally hold despite the multiplication of disasters under their watch including, eventually, catastrophic losses of life during the pandemic. This book argues that this political arrangement is intrinsically unstable, and it is likely to foster a destabilising politics of permanent crisis.

Examination of these circumstances led to the identification of three paradoxes of neoliberalism. First the *economic paradox*, that is, the delivery of unprecedentedly favourable conditions for accumulation under neoliberalism led to a marked slowdown of investment and GDP growth. This is followed by the *political paradox*, that the consolidation of neoliberal democracies excluded the economic domain from political debate, undermined the representation of the poor and severely limited the capacity of states to address social conflicts. Finally, the *paradox of authoritarianism*, that is, the economic and political crises in the system of accumulation fostered the personalisation of politics around 'spectacular' leaders and the emergence of authoritarian modes of governance as the newly dominant political form of neoliberalism. They drive a politics of crisis management through social divisions and the manipulation of resentments aiming to intensify exclusion, oppression and exploitation, that inevitably undermines their own base of support. These three paradoxes ultimately ensue from the hegemony of interest-bearing capital over the economic resources, institutions, the law and the (nominally democratic) political system under neoliberalism. In turn, neoliberal politics has been extensively eviscerated and fossilised into a set of unresponsive parties and institutions serving finance above any consideration of public welfare. In these circumstances, in which both the economy and the political system are regulated by the imperatives of exploitation, extraction and reproduction of exclusion, the interplay between the three paradoxes of neoliberalism is likely to open spaces for new forms of fascism.

These pressures culminated in the 'Great Stagnation' and the emergence of authoritarian neoliberalism after the GFC. In January 2020, the world was hit by the COVID-19 pandemic. In addition to its countless victims, the pandemic triggered a profound economic crisis that could be contained only by unprecedented levels of public sector intervention to support production and demand, compensate the contractionary impact of the lockdowns and settle the health and other costs of the pandemic itself. These interventions will have long-term consequences for the functioning of capitalism.

The pandemic hit a world already under stress because of the slowdown of the US economy, entrenched stagnation in the Eurozone and Japan, growing conflicts between the USA and China and the USA and Iran, severe instability in Central Asia, the Middle East and North Africa, and with countries and public health systems everywhere significantly less resilient after 40 years of neoliberal reforms disguised as 'competition' and 'efficiency gains'. The emergence of COVID-19 in a context of weak economies and weakened state capacities exposed the limitations of neoliberalism and, potentially, reinforced its exclusionary tendencies, with grave implications for long-term prosperity, democracy and the legitimacy of the system of accumulation.

In these charged circumstances, the pandemic brought to light the incompetence, mendacity and disregard for life of some of the most prominent politicians of our time. In particular, the 'spectacular' authoritarian leaders that emerged after the GFC, and who tended to thrive under political crises that they deliberately stoked, failed miserably. Despite their bombastic discourse and fantastical promises, those leaders were shown to be ill-equipped to protect lives and livelihoods and, when this became impossible, to express compassion, lead the nation in mourning, find ways to address the problem at hand and heal the collective wounds. Regardless of these staggering failures, the popularity of the 'spectacular' leaders never collapsed entirely; instead, it tended only to wobble at the margin. This outcome is too striking to be attributed to chance or to some hidden 'virtue' of those incompetent leaders. Instead, their continuing popularity is the reflection of the desperate search, by the losers, for solutions to problems of neoliberalism that they cannot find anywhere else. That is, the political traction of failed leaders is due to a deep malaise in neoliberalism, driven by its economic limitations, socially destructive consequences and worsening political gridlock.

The policy failures and the experiences of success addressing the pandemic suggest six key lessons.

First, neoliberal states can be efficient at protecting profits and the interests of the privileged, and they can rescue finance from self-inflicted disasters. However, these states can have great difficulty performing arguably more important functions of governance, especially protecting the population from the ravages of misfortune and securing jobs, incomes and basic services. This must be done for reasons of justice and distributive economic policy (see below); it can also support effective health policies, since job and income security will make the population healthier and, in a pandemic, they will make it possible for more people to stay at home, easing the load on the health system and accelerating the recovery. Costs should not be an obstacle: since the public authorities have provided hundreds of billions to banks, hedge funds and large corporations time and again, they can certainly support the vulnerable and fund a resilient and universal health system—if there is political will to do so.

Second, the more that neoliberal ideologues and policymakers had reconstructed the state along neoliberal lines, and the more they had enforced the marketisation of social reproduction, the lower became the capacity of these states to mobilise resources and expertise to respond to emergencies (Assa & Calderon, 2020). This limitation was strikingly obvious in the Quartet of Calamity.

Third, there is no clear trade-off between health and the economy. That is, the claim that countries must choose a position along a purported continuum between lockdown (with minimum loss of life in the short term but heavy economic costs) and a strategy of 'herd immunity' (with the opposite balance of costs and benefits) was a misleading guide to public policy (Levy Yeyati & Filippini 2021, p. 5). What was proven, instead, is that the economy cannot function if the population is either insecure or unhealthy. Experience also shows that, in the absence of a vaccine or effective treatment, countries that resisted lockdowns and flirted with 'herd immunity' tended to suffer much larger human catastrophes *as well as* deeper economic collapse. These outcomes reinforce the significance of integrated public policy, state capacity and a strong manufacturing base, in contrast with the systematic depredation of the economy and the public sector under neoliberalism.

Fourth, it was possible to eliminate the coronavirus in multiple ways. In particular, the supposed trade-off between democracy and successful combat against the virus was false, because countries have performed more or less well depending on their state capacity and public policies, rather than their political regimes. Since it was possible to address the pandemic successfully in a democratic framework (viz. Australia, Denmark, Finland, Iceland and New Zealand), the shift towards a more authoritarian political order in the wake of COVID-19 was a travesty: the primary goal, in many cases, was not to implement appropriate health policies, but to disguise policy failures in the short term and increase social control in the longer term. The 'successful' states deployed distinct combinations of state capacity, purposeful, centralised and coordinated action, economic resources, technology, testing, tracing, capillarity of health systems and social control. *These are the principles and features of successful industrial policy, applied to the field of health.*[2] In contrast, the 'failed' states tended to be disorganised, disarticulated and to have been more radically restructured by the neoliberal 'reforms', as well as having deindustrialised, fragmented their own supply chains in the name of 'globalisation', introduced 'competition' into their health systems, acted late and unwillingly, failed to test, imposed lockdowns reluctantly, and to lack PPE, ICU beds and ventilators. This is, then, very much a *pandemic with neoliberal characteristics*, in which the impositions of neoliberalism were directly responsible for tens of thousands of deaths.

Fifth, the pandemic revealed how the neoliberal cult of individual maximisation and competition fostered nationalism and racism, debased science, and fed the individualisation of the truth. This is profoundly corrosive, because if *any* truth is open to 'choice' there will be no possibility of dialogue between people with different viewpoints.

Sixth, the economic burden of COVID-19 will be much higher than that of the GFC. Most governments, especially in the AEs, spent huge sums during the pandemic, in addition to lowering interest rates whenever this was possible (given the exceptionally low rates already prevailing for a decade). Many governments expressed their intention to cover these costs by shifting to a 'new fiscal austerity' as soon as possible. This would be untenable. Fiscal austerity is unjustifiable in economic terms and it will be widely seen as illegitimate, given the boost to wealth due to government support to the asset markets. It is also impossible for the poor and the remaining public services to bear the burden of adjustment. Austerity policies could be imposed only by force, and these policies, their regressive implications and the repression that must accompany them, would undermine government legitimacy and damage its mass base, which would be especially problematic for the authoritarian administrations supported by the 'losers'. These limitations suggest the likelihood of a long period of crisis politics with unpredictable implications. The only just way to defray those costs and fund the transition to a democratic and sustainable economy is through progressive taxation, the confiscation of fortunes made during the pandemic, strategic nationalisations, default where necessary, and—essential for the long term—a bold 'green' growth strategy addressing climate change (Saad-Filho, 2021a).

The evidence and the lessons outlined above suggest that, throughout the pandemic, several neoliberal administrations focused on the protection of the short-term interests of capital instead of sheltering life. Although this is shocking, it should not be surprising since capitalism has always been about profits at the expense of people. Millions of deaths in the pandemic have highlighted, for those who care to look, the limitations of the system of accumulation: neoliberalism is regressive, its political forms are undemocratic, an outsized financial sector is worse than useless, and capitalism is inherently exploitative. In the heat of the pandemic, several authoritarian neoliberal regimes enforced a necropolitics drawing upon their own selfish (profit-seeking) interest in 'keeping the economy open', regardless of the loss of life. This was an unmitigated social harm tinged with reactionary and racist overtones, that victimised disproportionately the poor, minorities and the unprotected. This policy was symptomatic of the perversities of neoliberalism. This must never be forgotten, and never forgiven.

It follows that the overlapping crises in the economy, politics and health are *outcomes of neoliberalism*, and they cannot be addressed effectively by, or through, marginal adjustments in the system of accumulation, a reversal to 'fiscal austerity', or a renewed commitment to the 'free market'; even the attempt to do so will undermine what remains of democracy. Realisation of these shortcomings can have implications not only for the legitimacy of political leaders, but even for the viability of the mode of production. In this sense, the expansionary policies implemented by US President Joe Biden in early 2021 may offer global neoliberalism a more promising road to survival than the orthodox neoliberalism pursued in the UK and the EU, but both approaches remain limited by the regressive structures that they, ultimately, seek to protect.

The successful responses to the pandemic have shown that the state can take a progressive role, especially when it suspends the normal workings of finance and 'the markets' and mobilises resources directly to address social needs, for which democratic accountability is important both on principle and for efficiency reasons. After all, despite the strident claims of diehard neoliberals, who but the state can nurse the population, rescue airlines and other key industries, enforce lockdowns, contain the implosion of the stock markets and fund new vaccines? These lessons can guide efforts to address other crises in neoliberalism, not least those concerning food production, water and climate change (Saad-Filho, 2021a). They can also guide challenges against the dominant system of accumulation in general, and against the violence of authoritarian neoliberalism specifically. Finally, they can inform the search for a mode of living that privileges the protection of life, livelihoods and wellbeing, promotes economic and civic equality, restores state capacities and affirms collectivity and the irreducible sociability of the human species.[3]

The strains of the pandemic have shown, tentatively, that the economy is a social system characterised by strong interdependencies (we *are* the economy), that we are bound together as humans, and that the universal provision of basic services is far more efficient than privatised, for-profit and fragmented supply. It follows that, first, it is incumbent upon the state to secure access to universal basic services, jobs and incomes, opening the way to the transformation of dysfunctional (but highly profitable) essential sectors into public utilities. This can give a decisive contribution to the definancialisation of the economy and the transformation of the *crises in neoliberalism* into a *crisis of neoliberalism*, while also pointing to a progressive and democratic pathway to resolution (Gindin 2020; Henwood 2020; Saad-Filho, 2011). Second, responses to the crises in neoliberalism must be based on internationalist values, since only global solutions can be effective in an integrated world: we truly are 'in it together' (TNI 2020). These truths can pave the way for a politics of humanity and hope, organised around the defining concerns of the left with equality, collectivity and economic and political democracy, against (a, by now, clearly zombie form of) neoliberalism.[4]

In the immediate case of COVID-19, progressive policies must deliver medical and financial solidarity, and support the unrestricted dissemination of knowledge and technologies and the provision of healthcare for all according to need, in order to save lives everywhere. Without this global orientation, 'we risk reinforcing the ways that the virus has seamlessly fed into the discursive political rhetoric of nativist and xenophobic movements – a politics deeply seeped in authoritarianism, an obsession with border controls, and a "my-country first" national patriotism' (Hanieh 2020). Conversely, without this internationalist approach our societies will remain stuck in 'mutual assured vulnerability', since the circulation of the coronavirus in the Global South will drastically limit the scope for containment in the Global North while, also, turning the South into a cauldron where new variants will continuously emerge and will, inevitably, escape control.

Building alternatives to the dominant system of accumulation requires the integration of economic, political, health and other demands into a programme for the expansion of democracy, bringing to light the incompatibility between capitalism and democracy and the complementarities between political democracy, economic democracy and socialism. The aftermath of the most devastating pandemic in one hundred years is the right time to imagine new forms of social organisation, based on solidarity, human values and respect for nature, that will serve the majority and avoid the repetition of the sufferings experienced in 2020 and 2021. This book has shown that the tendency is for a prolonged economic stagnation and growing authoritarianism with racist and reactionary policies, potentially leading to new forms of fascism. Yet there are also powerful counter-tendencies pointing to the possibility of resurgence of the left.

Neoliberalism has never been so unstable or its hegemony so brittle, and its limitations and perversities have been startlingly revealed by the pandemic. With the combination of crises and systemic shocks becoming increasingly severe, capitalism could be facing its biggest crisis. Given these ravages and disasters, we might expect a wave of protests from those fighting for a more egalitarian, just and sustainable world. They are right, and they must win, for the sake of humanity and the planet.

The COVID-19 pandemic may have happened by chance but it was not unexpected, and it exposed neoliberal capitalism for its inhumanity and criminality. The pandemic has shown that there can be no health policy without solidarity, democracy, equality, state capacity and industrial policy, all of which are anathema to neoliberalism. The pandemic has revealed starkly both the limitations of authoritarian neoliberalism and the imperative to overcome them. I am cautiously optimistic that capitalism cannot wash this stain. It is now time to imagine what kind of society can serve the majority and avoid the repetition of the tragic outcomes that have been inflicted upon us.

## Notes

1. The term 'US empire' is used here in the sense of Panitch and Gindin (2012).

2. For a similar argument, see Ferrannini et al. (2021). For a counter-example of the consequences of fragmentation, see Peel (2020).
3. See, however, Macfarlane (2021).
4. For similar arguments, see Buscher et al. (2020) and Gupta et al. (2021).

## References


Assa, J., & Calderon, C. (2020). *Privatization and pandemic: A cross-country analysis of Covid-19 rates and health-care financing structures*. https://ideas.repec.org/p/new/wpaper/2008.html.

Buscher, B., Feola, G., Fischer, A., Fletcher, R., Gerber, J. F., Harcourt, W., Koster, M., Schneider, M., Scholtens, J., Spierenburg, M., Walstra, V., & Wiskerke, H. (2020). Planning for a world beyond COVID-19: Five pillars for post-neoliberal development. *World Development*. https://doi.org/10.1016/j.worlddev.2020.105357.

Ferrannini, A., Barbieri, E., Biggeri, M., & Di Tommaso, M. (2021). Industrial policy for sustainable human development in the post-Covid19 era. *World Development*, 137. https://www.sciencedirect.com/science/article/abs/pii/S0305750X20303429.

Gindin, S. (2020). *The coronavirus and the crisis this time*. https://socialistproject.ca/2020/04/coronavirus-and-the-crisis-this-time.

Gupta, J., Bavinck, M., Ros-Tonen, M., Asubonteng, K., Bosch, H., van Ewijk, E., Hordijk, M., Van Leynseele, Y., Cardozo, M. L., Miedema, E., & Pouw, N. (2021). COVID-19, Poverty and inclusive development. *World Development*. https://doi.org/10.1016/j.worlddev.2021.105527.

Henwood, D. (2020). *A few ambitious points on fighting the crisis*. https://lbo-news.com/2020/03/20/a-few-ambitious-points-on-fighting-the-crisis/?fbclid=IwAR2k5vz91AwG7hl_foOmbWVGEEPwn0WdQivEmXWGGfaeNBWBGPFloo0-UKY.

Hanieh, A. (2020). *This is a global pandemic—Let's treat it as such*. https://www.versobooks.com/blogs/4623-this-is-a-global-pandemic-let-s-treat-it-as-such.

Levy Yeyati, E., & Filippini, F. (2021). *Social and economic impact of COVID-19*. Paper commissioned by The Independent Panel for pandemic preparedness and response. https://theindependentpanel.org/documents/.

Macfarlane, L. (2021). *Covid has forced a neoliberal retreat. But state intervention isn't always progressive*. https://www.theguardian.com/commentisfree/2021/apr/29/neoliberalism-authoritarian-capitalism-covid-crisis-state-intervention.

Marx, K. (1976). *Capital*, vol. 1. Penguin.

Panitch, L., & Gindin, S. (2012). *The making of global capitalism: The political economy of American empire*. Verso.

Peel, M. (2020). *Belgium's fight against Covid hindered by regional rivalries*. https://www.ft.com/content/fb00d2ff-a56b-4327-9dfd-695dc4c741f7.

Saad-Filho, A. (2021a). *Progressive policies for economic development: Economic diversification and social inclusion after climate change*. Routledge.

Saad-Filho, A. (2011). Crisis in neoliberalism or crisis of neoliberalism? In *Socialist register* (pp. 242–259).

Saad-Filho, A., & Boffo, M. (2021). Authoritarian neoliberalism, Covid-19, and the future of democracy. In A. Regelmann (Ed.), *The crisis and the future of democracy*. Rosa Luxemburg Foundation.

TNI. (2020). *Coronavirus: The need for a progressive internationalist response*. https://www.tni.org/en/article/coronavirus-the-need-for-a-progressive-internationalist-response.

# References


247. (2020). *Prefeito bolsonarista, para quem a cura da Covid-19 viria de igrejas, é internado em hospital de luxo com a doença*. https://www.brasil247.com/regionais/sudeste/prefeito-bolsonarista-para-quem-a-cura-da-covid-19-viria-de-igrejas-e-internado-em-hospital-de-luxo-com-a-doenca

247. (2021a). *Desigualdade cresceu em todos os trimestres após o golpe contra Dilma*. https://www.brasil247.com/brasil/desigualdade-cresceu-em-todos-os-trimestres-apos-o-golpe-contra-dilma-nkkpcroh

247. (2021b). *A história secreta da cloroquina*. https://www.brasil247.com/midia/a-historia-secreta-da-cloroquina-o-novo-documentario-da-tv-247-xnz4f6r4

Abbasi, K. (2021). Covid-19: Social murder, they wrote—Elected, unaccountable, and unrepentant. *British Medical Journal, 372*(314). http://dx.doi.org/10.1136/bmj.n314

Achcar, G. (2021). *How can we revive herd immunity to fascism*. https://www.thenation.com/article/world/fascism-trump-neoliberalism-capitalism/

Agamben, G. (2020a). *The invention of an epidemic*. http://www.journal-psychoanalysis.eu/coronavirus-and-philosophers/

Agamben, G. (2020b). *Clarifications*. https://itself.blog/2020/03/17/giorgio-agamben-clarifications/

Agamben, G. (2020c). *Biosecurity and politics*. https://medium.com/@ddean3000/biosecurity-and-politics-giorgio-agamben-396f9ab3b6f4

Agamben, G. (2020d). *Requiem for the students*. https://medium.com/@ddean3000/requiem-for-the-students-giorgio-agamben-866670c11642

Agüero, J. M. (2021). COVID-19 and the rise of intimate partner violence. *World Development*, 137. https://doi.org/10.1016/j.worlddev.2020.105217





A. Saad-Filho, *The Age of Crisis*,
https://doi.org/10.1007/978-3-030-81608-7

Ahmed, A., & Kumar, M. (2020). *Exclusive: India set to cap stimulus package at $60 billion to protect credit rating, sources say*. https://www.reuters.com/article/us-health-coronavirus-india-economy-excl/exclusive-india-set-to-cap-stimulus-package-at-60-billion-to-protect-credit-rating-sources-say-idINKBN22D5JX?edition-redirect=in

Al Dahdah, M., & Javed Alam, M. (2020). *Tracing apps to fight Covid-19. Are surveillance technologies effective?* https://booksandideas.net/Tracing-Apps-to-Fight-Covid-19.html

Albo, G., & Fanelli, C. (2014). *Austerity against democracy: An authoritarian phase of neoliberalism?* https://socialistproject.ca/content/uploads/2014/08/AusterityAgainstDemocracy.pdf

Al-Gharbi, M. (2020). *Disposable people*. https://thebaffler.com/latest/disposable-people-algharbi

Alvaredo, F., Chancel, L., Piketty, T., Saez, E., & Zucman, G. (2018). *World inequality report*. https://wir2018.wid.world/

Alves, R. (2021). *Money-laundering scheme a Bolsonaro family business?* https://brazilian.report/power/2021/03/16/money-laundering-scheme-a-bolsonaro-family-business/

Amaro, S. (2020). *European Central Bank takes its pandemic bond buying to 1.35 trillion euros to try to prop up economy*. https://www.cnbc.com/2020/06/04/european-central-bank-ramps-up-its-pandemic-bond-buying-to-1point35-trillion-euros.html

Andersen, H. (2020). *Unlike the UK, many African nations have an effective test and trace system—This is why*. https://www.independent.co.uk/voices/africa-test-and-trace-covid-b1774982.html

Aratani, L. (2020). *US job losses pass 40m as coronavirus crisis sees claims rise 2.1m in a week*. https://www.theguardian.com/business/2020/may/28/us-job-losses-unemployment-coronavirus

Aschwanden, C. (2020). *Contact tracing, a key way to slow COVID-19, Is badly underused by the U.S.* https://www.scientificamerican.com/article/contact-tracing-a-key-way-to-slow-covid-19-is-badly-underused-by-the-u-s/

Ashman, S., & Fine, B. (2013). Neo-liberalism, varieties of capitalism, and the shifting contours of South Africa's financial system. *Transformation, 81*(2), 144–178.

Assa, J., & Calderon, C. (2020). *Privatization and pandemic: A cross-country analysis of COVID-19 rates and health-care financing structures*. https://ideas.repec.org/p/new/wpaper/2008.html

Atkinson, A. (2020). *George Osborne, architect of U.K. austerity, says new cuts needed post-crisis*. https://www.bloomberg.com/news/articles/2020-04-20/architect-of-u-k-austerity-says-retrenchment-needed-post-crisis

Avhad, P. (2020). *The Indian pharmaceutical industry: The 'pharmacy of the world'?* https://blogs.deloitte.co.uk/health/2020/03/the-indian-pharmaceutical-industry-the-pharmacy-of-the-world.html

Ayers, A., & Saad-Filho, A. (2015). Democracy against neoliberalism: Paradoxes, limitations, transcendence. *Critical Sociology, 41*(4–5), 597–618.

Ayers, A., & Saad-Filho, A. (2020). The twilight of formal democracy: Contradictions of accumulation and the political crisis of neoliberalism. *Journal of Australian Political Economy, 86*, 230–255.

Backhouse, R., & Boianovsky, M. (2016). Secular stagnation: The history of a macroeconomic heresy. *European Journal of the History of Economic Thought, 23*(6), 946–970.

Bahia, L., Chade, J., Dedecca, C. S., Domingues, J. M., Gonçalves, G. L., Herz, M., Lavinas, L., Ocké-Reis, C., Ortiz, M. E. R., & Santos, F. (2021). *A tragédia brasileira do coronavírus/covid-19: Uma análise do desgoverno do governo federal, 2020–2021.* https://www.clacso.org/en/a-tragedia-brasileira-do-coronavirus-covid-19/

Barrera-Algarín, E., Maestre, F. E., Sarasola, J. L., & Andrada, A. V. (2020). COVID-19 neoliberalismo y sistemas sanitarios en 30 países de europa: Repercusiones en el número de fallecidos. *Revista Española de Salud Pública* (94), 57. https://recyt.fecyt.es/index.php/RESP/article/view/85707

Baxter, H. (2020). *The Americans who think that coronavirus is a hoax.* https://www.independent.co.uk/independentpremium/long-reads/coronavirus-conspiracy-theory-trump-us-hoax-a9498081.html

BBC News. (2020a). *Coronavirus: hydroxychloroquine ineffective says Fauci.* https://www.bbc.co.uk/news/world-us-canada-53575964

BBC News. (2020b). *Covid "hate crimes" against Asian Americans on rise.* https://www.bbc.co.uk/news/world-us-canada-56218684

BBC News. (2020c).*Coronavirus: Sweden's Tegnell admits too many died.* https://www.bbc.co.uk/news/world-europe-52903717

BBC News. (2020d). *Brazil judge stymies plan to revoke mangrove protection.* https://www.bbc.com/news/world-latin-america-54350180

BBC News. (2021a). *India Covid: Anger as twitter ordered to remove critical virus posts.* https://www.bbc.co.uk/news/world-asia-56883483

BBC News. (2021b). *India coronavirus: Over-18s vaccination drive hit by shortages.* https://www.bbc.co.uk/news/world-asia-india-56345591

Beckett, L. (2020). *'All the psychoses of US history': How America is victim-blaming the coronavirus dead.* https://www.theguardian.com/world/2020/may/21/all-the-psychoses-of-us-history-how-america-is-victim-blaming-the-coronavirus-dead

Beer, T. (2020). *All the times trump compared Covid-19 to the Flu, even after he knew Covid-19 was far more deadly.* https://www.forbes.com/sites/tommybeer/2020/09/10/all-the-times-trump-compared-covid-19-to-the-flu-even-after-he-knew-covid-19-was-far-more-deadly/?sh=b613007f9d2f

Berberoglu, B. (Ed.). (2021). *The global rise of authoritarianism in the 21st century crisis of neoliberal globalization and the nationalist response*. Routledge.

Berengaut, A. A. (2020). *Democracies are better at fighting outbreaks*. https://www.theatlantic.com/ideas/archive/2020/02/why-democracies-are-better-fighting-outbreaks/606976/

Bessner, D., & A'Lee Frost, A. (2021). *How the QAnon cult stormed the capitol*. https://www.jacobinmag.com/2021/01/q-anon-cult-capitol-hill-riot-trump

Bialasiewicz, L., & Eckes, C. (2021). "Individual sovereignty" in pandemic times—A contradiction in terms? *Political Geography*, 85. https://doi.org/10.1016/j.polgeo.2020.102277

Bijl, M. (2020). *The Covid-19 crisis is exacerbating gender inequalities—But who cares?* https://www.socialeurope.eu/the-covid-19-crisis-is-exacerbating-gender-inequalities-but-who-cares

Bissett, A. N. (2020). *Elimination policy, business funds, and total transparency: Jacinda Ardern is showing how to lead a country through crisis*. https://www.independent.co.uk/news/world/australasia/jacinda-ardern-new-zealand-coronavirus-world-leaders-mental-health-cases-a9470531.html

Boffo, M., Saad-Filho, A., & Fine, B. (2019). Neoliberal capitalism: The authoritarian turn. In L. Panitch & G. Albo (Eds.), *Socialist register* (pp. 247–270).

Bonduki, N. (2020). *Bruno Covas: por que os shoppings estão abertos e os parques fechados?* https://www1.folha.uol.com.br/colunas/nabil-bonduki/2020/06/bruno-covas-por-que-os-shoppings-estao-abertos-e-os-parques-fechados.shtml

Bonefeld, W. (2017). *The strong state and the free economy*. Rowman & Littlefield.

Booth, R. (2021). *Delaying England's winter lockdown "caused up to 27,000 extra Covid deaths"*. https://www.theguardian.com/uk-news/2021/mar/18/delaying-englands-winter-lockdown-caused-up-to-27000-extra-covid-deaths

Bourgeron, T. (2021). 'Let the virus spread'. A doctrine of pandemic management for the libertarian-authoritarian capital accumulation regime. *Organization*. https://journals.sagepub.com/doi/10.1177/1350508421995741

Bowman, S., & Serodio, P. (2020). *Live free and die: Sweden's coronavirus experience*. https://thecritic.co.uk/live-free-and-die-swedens-coronavirus-experience/

Boyle, D. (2013). *Broke: Who killed the middle classes?* Fourth Estate.

Brenner, R. (2020). Escalating plunder. *New Left Review, 123*, 5–22.

Breuninger, K. (2020). *Trump refuses to accept election results, says it's 'far from over'*. https://www.cnbc.com/2020/11/07/trump-refuses-to-accept-election-results-says-it-is-far-from-over.html

Brodeur, A., Gray, D., Islam, A., & Bhuiyan, S. (2021). A literature review of the economics of COVID-19. *Journal of Economic Surveys*. https://doi.org/10.1111/joes.12423

Brooks, C. (2020). *Follow the money: Employers are behind the rush to reopen*. https://www.labornotes.org/2020/05/follow-money-employers-are-behind-rush-reopen

Brown, W. (2015). *Undoing the demos: Neoliberalism's stealth revolution*. Zone Books.

Bruff, I. (2014). The rise of authoritarian neoliberalism. *Rethinking Marxism, 26*(1), 113–129.

Bruff, I. (2016). Neoliberalism and authoritarianism. In S. Springer, K. Birch & J. MacLeavy (Eds.), *Handbook of Neoliberalism*. Routledge.

Bruff, I., & Tansel, C. B. (Eds.). (2020). *Authoritarian neoliberalism: Philosophies, practices, contestations*. Routledge.

Brum, E. (2021). *Pesquisa revela que Bolsonaro executou uma "estratégia institucional de propagação do coronavírus"*. https://brasil.elpais.com/brasil/2021-01-21/pesquisa-revela-que-bolsonaro-executou-uma-estrategia-institucional-de-propagacao-do-virus.html

Bueno de Mesquita, J., Kapilashrami, A., & Meier, B. M. (2021). *Human rights dimensions of the COVID-19 pandemic*, paper commissioned by The Independent Panel for pandemic preparedness and response. https://theindependentpanel.org/documents/

Burke, J., & Okiror, S. (2020). *Africa's fragile health systems rush to contain coronavirus*. https://www.theguardian.com/world/2020/mar/20/africas-fragile-health-systems-rush-to-contain-coronavirus

Buscher, B., Feola, G., Fischer, A., Fletcher, R., Gerber, J. F., Harcourt, W., Koster, M., Schneider, M., Scholtens, J., Spierenburg, M., Walstra, V., & Wiskerke, H. (2020). Planning for a world beyond COVID-19: Five pillars for post-neoliberal development. *World Development*. https://doi.org/10.1016/j.worlddev.2020.105357

Caduff, C. (2020). What went wrong: Corona and the world after the full stop. *Medical Anthropology Quarterly, 34*(4), 467–487.

Carlsen, A., Huang, P., Levitt, Z., & Wood, D. (2021). *How is the COVID-19 vaccination campaign going in your state?* https://www.npr.org/sections/health-shots/2021/01/28/960901166/how-is-the-covid-19-vaccination-campaign-going-in-your-state?t=1618592090650

CGD (Commission on Growth and Development). (2008). *The growth report: Strategies for sustained growth and inclusive development*. https://openknowledge.worldbank.org/handle/10986/6507

Chamayou, G. (2018). *La société ingouvernable: Une généalogie du libéralisme autoritaire*. La fabrique.

Chandrasekhar, C. P., & Ghosh, J. (2015). The financialization of finance? Demonetization and the dubious push to cashlessness in India. *Development and Change, 49*(2), 420–436.

Chandrasekhar, C. P., & Ghosh, J. (2020). *Economic contraction and the fiscal stance of the Indian government*. https://www.networkideas.org/featured-articles/2020/06/economic-contraction-and-the-fiscal-stance-of-the-indian-government/

Cheetham, J. (2020). *Navajo nation: The people battling America's worst coronavirus outbreak*. https://www.bbc.co.uk/news/world-us-canada-52941984

Chowdhury, A., & Sundaram, J. (2020). *Kerala Covid-19 response model for emulation*. http://www.ipsnews.net/2020/04/kerala-covid-19-response-model-emulation/

Chowdhury, S., & Narayanan, R. (2021). *A made-in-India shock doctrine, with a little help from Latin America*. https://mronline.org/2021/04/27/a-made-in-india-shock-doctrine-with-a-little-help-from-latin-america/

Christophers, B., & Fine, B. (2019). The value of financialization and the financialization of value. In P. Mader, D. Mertens & N. van der Zwan (Eds.), *The Routledge international handbook of financialization*. Routledge.

Claeson, M., & Hanson, S. (2021). The Swedish COVID-19 strategy revisited. *The Lancet*. https://doi.org/10.1016/S0140-6736(21)00885-01

Cliffe, J. (2020). *Coronavirus hits the Global South*. https://www.newstatesman.com/world/south-america/2020/04/coronavirus-hits-global-south

Coburg, T. (2020). *The £5.5bn PPE scandal that goes to the core of government incompetence—And that's just for starters*. https://www.thecanary.co/uk/analysis/2020/07/11/the-5-5bn-ppe-scandal-that-goes-to-the-core-of-government-incompetence-and-thats-just-for-starters/

Cockburn, P. (2020). *Britain will seek coronavirus 'herd immunity' covertly or by default—Thanks to the failure of lockdown*. https://www.independent.co.uk/voices/boris-johnson-coronavirus-testing-nhs-covid-app-herd-immunity-b599887.html

Cole, B. (2020). *Brazil government aide says COVID-19's toll on elderly will reduce pension deficit as country's outbreak escalates*. https://www.newsweek.com/brazil-government-aide-says-covid-19s-toll-elderly-will-reduce-pension-deficit-countrys-1506830

Collins, C., Ocampo, O., & Paslaski, S. (2020). *Billionaire Bonanza*. https://ips-dc.org/wp-content/uploads/2020/04/Billionaire-Bonanza-2020.pdf

Collinson, A. (2021). *The new class divide—How Covid-19 exposed and exacerbated workplace inequality in the UK*. https://www.tuc.org.uk/blogs/new-class-divide-how-covid-19-exposed-and-exacerbated-workplace-inequality-uk

Collucci, C. (2021). *Subnotificação esconde ao menos 30% das mortes, diz estudo*. https://www1.folha.uol.com.br/equilibrioesaude/2021/05/subnotificacao-dos-casos-de-covid-esconde-ate-30-das-mortes-mostra-estudo.shtml

Conley, J. (2020). *'The next crisis': Up to 43 million Americans could lose health insurance due to pandemic, study shows*. https://www.commondreams.org/news/2020/05/10/next-crisis-43-million-americans-could-lose-health-insurance-due-pandemic-study?amp&__twitter_impression=true

Conn, D., & Lewis, P. (2020). *Documents contradict UK government stance on Covid-19 "herd immunity"*. https://www.theguardian.com/world/2020/apr/12/documents-contradict-uk-government-stance-on-covid-19-herd-immunity

Conti, J. (2020). *Ricardo Darín em entrevista disse: "É muito difícil lutar contra a pandemia de imbecis"*. https://www.contioutra.com/ricardo-darin-em-entrevista-disse-e-muito-dificil-lutar-contra-a-pandemia-de-imbecis/

Cookson, C. (2020). *UK's original coronavirus plan risked 'hundreds of thousands' dead*. https://www.ft.com/content/249daf9a-67c3-11ea-800d-da70cff6e4d3

Crouch, C. (2019). Post-democracy and populism. *The Political Quarterly, 90*, 124–137.

Crouch, C. (2020). *Post-democracy after the crisis*. Polity Press.

Crowley, T. (2020). *"This is a revolution, sir"*. https://www.jacobinmag.com/2020/12/general-strike-india-modi-bjp-cpm-bihar

Csernatoni, R. (2020). New states of emergency: Normalizing techno-surveillance in the time of COVID-19. *Global Affairs, 6*(3), 301–310.

Cunningham, S. (2020). *Liverpool vs Atletico madrid: The champions league match that should never have happened*. https://inews.co.uk/sport/football/champions-league/liverpool-atletico-madrid-coronavirus-merseyside-spain-champions-league-fixture-march-2020-420585

Cuthbertson, A. (2020). *Coronavirus tracked: How Covid-19 deaths in the US compare by race and ethnicity*. https://www.independent.co.uk/news/world/americas/coronavirus-deaths-us-race-black-white-asian-latino-racism-a9544401.html

Dale, G. (2020). *Lockdown politics: A response to panagiotis sotiris*. https://www.historicalmaterialism.org/blog/lockdown-politics-response-to-panagiotis-sotiris

Dang, H.-A., & Nguyen, C. V. (2020). Gender inequality during the COVID-19 Pandemic: Income, expenditure, savings, and job loss. *World Development*, 140.

Dardot, P., & Laval, C. (2013). *The new way of the world: On neoliberal society*. Verso.

Davidson, N. (2017). Crisis neoliberalism and regimes of permanent exception. *Critical Sociology, 43*(4–5), 615–634.

Davidson, N., & Saull, R. (2017). Neoliberalism and the far-right: A contradictory embrace. *Critical Sociology, 43*(4–5), 707–724.

Davies, H. (2020). *Private firm running UK PPE stockpile was sold in middle of pandemic*. https://www.theguardian.com/world/2020/apr/22/revealed-private-firm-running-uk-ppe-stockpile-was-sold-in-middle-of-pandemic

Davis, M. (2020a). *The monster is finally at the door*. https://mronline.org/2020/03/19/mike-davis-on-covid-19-the-monster-is-finally-at-the-door/

Davis, M. (2020b). *The monster enters: COVID-19, avian flu, and the plagues of capitalism*. OR Books.

De Negri, F., Galliez, R.M., Miranda, P., Koeller, P., Zucoloto, G. F., Costa, J. S. D. M., Farias, C. M. D., Travassos, G. H. & Medronho, R. D. A. (2020). *Chances de óbito por COVID-19 entre os trabalhadores formais: Evidências do Estado do Rio de Janeiro*. http://repositorio.ipea.gov.br/handle/11058/10301

Decerf, B., Ferreira, F. H. G., Mahler, D. G., & Sterck, O. (2020). *Lives and livelihoods: Estimates of the global mortality and poverty effects of the Covid-19 pandemic*. http://eprints.lse.ac.uk/105825/

Dennis, S. (2021). *How Modi's failures led to India's covid catastrophe*. https://tribunemag.co.uk/2021/05/how-modis-failures-led-to-indias-covid-catastrophe

Dobbs, R., Lund, S., Woetzel, J., & Mutafchieva, M. (2015). *Debt and (not much) deleveraging*. Mckinsey Global Institute Report. https://www.mckinsey.com/featured-insights/employment-and-growth/debt-and-not-much-deleveraging

Doğantekin, V. (2020). *US "steals" medical supplies amid pandemic*. https://www.aa.com.tr/en/americas/us-steals-medical-supplies-amid-pandemic-expert/1800001

Doucleff, M. (2021). *People are talking about a 'double mutant' variant in India. What does that mean?* https://www.npr.org/sections/goatsandsoda/2021/04/24/988744811/people-are-talking-about-a-double-mutant-variant-in-india-what-does-that-mean

Douglas, B. (2018). *Number of Brazilians living in poverty rises 2 million in a year*. https://www.bloomberg.com/news/articles/2018-12-05/number-of-brazilians-living-in-poverty-rises-2-million-in-a-year,

Duménil, G., & Lévy, D. (2011). *The crisis of neoliberalism*. Harvard University Press.

Dutta, P. (2021). *Why Kerala is not facing oxygen crisis in Covid-19 second wave*. https://www.indiatoday.in/coronavirus-outbreak/story/kerala-oxygen-crisis-covid-19-second-wave-1795603-2021-04-27

Edgecliffe-Johnson, A. (2020). *Corporate America experiences 'K-shaped' recovery*. https://www.ft.com/content/258b74d8-6bac-47e5-a675-8f091b25db3e

Egger, P., & Zhu, J. (2021). How Covid-19 travels in—and outside of value chains and then affects the stock market: Evidence from China. *The World Economy*. https://doi.org/10.1111/TWEC.13134

Eichengreen, B. (2015). Secular stagnation: The long view. *American Economic Review, 105*(5), 66–70.

Elliott, L. (2020a). *Dozens of poorer nations seek IMF help amid coronavirus crisis*. https://www.theguardian.com/world/2020/mar/27/dozens-poorer-nations-seek-imf-help-coronavirus-crisis

Elliott, L. (2020b). *IMF estimates global Covid cost at $28tn in lost output*. https://www.theguardian.com/business/2020/oct/13/imf-covid-cost-world-economic-outlook

Ellis-Petersen, H. (2020c). *India's Covid-19 app fuels worries over authoritarianism and surveillance*. https://www.theguardian.com/world/2020/may/04/how-safe-is-it-really-privacy-fears-over-india-coronavirus-app

Ellis-Petersen, H., & Hassan. (2021). *Kumbh Mela: How a superspreader festival seeded Covid across India*. https://www.theguardian.com/world/2021/may/30/kumbh-mela-how-a-superspreader-festival-seeded-covid-across-india

Evans, T. (2015). *The crisis of finance-led capitalism in the United States of America* (Working Paper No. 51). Institute for International Political Economy.

Fabry, A. (2019). *The political economy of Hungary: From state capitalism to authoritarian neoliberalism*. Palgrave Pivot.

Farrer, M. (2021). *Why is India seeing such a huge surge in Covid-19 cases?* https://www.theguardian.com/world/2021/apr/21/why-is-india-seeing-such-a-huge-surge-in-covid-19-cases

Fedor, L., & Zhang, C. (2020). *Covid-19 pandemic hits black voters' incomes hardest, FT poll shows*. https://www.ft.com/content/e22636d7-8259-4b97-bcf8-19349cee61fd?shareType=nongift

Ferrannini, A., Barbieri, E., Biggeri, M., & Di Tommaso, M. (2021). Industrial policy for sustainable human development in the post-Covid19 era. *World Development* 137. https://www.sciencedirect.com/science/article/abs/pii/S0305750X20303429

Ferry, M., Venkatasubramanian, G., Guérin, I., & Al Dahdah, M. (2020). *Una tragedia humanitaria en ciernes*. https://vientosur.info/una-tragedia-humanitaria-en-ciernes/

Filgueiras, L. (2021). *Que País é Esse?* https://www.bnews.com.br/artigo/1431,que-pais-e-esse.html

Findlay, S., Peel, M., & Mancini, D. (2021). *India blocks vaccine exports in blow to dozens of nations*. https://www.ft.com/content/5349389c-8313-41e0-9a67-58274e24a019

Fine, B. (2013–14). Financialisation from a marxist perspective. *International Journal of Political Economy, 42*(4), 46–66.

Fine, B., & Saad-Filho, A. (2017). Thirteen things you need to know about neoliberalism. *Critical Sociology, 43*(4–5), 685–706.

Fitzpatrick, P. (2021). *How Taiwan beat COVID-19—New study reveals clues to its success*. https://theconversation.com/how-taiwan-beat-covid-19-new-study-reveals-clues-to-its-success-158900

FitzRoy, F., & Spencer, D. (2020). *Economic policy response to the pandemic: From COVID-19 emergency to economic democracy*. https://www.iza.org/publications/pp/160/economic-policy-response-to-the-pandemic-from-covid-19-emergency-to-economic-democracy

Foster, P., & Neville, S. (2020). *How poor planning left the UK without enough PPE*. https://www.ft.com/content/9680c20f-7b71-4f65-9bec-0e9554a8e0a7

France24. (2020). *Israel health minister under fire over ultra-orthodox COVID-19 crisis*. https://www.france24.com/en/20200408-israel-health-minister-under-fire-over-ultra-orthodox-covid-19-crisis

Freeman, H. (2020). *Billionaires, please back off—We can't all self-isolate on a giant yacht*. https://www.theguardian.com/fashion/2020/mar/30/self-isolate-giant-yacht-david-geffen-social-media

Frey, I. (2020a). *"Herd immunity" is epidemiological neoliberalism*. https://thequarantimes.wordpress.com/2020/03/19/herd-immunity-is-epidemiological-neoliberalism/?fbclid=IwAR1S6GyMrklnntU7c54CEEMceZOI92Ipf0rlWPCbY2nCKIEu3MCcARoGbOgThe

Frey, I. (2020b). *"Herd immunity" is epidemiological neoliberalism*. https://economicsociology.org/2020/04/24/herd-immunity-is-epidemiological-neoliberalism/

Friedman, L. (2020). *E.P.A., citing coronavirus, drastically relaxes rules for polluters*. https://www.nytimes.com/2020/03/26/climate/epa-coronavirus-pollution-rules.html

Fritze, J., & Collins, M. (2020). *As Trump touts increased production, coronavirus swabs made during his Maine factory tour will be tossed in the trash*. https://eu.usatoday.com/story/news/politics/2020/06/05/trump-maine-puritan-throw-away-coronavirus-swabs/3153622001/

Garcia, L. P., & Silva, G. D. M. (2016). *Doenças Transmissíveis e Situação Socioeconômica no Brasil: Análise Espacial*. https://www.ipea.gov.br/portal/index.php?option=com_content&view=article&id=29193%3Atd-2263-doencas-transmissiveis-e-situacao-socioeconomica-no-brasil-analise-espacial&catid=390%3A2016&directory=1&Itemid=1.

Gent, C. (2020). *When logistics run out of time*. https://novaramedia.com/2020/03/23/when-logistics-run-out-of-time/

Gentilini, U., Almenfi, M., Orton, I., & Dale, P. (2020). *Social protection and jobs responses to COVID-19: A real-time review of country measures*. https://openknowledge.worldbank.org/handle/10986/33635

Geoghegan, P. (2020). *Cronyism and clientelism*. https://www.lrb.co.uk/the-paper/v42/n21/peter-geoghegan/cronyism-and-clientelism

Gettleman, J., Kumar, H., Raj, S., & Yasir, S. (2021). *As Covid-19 devastates India, deaths go undercounted*. https://www.nytimes.com/2021/04/24/world/asia/india-coronavirus-deaths.html?referringSource=articleShare

Ghosh, J. (2020a). *The pandemic and the global economy*. https://www.dissentmagazine.org/online_articles/the-pandemic-and-the-global-economy

Ghosh, J. (2020b). A critique of the Indian government's response to the COVID-19 pandemic. *Journal of Industrial and Business Economics, 47*, 519–530.

Ghosh, J. (2021). *Covid-19 in India—Profits before people*. https://www.socialeurope.eu/covid-19-in-india-profits-before-people

Giles, G. (2020). *Deaths from coronavirus far higher in England than first reported*. https://www.ft.com/content/c07e267b-7bca-418f-ad9e-8631a29854cb

Gindin, S. (2020). *The coronavirus and the crisis this time*. https://socialistproject.ca/2020/04/coronavirus-and-the-crisis-this-time

Gisselquist, R. M., & Solanki, D. (2020). *Coronavirus: Five ways some states have used the pandemic to curtail human rights and democracy*. https://theconversation.com/coronavirus-five-ways-some-states-have-used-the-pandemic-to-curtail-human-rights-and-democracy-151618

Glasser, S. B. (2020). *How did the U.S. end up with nurses wearing garbage bags?* https://www.newyorker.com/news/letter-from-trumps-washington/the-coronavirus-and-how-the-united-states-ended-up-with-nurses-wearing-garbage-bags

Glenza, J. (2020). *States use coronavirus to ban abortions, leaving women desperate: 'You can't pause a pregnancy'*. https://www.theguardian.com/world/2020/apr/30/us-states-ban-abortions-coronavirus-leave-women-desperate

Gonzalez, M. (2020). *Coronavirus in Latin America*. https://www.rs21.org.uk/2020/05/02/coronavirus-in-latin-america/

Gordon, R. J. (2015). Secular stagnation: A supply-side view. *American Economic Review, 105*(5), 54–59.

Gourinchas, P.-O. (2020). *Flattening the pandemic and recession curves*. https://clausen.berkeley.edu/flattening-the-pandemic-and-recession-curves/

Gowan, P. (1999). *The global gamble: Washington's faustian bid for world dominance*. Verso.

Grey, S., & MacAskill, A. (2020). *Johnson listened to his scientists about coronavirus—But they were slow to sound the alarm*. https://www.reuters.com/article/us-health-coronavirus-britain-path-speci-idUSKBN21P1VF

Guida, V. (2020). *Companies shed workers, paid dividends after getting fed aid, panel finds*. https://www.politico.com/news/2020/09/23/companies-shed-workers-paid-dividends-after-getting-fed-aid-panel-finds-420537

Gul, R. (2020). *Explained: The legal framework behind the lockdown*. https://www.nationalheraldindia.com/india/explained-the-legal-framework-behind-the-lockdown

Gupta, J., Bavinck, M., Ros-Tonen, M., Asubonteng, K., Bosch, H., van Ewijk, E., Hordijk, M., Van Leynseele, Y., Cardozo, M. L., Miedema, E., & Pouw, N. (2021). COVID-19, Poverty and inclusive development. *World Development*. https://doi.org/10.1016/j.worlddev.2021.105527

Gussen, A. F. (2021). *O que há por trás do lobby de Bolsonaro pelo uso da cloroquina*. https://www.cartacapital.com.br/politica/o-que-ha-por-tras-do-lobby-de-bolsonaro-pelo-uso-da-cloroquina/

Hall, D., Lister, J., & Mercer, H. (2020). *Privatised and unprepared: The NHS supply chain*. https://gala.gre.ac.uk/28230

Hanieh, A. (2020). *This is a global pandemic—Let's treat it as such*. https://www.versobooks.com/blogs/4623-this-is-a-global-pandemic-let-s-treat-it-as-such

Harris, B., & Schipani, A. (2020). *Jair Bolsonaro triggers furore by firing Brazil's health minister*. https://www.ft.com/content/5c362cbc-aadf-4849-94a6-ed9b19ef0a29

Harris, J. (2021). *Homeworking sounds good—Until your job takes over your life*. https://www.theguardian.com/commentisfree/2021/mar/07/homeworking-job-takes-over-life-office-grind-remote-working

Harvey, D. (2009). Interview: Exploring the logic of capital. *Socialist Review*. http://www.socialistreview.org.uk/article.php?articlenumber=10801

Hattenstone, S. (2020). *"The virus piggybacked on racism": Why did Covid-19 hit BAME families so hard?* https://www.theguardian.com/world/2020/aug/08/the-virus-piggybacked-on-racism-why-did-covid-19-hit-bame-families-so-hard

Hausermann, S., Kitschelt, H., Abou-Chadi, T., Ares, M., Bischof, D., Kurer, T., van Ditmars, M., & Wagner, M. (2021). *Transformation of the left: The myth of voter losses to the radical right*. http://www.fes.de/cgi-bin/gbv.cgi?id=17385&ty=pdf

Healy, J. (2020). *Workers fearful of the coronavirus are getting fired and losing their benefits*. https://www.nytimes.com/2020/06/04/us/virus-unemployment-fired.html?referringSource=articleShare

Heffer, G. (2020). *Coronavirus: Experts once said 20,000 deaths was a 'good outcome'—So where is the UK headed now?* https://news.sky.com/story/coronavirus-experts-once-said-20-000-deaths-was-a-good-outcome-so-where-is-the-uk-headed-now-11978609

Hendrikse, R. (2018). Neo-illiberalism. *Geoforum, 95*, 169–172.

Henley, J. (2020). *Female-led countries handled coronavirus better, study suggests*. https://www.theguardian.com/world/2020/aug/18/female-led-countries-handled-coronavirus-better-study-jacinda-ardern-angela-merkel

Henwood, D. (2020). *A few ambitious points on fighting the crisis*. https://lbo-news.com/2020/03/20/a-few-ambitious-points-on-fighting-the-crisis/?fbclid=IwAR2k5vz91AwG7hl_foOmbWVGEEPwn0WdQivEmXWGGfaeNBWBGPFloo0-UKY

Herman, B. (2020). *Coronavirus likely forced 27 million off their health insurance*. https://www.axios.com/coronavirus-27-million-lost-employer-health-insurance-c77fe46a-691d-49b3-9cd2-3ad6d19df159.html

Hoen, E., Garrison, C., Boulet, P., Mara, K., & Perehudoff, K. (2021). *Scaling-up vaccine production capacity: Legal challenges and recommendations*, paper commissioned by The Independent Panel for pandemic preparedness and response. https://theindependentpanel.org/documents/

Holpuch, A. (2021). *'I don't make enough': The financial cost of having Covid in the US*. https://www.theguardian.com/us-news/2021/feb/12/us-financial-cost-covid-coronavirus

Hook, L., & Kuchler, H. (2020). *How coronavirus broke America's healthcare system*. https://www.ft.com/content/3bbb4f7c-890e-11ea-a01c-a28a3e3fbd33

Hopkins, N. (2020). *Revealed: UK ministers were warned last year of risks of coronavirus pandemic*. https://www.theguardian.com/world/2020/apr/24/revealed-uk-ministers-were-warned-last-year-of-risks-of-coronavirus-pandemic

ICG. (2020). *COVID-19 and conflict: Seven trends to watch*. Crisis Group Special Briefing No.4. https://d2071andvip0wj.cloudfront.net/B004-covid-19-seven-trends.pdf

ILO. (2020). Covid-19 and the world of work: Impact and policy responses. *ILO Monitor*. https://www.ilo.org/wcmsp5/groups/public/---dgreports/---dcomm/documents/briefingnote/wcms_738753.pdf

IMF. (2021a, January). *World economic outlook*. Washington, DC.

IMF. (2021b). *Fiscal monitor April 2021: A fair shot*. Washington, DC.

Irish Times. (2020). *'One day, it's like a miracle, it will disappear': Trump on Covid-19*. https://www.irishtimes.com/news/world/us/one-day-it-s-like-a-miracle-it-will-disappear-trump-on-covid-19-1.4370294

I-SAGE. (2020a). *A closer look at Sweden's response to COVID-19: Independent SAGE Report 15*. https://www.independentsage.org/wp-content/uploads/2020/09/Sweden_case-study-v2.pdf

I-SAGE. (2020b). *COVID-19 and health inequality: Independent SAGE Report 21*. https://www.independentsage.org/covid-19-and-health-inequality/

Itkowitz, C. (2020). *Trump again uses racially insensitive term to describe coronavirus*. https://www.washingtonpost.com/politics/trump-again-uses-kung-flu-to-describe-coronavirus/2020/06/23/0ab5a8d8-b5a9-11ea-aca5-ebb63d27e1ff_story.html

Jacobs, A. (2020). *Despite claims, trump rarely uses wartime law in battle against Covid*. https://www.nytimes.com/2020/09/22/health/Covid-Trump-Defense-Production-Act.html

Jacob, J. (2021). *Why Kerala is not following Covid protocols*. https://www.indiatoday.in/india-today-insight/story/why-kerala-is-not-following-covid-protocols-1795236-2021-04-26

Jeffery, L. (2020). *German, French officials accuse U.S. of diverting supplies*. https://www.npr.org/2020/04/04/827321294/german-french-officials-accuse-u-s-of-diverting-supplies?t=1586817225869

Jenkins, D., & Ram, L. (2020). *Kerala's pandemic response owes its success to participatory politics*. https://novaramedia.com/2020/08/07/keralas-pandemic-response-owes-its-success-to-participatory-politics/

Johnson, S. (2021). *Cambodia accused of using Covid to edge towards 'totalitarian dictatorship'*. https://www.theguardian.com/global-development/2021/apr/19/cambodia-accused-of-using-covid-to-edge-towards-totalitarian-dictatorship

Jolley, R. (2020). *The regimes using coronavirus as an excuse to attack press freedom*. https://www.newstatesman.com/world/africa/2020/03/regimes-using-coronavirus-excuse-attack-press-freedom

Jones, O. (2021). *It's not 'greed' behind the Covid vaccine success. It's state finance and the NHS*. https://www.theguardian.com/commentisfree/2021/mar/24/greed-covid-vaccine-success-state-finance-nhs

Jorge, M. R. (2020). *Bolsonaro's Brazil in times of COVID-19: A necropolitical Pharmakon*. https://www.e-ir.info/2020/05/19/bolsonaros-brazil-in-times-of-covid-19-a-necropolitical-pharmakon/

Jornal da USP. (2020). *Com poucos testes de covid-19, mortes por todas as causas viram dado crucial*. https://jornal.usp.br/atualidades/calculo-do-pico-da-covid-19-deve-levar-em-conta-quantidade-de-mortes/

Kaul, N. (2021). *COVID in India: A tragedy with its roots in Narendra Modi's leadership style*. https://theconversation.com/covid-in-india-a-tragedy-with-its-roots-in-narendra-modis-leadership-style-160552

Kavanagh, M. M., & Singh, R. (2020). Democracy, capacity, and coercion in pandemic response: COVID-19 in comparative political perspective. *Journal of Health Politics, Policy and Law, 45*(6), 997–1012.

Kendi, I. X. (2020). *What the racial data show*. https://www.theatlantic.com/ideas/archive/2020/04/coronavirus-exposing-our-racial-divides/609526/

Kermani, S. (2020). *Coronavirus: Whitty and vallance faced 'herd immunity' backlash, emails show*. https://www.bbc.co.uk/news/uk-politics-54252272

Kiely, R. (2018). *The neoliberal paradox*. Edward Elgar.

Kinder, T., & Plimmer, G. (2020). *UK government paid £1.7bn to private groups for coronavirus contracts*. https://www.ft.com/content/7fe7c2d5-24df-431b-9149-50417fa0236a

Klein, N. (2015). *This changes everything: Capitalism vs. the climate*. Simon and Schuster.

Klein, A. (2020). *Why New Zealand decided to go for full elimination of the coronavirus*. https://www.newscientist.com/article/2246858-why-new-zealand-decided-to-go-for-full-elimination-of-the-coronavirus

Kolhatkar, S. (2021). *India's pandemic disaster: The responsibility of Modi and the BJP*. https://socialistproject.ca/2021/05/india-pandemic-disaster-modi-bjp/

Kollewe, J. (2021). *Pfizer forecasts $26bn from annual sales of Covid-19 vaccine*. https://www.theguardian.com/business/2021/may/04/pfizer-forecasts-26bn-annual-sales-covid-vaccine

Konings, M. (2018). From hayek to Trump: The logic of neoliberal democracy. *Socialist Register, 54*, 48–73.

Kontopantelis, E., Kontopantelis, E., Mamas, M. A., Deanfield, J., Asaria, M., & Doran, T. (2020). Excess mortality in England and Wales during the first wave of the COVID-19 pandemic. *Journal of Epidemiology and Community Health*. https://www.google.com/search?client=firefox-b-d&q=10.1136%2Fjech-2020-214764

Krippner, G. (2005). The financialization of the American economy. *Socio-Economic Review, 3*, 173–208.

Krippner, G. (2011). *Capitalizing on crisis: The political origins of the rise of finance*. Harvard University Press.

Krishna, Y. (2020). *India's Kerala is combating COVID-19 through participatory governance*. https://socialistproject.ca/2020/05/india-kerala-combating-covid19-participatory-governance/

Krishnan, M. (2020). *Police excesses for lockdown violation led to 12 deaths: Study*. https://www.hindustantimes.com/india-news/police-excesses-for-lockdown-violation-led-to-12-deaths-study/story-qj5dZ68nxPBc3B0HbSBg3L.html

Kurian, O. (2020). *How the Indian state of Kerala flattened the coronavirus curve*. https://www.theguardian.com/commentisfree/2020/apr/21/kerala-indian-state-flattened-coronavirus-curve

Lakhani, S. (2020). *Shaheen Bagh sit-in protest cleared amid coronavirus lockdown*. https://indianexpress.com/article/cities/delhi/shaheen-bagh-protests-delhi-coronavirus-6328815/

Lasco, G. (2020). Medical populism and the COVID-19 pandemic. *Global Public Health, 15*(10), 1417–1429.

Lawrence, F., Gardside, J., & Pegg, D. (2020). *How a decade of privatisation and cuts exposed England to coronavirus*. https://www.theguardian.com/world/2020/may/31/how-a-decade-of-privatisation-and-cuts-exposed-england-to-coronavirus

LeBlanc, P. (2020). *GOP congressman says letting more Americans die of coronavirus is lesser of two evils compared to economy tanking*. https://edition.cnn.com/2020/04/14/politics/trey-hollingsworth-coronavirus/index.html

Lee, B. Y. (2020). *Steve Bannon suggests beheading Fauci, what to do about threats to health experts*. https://www.forbes.com/sites/brucelee/2020/11/06/twitter-bans-steve-bannon-account-after-talk-of-a-beheaded-anthony-fauci-wray/?sh=358ea96a4ac8

Lerner, S. (2020). *Coronavirus numbers reflect New York City's deep economic divide*. https://theintercept.com/2020/04/09/nyc-coronavirus-deaths-race-economic-divide/

Levenson, T. (2020a). *The truth about Isaac Newton's productive plague*. https://www.newyorker.com/culture/cultural-comment/the-truth-about-isaac-newtons-productive-plague

Levenson, Z. (2020b). *An organic crisis is upon us*. https://spectrejournal.com/an-organic-crisis-is-upon-us/

Levey, N. N., Christensen, K., & Phillips, A. M. (2020). *A disaster foretold: Shortages of ventilators and other medical supplies have long been warned about*. https://www.latimes.com/politics/story/2020-03-20/disaster-foretold-shortages-ventilators-medical-supplies-warned-about

Levy Yeyati, E., & Filippini, F. (2021). *Social and economic impact of COVID-19*, paper commissioned by The Independent Panel for pandemic preparedness and response. https://theindependentpanel.org/documents/

Lewis, P., & Conn, D. (2020). *UK scientists condemn 'stalinist' attempt to censor Covid-19 advice*. https://www.theguardian.com/world/2020/may/08/revealed-uk-scientists-fury-over-attempt-to-censor-covid-19-advice

Lewis, T. (2021). *How the U.S. pandemic response went wrong—And what went right—During a year of Covid*. https://www.scientificamerican.com/article/how-the-u-s-pandemic-response-went-wrong-and-what-went-right-during-a-year-of-covid/

Leys, C. (2020). *How market reforms made the NHS vulnerable to pandemics*. https://socialistproject.ca/2020/03/how-market-reforms-made-the-nhs-vulnerable-to-pandemics

Leys, C. (2021). *100,000 Deaths and a white paper: What we need instead in Britain*. https://socialistproject.ca/2021/03/100000-deaths-and-a-white-paper/

Leys, C., & Player, S. (2011). *The plot against the NHS*. Merlin Press.

Lin, F., Wang, X., & Zhou, M. (2021). How trade affects pandemics? Evidence from severe acute respiratory syndromes in 2003. *The World Economy*. https://doi.org/10.1111/twec.13127

Lintern, S. (2020). *Chief nurse dropped from downing Street coronavirus briefing 'after refusing to back Dominic Cummings'*. https://www.independent.co.uk/news/uk/politics/coronavirus-chief-nurse-dominic-cummings-ruth-may-daily-briefing-downing-street-a9562741.html

Lipton, E., Sanger, D., Haberman, M., Shear, M., Mazzetti, M., & Barnes, J. (2020a). *He could have seen what was coming: Behind Trump's failure on the virus*. https://www.google.com/search?client=firefox-b-d&q=He+could+have+seen+what+was+coming%3A+Behind+Trump%E2%80%99s+failure+on+the+virus

Lipton, E., Sanger, D., Haberman, M., Shear, M., Mazzetti, M., Barnes, J., Londoño E., & Simões, M. (2020b). *Brazil president embraces unproven "cure" as pandemic surges*. https://www.nytimes.com/2020/06/13/world/americas/virus-brazil-bolsonaro-chloroquine.html

Loh, J. U., Wilson, K., & Purewal, N. (2020). *Weaponising the COVID-19 crisis in India*. https://femrev.wordpress.com/2020/05/08/weaponising-the-covid-19-crisis-in-india-a-view-from-feminist-review-issue-119/

Londoño, E., Andreoni, M., & Casado, L. (2020). *"A family business:" Graft investigation threatens Brazil's Bolsonaro*. https://www.nytimes.com/2020/08/28/world/americas/brazil-bosonaro-corruption.html

Londres, M., & Aguiar, P. (2021). *Congresso Nacional aprova a PEC que recria auxílio emergencial*. https://noticias.r7.com/prisma/r7-planalto/congresso-nacional-aprova-a-pec-que-recria-auxilio-emergencial-12032021

Loureiro, P. M., & Saad-Filho, A. (2019). The limits of pragmatism: The rise and fall of the Brazilian workers' party (2002–2016). *Latin American Perspectives, 46*(1), 66–84.

Luce, E. (2020). *Inside Trump's coronavirus meltdown*. https://www.ft.com/content/97dc7de6-940b-11ea-abcd-371e24b679ed

Macfarlane, L. (2021). *Covid has forced a neoliberal retreat. But state intervention isn't always progressive*. https://www.theguardian.com/commentisfree/2021/apr/29/neoliberalism-authoritarian-capitalism-covid-crisis-state-intervention

MacKenzie, D. (2020). *COVID-19: The pandemic that never should have happened, and how to stop the next one*. The Bridge Street Press.

Mackey, K., Ayers, C. K., Kondo, K. K., Saha, S., Advani, S. M., Young, S., Spencer, H., Rusek, M., Anderson, J., Veazie, S., & Smith, M. (2021). Racial and ethnic disparities in COVID-19-related infections, hospitalizations, and deaths: A systematic review. *Annals of Internal Medicine, 174*(3), 362–386.

Madad, S. Nuzzo, J., & Bourdeaux, M. (2020). *The missing piece in America's COVID-19 isolation and quarantine strategy: Wraparound services*. https://www.healthaffairs.org/do/10.1377/hblog20201207.458415/full/

Maia, G. (2020). *Quem tem 'bom preparo' não tem que se preocupar com Covid-19, diz Bolsonaro*. https://oglobo.globo.com/sociedade/quem-tem-bom-preparo-nao-tem-que-se-preocupar-com-covid-19-diz-bolsonaro-24620080

Maltur, R., Rentsch, C. T., Morton, C. E., Hulme, W. J., Schultze, A., MacKenna, B., Eggo, R. M., Bhaskaran, K., Wong, A. Y., Williamson, E. J., & Forbes, H. (2021). Ethnic differences in SARS-CoV-2 infection and COVID-19-related hospitalisation, intensive care unit admission, and death in 17 million adults in England: an observational cohort study using the open safely platform. *The Lancet, 397*(10286), 1711–1724.

Maqbool, A. (2020). *Coronavirus: Pastor who decried 'hysteria' dies after attending Mardi Gras*. https://www.bbc.co.uk/news/world-us-canada-52157824

Marazzi, C. (2010). *The violence of financial capitalism*. Semiotext(e).

Marcetic, B. (2020). *Give me liberty—No, wait, give me death*. https://jacobinmag.com/2020/05/republicans-conservatives-coronavirus-economy-terrorism

Marino, A., Klintowitz, D., Brito, G., Rolnik, R., Santoro, P., & Mendonça, P. (2020). *Circulação para trabalho explica concentração de casos de Covid-19*. https://www.cartamaior.com.br/?/Editoria/Sociedade-e-Cultura/Circulacao-para-trabalho-explica-concentracao-de-casos-de-Covid-19/52/48008

Marino, F., Klintowitz, D., Brito, G., Rolnik, R., Santoro, P., & Mendonça, P. (2021). *Disparidades raciais no excesso de mortalidade em tempos de Covid-19 em São Paulo*. https://cebrap.org.br/pesquisas/desigualdades-raciais-e-covid-19/

Marmot, M., Allen, J., Boyce, T., Goldblatt, P., & Morrison, J. (2010). *Fair society, healthy lives: The Marmot review*. https://www.parliament.uk/globalassets/documents/fair-society-healthy-lives-full-report.pdf

Marmot, M., Allen, J., Boyce, T., Goldblatt, P., & Morrison, J. (2020a). *Health equity in England: The Marmot review 10 years on*. https://www.health.org.uk/publications/reports/the-marmot-review-10-years-on

Marmot, M., Allen, J., Boyce, T., Goldblatt, P., & Morrison, J. (2020b) *Build back fairer: The COVID-19 Marmot Review*. https://www.health.org.uk/publications/build-back-fairer-the-covid-19-marmot-review

Mars, A., & Guimón, P. (2020). *Los 100.000 muertos de Estados Unidos: así ha fracasado el país más poderoso del mundo*. https://elpais.com/internacional/2020-05-26/los-100000-muertos-de-estados-unidos-asi-ha-fracasado-el-pais-mas-poderoso-del-mundo.html?s%E2%80%A6

Marx, K. (1852). *The eighteenth Brumaire of Louis Bonaparte*. https://www.marxists.org/archive/marx/works/1852/18th-brumaire/

Marx, K. (1976). *Capital* (Vol. 1). Penguin.
Marx, K. (1981). *Capital* (Vol. 3). Penguin.
Mathrubhumi. (2021). *COVID vaccination: Kerala focuses on frontline workers in 2nd phase*. https://english.mathrubhumi.com/news/kerala/covid-vaccination-kerala-focuses-on-frontline-workers-in-2nd-phase-1.5429845
Mattoso, C. (2021). *Vice do Amazonas diz que política de imunidade de rebanho apoiada por Bolsonaro levou Manaus ao colapso*. https://www1.folha.uol.com.br/colunas/painel/2021/05/vice-do-amazonas-diz-que-politica-de-imunidade-de-rebanho-apoiada-por-bolsonaro-levou-manaus-ao-colapso.shtml
Maxmen, A. (2021). *How the world failed to curb COVID-19*. https://www.nature.com/articles/d41586-021-01284-5
Mbembe, A. (2003). Necropolitics. *Public Culture, 15*(1), 11–40.
Mbembe, A. (2019). *Necropolitics*. Duke University Press.
McCarthy, T. (2020a). *Trump claims 'total authority' and attacks media in chaotic coronavirus briefing*. https://www.theguardian.com/world/2020/apr/13/trump-us-coronavirus-briefing-latest-media
McCarthy, T. (2020b). *No leadership and no plan: Is Trump about to fail the US on coronavirus testing?* https://www.theguardian.com/us-news/2020/may/02/donald-trump-us-coronavirus-testing
McNally, D. (2009). From financial crisis to world-slump: Accumulation, financialisation, and the global slowdown. *Historical Materialism, 17*(2), 35–83.
McNally, D. (2011). *Global slump: The economics and politics of crisis and resistance*. PM Press.
McNally, A. (2020). *Backers of 'herd immunity' shouldn't have been allowed near Boris Johnson*. https://www.theguardian.com/commentisfree/2020/dec/14/herd-immunity-boris-johnson-coronavirus
Menon, S. (2021). https://www.bbc.co.uk/news/world-asia-india-55571793. https://www.bbc.co.uk/news/world-asia-india-55571793
Mercier, D., & Gortázar, N. G. (2020). *Bolsonaro da alas al golpismo en un acto contra la cuarentena*. https://elpais.com/internacional/2020-04-20/el-presidente-bolsonaro-da-alas-al-golpismo-en-un-acto-con-seguidores.html
Merrick, J. (2020). *Health experts 'banished' from downing street briefing after failing to toe government line*. https://inews.co.uk/news/politics/coronavirus-latest-health-experts-banished-downing-street-briefings-explained-dominic-cummings-445004
Merrick, R., & Woodcock, A. (2021). *Downing street fails to deny report that Boris Johnson said UK should 'ignore' threat from Covid*. https://www.independent.co.uk/news/uk/politics/covid-boris-johnson-ignore-pandemic-b1817719.html
Michell, J. (2020). *Coronavirus reveals the cost of austerity*. https://tribunemag.co.uk/2020/04/coronavirus-reveals-the-cost-of-austerity

Michie, S. (2021). *This UK lockdown must be the last. Here's how we can achieve that.* https://www.theguardian.com/commentisfree/2021/feb/21/uk-lockdown-health-livelihoods-2021-sage-committee

Mikhailova, A., Hope, C., gillard, M., & Wells, L. (2020). *Government scientist Neil Ferguson resigns after breaking lockdown rules to meet his married lover.* https://www.telegraph.co.uk/news/2020/05/05/exclusive-government-scientist-neil-ferguson-resigns-breaking/

Milan, S., & Treré, E. (2020). *A widening data divide: COVID-19 and the Global South.* https://www.opendemocracy.net/en/openmovements/widening-data-divide-covid-19-and-global-south/

Milman, O. (2020). *Scientists alarmed as Trump embraces fringe views and extreme theories amid pandemic.* https://www.theguardian.com/us-news/2020/jun/03/trump-coronavirus-conspiracy-theories-pandemic

Mirowski, P. (2013). *Never let a serious crisis go to waste. How neoliberalism survived the financial meltdown.* Verso.

Mirowski, P., & Plehwe, D. (Eds.). (2009). *The road from Mont Pèlerin: The making of the neoliberal thought collective.* Harvard University Press.

Montgomerie, J. (2009). The pursuit of (past) happiness? middle-class indebtedness and American financialisation. *New Political Economy, 14*(1), 1–24.

Moody, K. (2020). *How "just in time" capitalism spread COVID-19.* https://spectrejournal.com/how-just-in-time-capitalism-spread-covid-19/

Morales, D. R., & Ali, S. N. (2021). COVID-19 and disparities affecting ethnic minorities. *The Lancet, 397*(10286), 1684–1685.

Mormina, M., & Nsofor, I. M. (2020). *What developing countries can teach rich countries about how to respond to a pandemic.* https://theconversation.com/what-developing-countries-can-teach-rich-countries-about-how-to-respond-to-a-pandemic-146784?

Mugabi, I. (2020). *COVID-19: Security forces in Africa brutalizing civilians under lockdown.* https://www.dw.com/en/covid-19-security-forces-in-africa-brutalizing-civilians-under-lockdown/a-53192163

Mumbai Mirror. (2021). *PM Narendra Modi: Amid Covid-19 pandemic, India has become world's pharmacy.* https://mumbaimirror.indiatimes.com/news/india/pm-narendra-modi-amid-covid-19-pandemic-india-has-become-worlds-pharmacy/articleshow/81375010.cms

NAO. (2021). *The government's approach to test and trace in England—Interim report.* https://www.nao.org.uk/report/the-governments-approach-to-test-and-trace-in-england-interim-report/

Nassif-Pires, L., Carvalho, L., & Rawed, E. (2020). *Multidimensional inequality and COVID-19 in Brazil.* Levy Economics Institute of Bard College Public Policy Brief. http://www.levyinstitute.org/files/download.php?file=ppb_153.pdf&pubid=2690

Nedergaard, P., & Snaith, H. (2015). "As i drifted on a river i could not control": The unintended ordoliberal consequences of the eurozone crisis. *Journal of Common Market Studies, 53*(5), 1094–1109.

Neri, M., & Soares, W. (2002). Desigualdade social e saúde no Brasil. *Cadernos de Saúde Publica, 18*. https://www.scielo.br/scielo.php?script=sci_arttext&pid=S0102-311X2002000700009

Newsclick. (2020). *COVID 19 lockdown has exposed major gaps in social protection systems, says report*. https://www.newsclick.in/India-Lockdown-COVID-19-Migrant-Workers-Housing-Land-Rights

Newton, F. (2021). Britain's chumocracy. *Tribune* (winter), 14–15.

Nicolelis, M. (2021). *Brazil's pandemic is a 'biological fukushima' that threatens the entire planet*. https://www.scientificamerican.com/article/brazils-pandemic-is-a-lsquo-biological-fukushima-rsquo-that-threatens-the-entire-planet/

Noko, K. (2020). *In Africa, social 'distancing is a privilege few can afford*. https://www.aljazeera.com/indepth/opinion/africa-social-distancing-privilege-afford-200318151958670.html

Nolan, H. (2020). *There is no plan (for you)*. https://inthesetimes.com/article/covid-19-coronavirus-unemployment-eviction-healthcare-united-states

Nordling, L. (2020). *A ticking time bomb: Scientists worry about coronavirus spread in Africa*. https://www.sciencemag.org/news/2020/03/ticking-time-bomb-scientists-worry-about-coronavirus-spread-africa

Nunes, J. (2020). The COVID-19 pandemic: Securitization, neoliberal crisis, and global vulnerabilization. *Cadernos de Saúde Pública, 36*(5).

O'Brien, H. (2020). *What's behind the headlines demanding a return to the office?* https://www.theguardian.com/commentisfree/2020/sep/01/office-workers

Oladipo, G. (2020). *'It's like they're waiting for us to die': Why Covid-19 is battering Black Chicagoans*. https://www.theguardian.com/us-news/2020/oct/23/covid-19-battering-black-chicagoans

Oliu-Barton, M., Pradelski, B. S. R., Aghion, P., Artus, P., Kickbusch, I., Lazarus, J. V., Sridhar, D., & Vanderslott, S. (2021). *SARS-CoV-2 elimination, not mitigation, creates best outcomes for health, the economy, and civil liberties*. https://www.thelancet.com/journals/lancet/article/PIIS0140-6736(21)00978-8/fulltext

Olsen, N., & Zamora, D. (2020). *Pandemics show how the free market fails us*. https://jacobinmag.com/2020/03/coronavirus-covid-19-capitalism-free-market-crisis

Olson, W. (2020). *Are the lockdown orders constitutional?* https://www.cato.org/publications/commentary/are-lockdown-orders-constitutional

Oltermann, P. (2020a). *Angela Merkel draws on science background in Covid-19 explainer*. https://www.theguardian.com/world/2020/apr/16/angela-merkel-draws-on-science-background-in-covid-19-explainer-lockdown-exit

Oltermann, P. (2020b). *"Everyone was drenched in the virus": Was this Austrian Ski Resort a COVID-19 ground zero?* https://www.theguardian.com/world/2020/sep/05/everyone-was-drenched-in-the-virus-was-this-austrian-ski-resort-a-covid-19-ground-zero

ONS [Office for National Statistics]. (2021). *Coronavirus (COVID-19) related deaths by occupation, England and Wales: deaths registered between 9 March and 28 December 2020*. https://www.gov.uk/government/statistics/coronavirus-covid-19-related-deaths-by-occupation-england-and-wales-deaths-registered-between-9-march-and-28-december-2020

Oppel Jr., A., Gebeloff, R., Lai, K. K. R., Wright, W., & Smith, M. (2020). *The fullest look yet at the racial inequity of Coronavirus*. https://www.nytimes.com/interactive/2020/07/05/us/coronavirus-latinos-african-americans-cdc-data.html

Oprysko, C. (2020). *'I don't take responsibility at all': Trump deflects blame for coronavirus testing fumble*. https://www.politico.com/news/2020/03/13/trump-coronavirus-testing-128971

Ortega, F., & Orsini, M. (2020). Governing COVID-19 without government in Brazil: Ignorance, neoliberal authoritarianism, and the collapse of public health leadership. *Global Public Health, 15*(9), 1257–1277.

Oxfam Brasil. (2020). *Pandemia de coronavírus escancara desigualdades brasileiras*. https://www.oxfam.org.br/noticias/pandemia-de-coronavirus-escancara-desigualdades-brasileiras/

Pandey, G. (2020). *Coronavirus: Is social distancing an oxymoron in India?* https://www.bbc.co.uk/news/world-asia-india-52393382

Panitch, L., & Gindin, S. (2012). *The making of global capitalism: The political economy of American empire*. Verso.

Panitch, L., Gindin, S., & Albo, G. (2010). *In and out of crisis: The global financial meltdown and left alternatives*. PM Press.

Parton, H. D. (2020). *How Trump's chaotic incompetence—And the "deconstruction" of the "deep state"—Got us here*. https://www.rawstory.com/2020/03/how-trumps-chaotic-incompetence-and-the-deconstruction-of-the-deep-state-got-us-here/

Payne, A. (2020). *Boris Johnson told Italy's prime minister the UK had been aiming for coronavirus herd immunity, new documentary reveals*. https://www.businessinsider.com/boris-johnson-told-italian-pm-conte-coronavirus-herd-immunity-plan-2020-6?r=US&IR=T

Peck, J., & Tickell, A. (2002). Neoliberalizing space. *Antipode, 34*(3), 380–404.

Peel, M. (2020). *Belgium's fight against Covid hindered by regional rivalries*. https://www.ft.com/content/fb00d2ff-a56b-4327-9dfd-695dc4c741f7

Pegg, D., Booth, R., & Conn, D. (2020). *Revealed: The secret report that gave ministers warning of care home coronavirus crisis.* https://www.theguardian.com/world/2020/may/07/revealed-the-secret-report-that-gave-ministers-warning-of-care-home-coronavirus-crisis

Pellegrini, A. (2021). *O cenário trágico nos hospitais do Brasil que chega a 300 mil mortos.* https://www.nexojornal.com.br/expresso/2021/03/24/O-cen%C3%A1rio-tr%C3%A1gico-nos-hospitais-do-Brasil-que-chega-a-300-mil-mortos

Pereira, F. (2021). *Bolsonaro: "Tem idiota que diz 'vai comprar vacina'. Só se for na casa da tua mãe!".* https://www.opovo.com.br/noticias/politica/2021/03/04/bolsonaro---tem-idiota-que-diz--vai-comprar-vacina---so-se-for-na-casa-da-tua-mae.html

Pereznieto, P., & Oehler, I. (2021). *Social costs of the COVID-19 pandemic,* paper commissioned by The Independent Panel for pandemic preparedness and response. https://theindependentpanel.org/documents/

PHE [Public Health England]. (2020). *Disparities in the risk and outcomes of COVID-19.* https://www.gov.uk/government/publications/covid-19-review-of-disparities-in-risks-and-outcomes

Phillips, T., & Phillips, D. (2020). *Bolsonaro dragging Brazil towards Coronavirus calamity, experts fear.* https://www.theguardian.com/world/2020/apr/12/bolsonaro-dragging-brazil-towards-coronavirus-calamity-experts-fear

Politi, J., Fontanella-Khan, J., & Aliaj, O. (2020). *Why the US pandemic response risks widening the economic divide.* https://www.ft.com/content/d211f044-ecf9-4531-91aa-b6f7815a98e3

Pollock, A. (2021). *Test-and-trace workers are paying the price for the government's outsourcing zeal.* https://www.theguardian.com/commentisfree/2021/may/12/test-trace-workers-government-outsourcing

Press Trust of India. (2021). *We are in the endgame of Covid-19 pandemic in India: Health minister Harsh Vardhan.* https://www.indiatoday.in/coronavirus-outbreak/story/we-are-in-the-endgame-of-covid-19-pandemic-in-india-vardhan-1776697-2021-03-07

Purdy, J. (2012). *The Roberts Court vs. America.* https://democracyjournal.org/magazine/23/the-roberts-court-v-america/

Purewal, N. (2021). *COVID in India: How the Modi government prioritised politics over public health.* https://theconversation.com/covid-in-india-how-the-modi-government-prioritised-politics-over-public-health-160016?fbclid=IwAR23zk8dHlfhI7g5JsWrNjRAOqEsd6CLRGo51QVovodtLE-gDQH3i6pg-TM

Qureshi, K., Kasstan, B., Meer, N., & Hill, S. (2020). *Submission of evidence on the disproportionate impact of COVID-19, and the UK government response, on ethnic minorities in the UK.* https://ghpu.sps.ed.ac.uk/ethnic-minorities-covid-19-uk/

Rachman, G. (2021). *Narendra Modi and the perils of Covid hubris*. https://www.ft.com/content/fa3096ff-4325-4a02-97fd-89095e44d5c1

Randall, I. (2021). *Countries led by women have NOT fared significantly better in the COVID-19 pandemic than those led by men, study finds*. https://www.dailymail.co.uk/sciencetech/article-9102585/COVID-19-Countries-led-women-NOT-fared-significantly-better-pandemic.html

Rao, A. (2021). *India is hiding its Covid crisis—and the whole world will suffer for it*. https://www.theguardian.com/commentisfree/2021/may/06/india-covid-crisis-narenda-modi-government-hiding

Redação, (2020). *Família ameaça médico que anotou suspeita de COVID-19 em óbito*. https://catracalivre.com.br/cidadania/familia-ameaca-medico-que-anotou-suspeita-de-COVID-19-em-obito/

Reich, R. (2020). *Donald Trump rushed to reopen America—Now Covid is closing in on him*. https://www.theguardian.com/commentisfree/2020/jul/05/donald-trump-reopen-america-covid-19-coronavirus

Ribeiro Scaldaferri, L. (2020). *Bolsonaro promove genocídio contra os povos indígenas*. https://esquerdaonline.com.br/2020/08/06/bolsonaro-promove-genocidio-contra-os-povos-indigenas/

Ribeiro, M. (2021). *Brasil, 200 mil mortes por Covid: 200 frases de Bolsonaro minimizando a pandemia*. https://br.noticias.yahoo.com/200-frases-de-bolsonaro-minimizando-a-pandemia-do-coronavirus-203647435.html

Ricardo, L. (2020). *Sinpro condena falta de investimento do governo na saúde pública*. https://www.sinprodf.org.br/sinpro-condena-falta-de-investimento-do-governo-na-saude-publica/

Richmond, M. A. (2020). *"A little flu" could be fatal for Jair Bolsonaro*. https://jacobinmag.com/2020/03/jair-bolsonaro-coronavirus-covid-political-crisis

Riess, R. (2020). *Bishop who said "God is larger than" Covid-19 has died from the disease*. https://edition.cnn.com/2020/04/14/us/bishop-gerald-glenn-god-larger-coronavirus-dies/index.html

Roberts, M. (2016). *The long depression*. Haymarket Books.

Roberts, M. (2020). *The virus, capitalism, and the long depression*. Interviewed by Ashley Smith. https://spectrejournal.com/the-virus-capitalism-and-the-long-depression/

Robinson, W. I. (2019). Global capitalist crisis and twenty-first century fascism: Beyond the Trump Hype. *Science and Society, 83*(2), 481–509.

Rocha, C. (2020). *Os vetos de Bolsonaro à lei de proteção de indígenas e quilombolas*. https://www.nexojornal.com.br/expresso/2020/07/08/Os-vetos-de-Bolsonaro-%C3%A0-lei-de-prote%C3%A7%C3%A3o-de-ind%C3%ADgenas-e-quilombolas

Rocha, R., Rocha, R., Atun, R., Massuda, A., Rache, B., Spinola, P., Nunes, L., Lago, M., & Castro, M. C. (2021). *Effect of socioeconomic inequalities and vulnerabilities on health-system preparedness and response to COVID-19 in Brazil: A comprehensive analysis*. https://www.thelancet.com/journals/langlo/article/PIIS2214-109X(21)00081-4/fulltext

Roediger, D. R. (2020). *The sinking middle class: A political history*. OR Books.

Romei, V. (2020). *How the pandemic is worsening inequality*. https://www.ft.com/content/cd075d91-fafa-47c8-a295-85bbd7a36b50

Romei, V., & Giles, C. (2021). *UK suffers biggest drop in economic output in 300 years*. https://www.ft.com/content/96e19afd-88b3-4e8d-bc3e-a72bd1f60d3c

Rosa, S. K. (2020). *Two-thirds of coronavirus deaths are of people with disabilities*. https://novaramedia.com/2020/07/24/two-thirds-of-coronavirus-deaths-are-people-with-a-disability/

Rossi, A., & Buono, R. (2020). *As mortes incógnitas da pandemia*. https://piaui.folha.uol.com.br/as-mortes-incognitas-da-pandemia/

Rothwell, J. (2020). *The unequal distribution of economic damage from COVID-19*. https://news.gallup.com/opinion/gallup/311714/unequal-distribution-economic-damage-covid.aspx

Roubini, N. (2020). *Coronavirus pandemic has delivered the fastest, deepest economic shock in history*. https://www.theguardian.com/business/2020/mar/25/coronavirus-pandemic-has-delivered-the-fastest-deepest-economic-shock-in-history

Roy, A. (2021). *We are witnessing a crime against humanity*. https://www.theguardian.com/news/2021/apr/28/crime-against-humanity-arundhati-roy-india-covid-catastrophe?CMP=Share_AndroidApp_Other

Rudan, I. (2020). A cascade of causes that led to the COVID-19 tragedy in Italy and in other European Union countries. *Journal of Global Health, 10*(1). https://www.ncbi.nlm.nih.gov/pmc/articles/PMC7125421/

Rude, C. (2005). The role of financial discipline in imperial strategy. In L. Panitch & M. Konings (Eds.), *American empire and the political economy of global finance*. Palgrave Macmillan.

Rukmini, S. (2020). *India had one of the world's strictest lockdowns. Why are cases still rising?* https://www.theguardian.com/commentisfree/2020/jul/04/india-lockdowns-cases-rising-

Rushe, D. (2020). *Making billions v making ends meet: How the pandemic has split the US economy in two*. https://www.theguardian.com/us-news/2020/aug/16/us-inequality-coronavirus-pandemic-unemployment

Ryner, M. (2015). Europe's ordoliberal iron cage: Critical political economy, the Euro area crisis and its management. *Journal of European Public Policy, 22*(2), 275–294.

Saad-Filho, A. (2007). Monetary policy in the neoliberal transition: A political economy review of keynesianism, monetarism and inflation targeting. In R. Albritton, R. Jessop & R. Westra (Eds.), *Political economy and global capitalism*. Anthem Press.

Saad-Filho, A. (2008). Marxian and keynesian critiques of neoliberalism. *Socialist Register, 44*, 337–345.
Saad-Filho, A. (2011). Crisis *in* neoliberalism or crisis *of* neoliberalism? *Socialist Register* (pp. 242–259).
Saad-Filho, A. (2017). Neoliberalism. In D. M. Brennan, D. Kristjanson-Gural, C. Mulder & E. Olsen (Eds.), *The Routledge handbook of Marxian economics*. Routledge.
Saad-Filho, A. (2018). Monetary policy and neoliberalism. In D. Cahill, M. Cooper and M. Konings (Eds.), *SAGE handbook of neoliberalism*. Sage.
Saad-Filho, A. (2019). *Value and crisis: Essays on labour, money and contemporary capitalism*. Haymarket.
Saad-Filho, A. (2020a). *Coronavirus, crisis, and the end of neoliberalism*. https://socialistproject.ca/2020/04/coronavirus-crisis-and-the-end-of-neoliberalism/#more
Saad-Filho, A. (2020b). From COVID-19 to the end of neoliberalism. *Critical Sociology, 46*(4–5), 477–485.
Saad-Filho, A. (2020c). *How is the pandemic going for you? Trump, Johnson and Bolsonaro in the swamp*. https://www.ppesydney.net/how-is-the-pandemic-going-for-you-trump-johnson-and-bolsonaro-in-the-swamp/
Saad-Filho, A. (2020d). *Coronavirus: How Brazil became the second worst affected country in the world*. https://theconversation.com/coronavirus-how-brazil-became-the-second-worst-affected-country-in-the-world-141102
Saad-Filho, A. (2021a). *Progressive policies for economic development: Economic diversification and social inclusion after climate change*. Routledge.
Saad-Filho, A. (2021b). *Growth and change in neoliberal capitalism: Essays in the political economy of late development*. Brill.
Saad-Filho, A. (2021c). Endgame: From crisis in neoliberalism to crises of neoliberalism. *Human Geography, 14*(1), 133–137.
Saad-Filho, A., & Ayers, A. (2020). A ticking time bomb: The global south in a time of coronavirus. *Journal of Australian Political Economy, 85*, 84–93.
Saad-Filho, A., & Boffo, M. (2020). The corruption of democracy: Corruption scandals, class alliances, and political authoritarianism in Brazil. *Geoforum*. https://www.sciencedirect.com/science/article/pii/S0016718520300373
Saad-Filho, A., & Boffo, M. (2021). Authoritarian neoliberalism, Covid-19, and the future of democracy. In A. Regelmann (Ed.), *The crisis and the future of democracy*. Rosa Luxemburg Foundation.
Saad-Filho, A., & Feil, F. (2020). *COVID-19 in Brazil: How Jair Bolsonaro created a calamity*. https://theconversation.com/covid-19-in-brazil-how-jair-bolsonaro-created-a-calamity-159066
Saad-Filho, A., & Morais, L. (2018). *Brazil: Neoliberalism versus democracy*. Pluto.

Safi, M. (2021). *Oxford/AstraZeneca Covid vaccine research 'was 97% publicly funded'*. https://www.theguardian.com/science/2021/apr/15/oxfordastrazeneca-covid-vaccine-research-was-97-publicly-funded

Safi, M., & Dhillon, A. (2021). *Ganges crowds highlight distancing challenges as Covid cases soar in India*. https://www.theguardian.com/world/2021/apr/12/ganges-crowds-highlight-distancing-challenges-as-covid-cases-soar-in-india

Sakamoto, L. (2020). *Coronavírus: Brasil mostra que é projetado para matar pobre em pandemia*. https://noticias.uol.com.br/colunas/leonardo-sakamoto/2020/05/06/coronavirus-brasil-mostra-que-e-projetado-para-matar-pobre-em-pandemia.htm?cmpid=copiaecola

Saletan, W. (2020). *The Trump pandemic*. https://slate.com/news-and-politics/2020/08/trump-coronavirus-deaths-timeline.html

Salluh, J. I. F., & Lisboa, T. (2016). Critical care in Brazil. *ICU management and practice*.https://healthmanagement.org/c/icu/issuearticle/critical-care-in-brazil-1

Sample, I., & Davis, N. (2021). *What do we know about the Indian coronavirus variant?* https://www.theguardian.com/world/2021/apr/19/what-do-we-know-about-the-indian-coronavirus-variant

Sandbu, M. (2020). *Huge fiscal spending is needed to fight the Coronavirus downturn*. https://www.ft.com/content/9963f71e-67b2-11ea-800d-da70cff6e4d3

Saphir, A., & Dunsmuir, L. (2020). *Timeline: Fed's response—Pandemic downturn vs financial crisis*. https://www.reuters.com/article/us-health-coronavirus-fed-timeline/timeline-feds-response-pandemic-downturn-vs-financial-crisis-idUSKCN21R2BC

Saunders, R. (2020). *"There is such a thing as society": Has Boris Johnson repudiated thatcherism?* https://www.newstatesman.com/politics/uk/2020/03/boris-johnson-thatcher-society-no-such-thing-policies

Scheiber, N., Schwartz, N. D., & Hsu, T. (2020). *"White collar quarantine" over virus spotlights class divide*. https://www.nytimes.com/2020/03/27/business/economy/coronavirus-inequality.html

Schipani, A., & Harris, B. (2020). *Drug gangs in Brazil's favelas enforce coronavirus lockdown*. https://www.ft.com/content/aaef1591-2fc5-4e6f-ab84-0e83b5a146ca

Schwartsman, H. (2021). *Bolsonaro é louco?* https://www1.folha.uol.com.br/colunas/helioschwartsman/2021/01/bolsonaro-e-louco.shtml

Sebenius, I., & Sebenius, J. K. (2020). *How many needless Covid-19 deaths were caused by delays in responding? Most of them*. https://www.statnews.com/2020/06/19/faster-response-prevented-most-us-covid-19-deaths/

Sell. (2020). What COVID-19 reveals about twenty-first century capitalism: Adversity and opportunity. *Development, 63*, 150–156.

Sevastopulo, D., & Shubber, K. (2020). *Trump cheers as anti-lockdown protests spread*. https://www.ft.com/content/c8f6f413-39c4-47ce-b1ff-0e02969cb612

Sharma, R. (2021). *The billionaire boom: How the super-rich soaked up Covid cash*. https://www.ft.com/content/747a76dd-f018-4d0d-a9f3-4069bf2f5a93

Shear, M. D., & Mervosh, S. (2020). *Trump encourages protest against governors who have imposed virus restrictions*. https://www.nytimes.com/2020/04/17/us/politics/trump-coronavirus-governors.html

Sheridan, D. (2020). *No 10 forced to deny claims Dominic Cummings said 'if some pensioners die, too bad'*. https://www.telegraph.co.uk/politics/2020/03/22/no-10-forced-deny-claims-dominic-cummings-said-pensioners-die/

Siddique, H. (2020). *Despite PM's praise of nurses, It's tory policies that made them suffer*. https://www.theguardian.com/society/2020/apr/13/despite-pms-praise-of-nurses-its-tory-policies-that-made-them-suffer

Sidera, A. (2020). *Bérgamo, la Masacre que la Patronal No Quiso Evitar*. https://ctxt.es/es/20200401/Politica/31884/Alba-Sidera-Italia-coronavirus-lombardia-patronal-economia-muertes.htm

Silva, R., & Pasti, D. (2020). *Da "gripezinha" ao "e daí?": as falas de Bolsonaro em cada fase da pandemia*. https://www.agazeta.com.br/es/politica/da-gripezinha-ao-e-dai-as-falas-de-bolsonaro-em-cada-fase-da-pandemia-0520

Sinclair, I., & Read, R. (2020). *"A national scandal": A timeline of the UK government's woeful response to the coronavirus crisis*. https://bylinetimes.com/2020/04/11/a-national-scandal-a-timeline-of-the-uk-governments-woeful-response-to-the-coronavirus-crisis/

Sirota, D. (2020). *The US public paid to develop this COVID-19 drug. It will cost $3,000 a dose*. https://www.jacobinmag.com/2020/06/gilead-remdesivir-drug-coronavirus-treatment-cost-pharma

Sivakumaran, S., Davies, G., & Al Sallakh, M. (2020). *Coronavirus can cause lasting lung damage—But the effects may ease over time*. https://theconversation.com/coronavirus-can-cause-lasting-lung-damage-but-the-effects-may-ease-over-time-140398

Slattery, G., Eisenhammer, S., & Perobelli, A. (2020). *Imported by the rich, coronavirus now devastating Brazil's poor*. https://www.reuters.com/article/us-health-coronavirus-brazil-poor/imported-by-the-rich-coronavirus-now-devastating-brazils-poor-idUSKBN22D549

Slobodian, Q. (2018). *Globalists: The end of empire and the birth of neoliberalism*. Harvard University Press.

Smith, D. (2020). *Trump reverts to media-bashing and blame-casting in latest press conference*. https://www.theguardian.com/us-news/2020/mar/19/trump-us-coronavirus-briefing-media

Snowden, F. M. (2020). *Epidemics and society: From the black death to the present*. Yale University Press.

Solty, I. (2020). *The bio-economic pandemic and the Western working classes*. https://socialistproject.ca/2020/03/bioeconomic-pandemic-and-western-working-classes/

Sotiris, P. (2020). Thinking beyond the lockdown: On the possibility of a democratic biopolitics. *Historical Materialism, 28*(3), 3–38.

Speed, E., & Mannion, R. (2020). Populism and health policy: Three international case studies of right-wing populist policy frames. *Sociology of Health & Illness, 42*(8), 1967–1981.

Spinney, L. (2020). *The coronavirus slayer! How Kerala's rock star health minister helped save it from Covid-19*. https://www.theguardian.com/world/2020/may/14/the-coronavirus-slayer-how-keralas-rock-star-health-minister-helped-save-it-from-covid-19?CMP=share_btn_tw

Spring, J. (2020). *Brazil minister calls for environmental deregulation while public distracted by COVID*. https://www.reuters.com/article/us-brazil-politics-environment-idUSKBN22Y30Y

Sridhar, D. (2021). *Here are five ways the government could have avoided 100,000 Covid deaths*. https://www.theguardian.com/commentisfree/2021/jan/27/five-ways-the-government-could-have-avoided-100000-covid-deaths

Stasavage, D. (2020). Democracy, autocracy, and emergency threats: Lessons for COVID-19 from the last thousand years. *International Organization, 74*, 1–17.

Stein, R., Wroth, C., & Hurt, A. (2020). *U.S. coronavirus testing still falls short. How's your state doing?* https://www.npr.org/sections/health-shots/2020/05/07/851610771/u-s-coronavirus-testing-still-falls-short-hows-your-state-doing?t=1591694986359

Stevano, S., Ali, R., & Jamieson, M. (2020). Essential for what? A global social reproduction view on the re-organisation of work during the COVID-19 pandemic. *Canadian Journal of Development Studies*. https://doi.org/10.1080/02255189.2020.1834362

Stone, J. (2020). *The people's vaccine—Moderna's coronavirus vaccine was largely funded by taxpayer dollars*. https://www.forbes.com/sites/judystone/2020/12/03/the-peoples-vaccine-modernas-coronavirus-vaccine-was-largely-funded-by-taxpayer-dollars/?sh=3ccf47146303

Stubbs, P., & Lendvai-Bainton, N. (2019). Authoritarian neoliberalism, radical conservatism and social policy within the European Union: Croatia, Hungary and Poland. *Development and Change, 51*(2), 540–560.

Stubbs, T., Kring, W., Laskaridis, C., Kentikelenis, A., & Gallagher, K. (2020). Whatever it takes? The global financial safety net, Covid-19, and developing countries. *World Development, 137*, 105171.

Stubley, P. (2020). *Coronavirus: Indians self-isolate in trees to protect relatives*. https://www.independent.co.uk/news/world/asia/coronavirus-india-trees-quarantine-lockdown-vangidi-purulia-bengal-modi-a9434966.html

Summers, L. H. (2015). Demand side secular stagnation. *American Economic Review, 105*(5), 60–65.

Summers, L. H. (2016). The age of secular stagnation. What it is and what to do about it. *Foreign Affairs*. https://www.foreignaffairs.com/articles/united-states/2016-02-15/age-secular-stagnation.

Summers, H. (2021). *UK government 'failed to consider gender' in its response to Covid pandemic*. https://www.theguardian.com/world/2021/may/08/uk-government-failed-to-consider-gender-in-its-response-to-covid-pandemic

Sumner, A., & Ortiz-Juarez, E. (2021). *Global monetary Poverty, 1981–2030*. Paper prepared for the United Nations Virtual Inter-Agency Expert Group Meeting on the Implementation of the Third United Nations Decade for the Eradication of Poverty, May. UNDESA.

Sumner, A. Ortiz-Juarez, E., & Hoy, C. (2020). *Estimates of the impact of COVID-19 on global poverty* (WIDER Working Paper 2020/43). https://www.wider.unu.edu/sites/default/files/Publications/Working-paper/PDF/wp2020-43.pdf

Sur, P., & Mitra, E. (2020). *Social distancing is a privilege of the middle class: For India's slum dwellers it will be impossible*. https://edition.cnn.com/2020/03/30/india/india-coronavirus-social-distancing-intl-hnk/index.html

Syal, R. (2020a). *Chief nurse was dropped from briefings after refusing to back Cummings*. https://www.theguardian.com/politics/2020/jul/20/englands-chief-nurse-dropped-from-covid-19-briefing-after-refusing-to-back-cummings-ruth-may

Syal, R. (2020b). *Government ignored warning to stockpile PPE as Covid-19 spread*. https://www.theguardian.com/world/2020/jun/12/government-ignored-warning-to-stockpile-ppe-as-covid-19-spread

Taneja, P., & Singh Bali, A. (2021). *India's staggering COVID crisis could have been avoided. But the government dropped its guard too soon*. https://theconversation.com/indias-staggering-covid-crisis-could-have-been-avoided-but-the-government-dropped-its-guard-too-soon-159538

Tansel, C. B. (Ed.). (2017). *States of discipline: Authoritarian neoliberalism and the contested reproduction of capitalist order*. Rowman & Littlefield.

Tcherneva, P. (2015). *When a rising tide sinks most boats: Trends in U.S. income inequality*. Policy Note 2015/4, Levy Economics Institute.

Tejani, S., & Fukuda-Parr, S. (2021). *Gender and Covid-19: Workers in global value chains*. https://ideas.repec.org/p/new/wpaper/2104.html

Tett, G. (2009). *Fool's gold: How unrestrained greed corrupted a dream*. Little, Brown & Co.

Teulings, C., & Baldwin, R. (Eds.) (2014). *Secular stagnation: Facts, causes and cures. Centre for economic policy research*. https://voxeu.org/content/secular-stagnation-facts-causes-and-cures

*The Economist*. (2008). Capitalism at bay. https://www.economist.com/node/12429544

*The Economist*. (2020). India's bureaucrats are fighting covid-19 with red tape. https://www.economist.com/asia/2020/06/11/indias-bureaucrats-are-fighting-covid-19-with-red-tape?utm_campaign=coronavirus-special-edition&u%E2%80%A6

*The Economist*. (2021). India is struggling with a catastrophic second wave. https://www.economist.com/asia/2021/04/24/india-is-struggling-with-a-catastrophic-second-wave

*The Guardian*. (2021a). Our key findings about US healthcare worker deaths in the pandemic's first year. https://www.theguardian.com/us-news/ng-interactive/2020/dec/22/lost-on-the-frontline-our-findings-to-date

*The Guardian*. (2021b). The Guardian view on Jair Bolsonaro: A danger to Brazil, and the world. https://www.theguardian.com/commentisfree/2021/apr/05/the-guardian-view-on-jair-bolsonaro-a-danger-to-brazil-and-the-world

*The Guardian*. (2021c). The Guardian view on Modi's mistakes: A pandemic that is out of control. https://www.theguardian.com/world/commentisfree/2021/apr/23/the-guardian-view-on-modis-mistakes-a-pandemic-that-is-out-of-control

The Independent. (2020). *Will the US ever have a national COVID-19 testing strategy?* https://www.independent.co.uk/news/will-the-us-ever-have-a-national-covid19-testing-strategy-donald-trump-strategy-people-joe-biden-us-b1767005.html

The Independent Panel. (2021a). *COVID-19: Make it the last pandemic*, paper commissioned by The Independent Panel for pandemic preparedness and response. https://theindependentpanel.org/documents/

The Independent Panel. (2021b). *COVID-19: The authoritative chronology, December 2019–March 2020*, paper commissioned by The Independent Panel for pandemic preparedness and response. https://theindependentpanel.org/documents/

Thorbecke, C., & Mitropoulos, A. (2020). *'Extreme inequality was the preexisting condition': How COVID-19 widened America's wealth gap*. https://abcnews.go.com/Business/extreme-inequality-preexisting-condition-covid-19-widened-americas/story?id=71401975&cid=social_twitter_abcn

Tilley, L. (2020). *Saying the quiet part out loud: Eugenics and the 'aging population' in conservative pandemic governance*. https://archive.discoversociety.org/2020/04/06/saying-the-quiet-part-out-loud-eugenics-and-the-aging-population-in-conservative-pandemic-governance/

TNI. (2020). *Coronavirus: The need for a progressive internationalist response*. https://www.tni.org/en/article/coronavirus-the-need-for-a-progressive-internationalist-response

Tooze, A. (2018). *Crashed: How a decade of financial crises changed the world*. Viking.

Tooze, A. (2020). *Shockwave*. https://www.lrb.co.uk/the-paper/v42/n08/adam-tooze/shockwave

Torres, E. (2020). *30-year-old dies after attending 'COVID party' thinking virus was a 'hoax'*. https://www.abc15.com/news/coronavirus/30-year-old-dies-after-attending-covid-party-thinking-virus-was-a-hoax

Toussaint, E. (2020). *The capitalist pandemic, coronavirus and the economic crisis*. http://internationalviewpoint.org/spip.php?article6458

TUC. (2021). *COVID-19 and insecure work*. https://www.tuc.org.uk/sites/default/files/2021-04/Covid-19%20and%20Insecure%20Work%20TUC%20template%20report%20130421.pdf

Turse, N. (2020). *"Exceptionally dire": Secondary impacts of Covid-19 could increase global poverty and hunger*. https://theintercept.com/2020/05/03/exceptionally-dire-secondary-impacts-of-covid-19-could-increase-global-poverty-and-hunger/

UK Home Office. (2020, August). *Statistics relating to passenger arrivals since the COVID-19 outbreak*. https://www.gov.uk/government/statistics/statistics-relating-to-passenger-arrivals-since-the-covid-19-outbreak-august-2020/statistics-relating-to-passenger-arrivals-since-the-covid-19-outbreak-august-2020

UNECA. (2020). *COVID-19 in Africa: Protecting lives and economies*. https://www.uneca.org/sites/default/files/PublicationFiles/eca_covid_report_en_24apr_web1.pdf

UOL. (2020). *Bolsonaro: Brasileiro tem que ser estudado. Pula no esgoto e nada acontece*. https://noticias.uol.com.br/politica/ultimas-noticias/2020/03/26/bolsonaro-brasileiro-tem-que-ser-estudado-cai-no-esgoto-e-nada-acontece.htm

Upadhyay, H. (2020). *Aarogya Setu app enters 150 Mn user club in 4 months*. https://entrackr.com/2020/08/aarogya-setu-app-enters-150-mn-user-club-in-4-months/

Usborne, S. (2020). *End of the office: The quiet, grinding loneliness of working from home*. https://www.theguardian.com/money/2020/jul/14/end-of-the-office-the-quiet-grinding-loneliness-of-working-from-home

Valentino-DeVries, J., Lu, D., & Dance, G. (2020). *Location data says it all: Staying at home during coronavirus is a luxury*. https://www.nytimes.com/interactive/2020/04/03/us/coronavirus-stay-home-rich-poor.html

Van Wagtendonk, A. (2020). *The UK backs away from "herd immunity" coronavirus proposal amid blowback*. https://www.vox.com/world/2020/3/15/21180414/coronavirus-uk-herd-immunity-vallance-johnson

Vanaik, A. (2009). India's paradigmatic communal violence. *Socialist Register, 45*, 141–162.

Varghese, S. (2020). *Why has Kerala been so successful in tackling coronavirus?* https://www.newstatesman.com/world/asia/2020/05/kerala-coronavirus-cases-response-india-KK-Shailaja

Vidal, J. (2020). *Human impact on wildlife to blame for spread of viruses, says study*. https://www.theguardian.com/environment/2020/apr/08/human-impact-on-wildlife-to-blame-for-spread-of-viruses-says-study-aoe

Vikram, K. (2021). *Not many takers for Aarogya Setu app, Delhi and Chandigarh see highest users*. https://www.newindianexpress.com/nation/2021/mar/21/not-many-takers-for-aarogya-setu-appdelhi-and-chandigarh-see-highest-users-2279311.html

Vyas, M. (2020). *The jobs bloodbath of April 2020*. https://cmie.com/kommon/bin/sr.php?kall=warticle&dt=2020-05-05%2008:22:21&msec=776

Wacquant, L. (2009). *Punishing the poor: The neoliberal government of social insecurity*. Duke University Press.

Wade, N. (2021). *The origin of COVID: Did people or nature open pandora's box at Wuhan?* https://thebulletin.org/2021/05/the-origin-of-covid-did-people-or-nature-open-pandoras-box-at-wuhan/

Walker, P. (2021). *Call centre staff to be monitored via webcam for home-working "infractions"*. https://www.theguardian.com/business/2021/mar/26/teleperformance-call-centre-staff-monitored-via-webcam-home-working-infractions

Walker, S., & Smith, H. (2020). *Why has Eastern Europe suffered less from the coronavirus that the West?* https://www.theguardian.com/world/2020/may/05/why-has-eastern-europe-suffered-less-from-coronavirus-than-the-west

Wallace, R. (2016). *Big farms make big flu: Dispatches on infectious disease, agribusiness, and the nature of science*. Monthly Review Press.

Wallace, R. (2020). *Dead epidemiologists: On the origins of COVID-19*. Monthly Review Press.

Wallace, R., Liebman, A., Chaves, L. F., & Wallace, R. (2020). *COVID-19 and the circuits of capital*. https://monthlyreview.org/2020/05/01/covid-19-and-circuits-of-capital/

Wallace-Wells, D. (2020). *We had the vaccine the whole time*. https://nymag.com/intelligencer/2020/12/moderna-covid-19-vaccine-design.html

Walsh, N. P., & Krever, M. (2020). *The UK's "coronavirus dashboard" may be under-reporting deaths significantly*. https://edition.cnn.com/2020/04/07/uk/coronavirus-uk-deaths-intl-gbr/index.html

Wang, M., Di, B., Zhou, D. H., Zheng, B. J., Jing, H., Lin, Y. P., Liu, Y.-F., Wu, X.-W., Qin, P.-Z., Wang, Y.-L., Jian, L.-Y., Li, X.-Z., Xu, J.-X., Lu, E.-J., Li, T.-G., & Xu, J. (2006). Food markets with live birds as source of avian influenza. *Emerging Infectious Diseases, 12*(11), 1773–1775.

Wearmouth, R. (2020). *Lockdown a week earlier would have halved UK coronavirus death toll, says Neil Ferguson*. https://www.huffingtonpost.co.uk/entry/lockdown-week-earlier-coronavirus-death-neil-ferguson_uk_5ee0f82ec5b66552b9a6e912

Wenham, C. (2020). *The UK was a global leader in preparing for pandemics. What went wrong with coronavirus?* https://www.theguardian.com/commentisfree/2020/may/01/uk-global-leader-pandemics-coronavirus-covid-19-crisis-britain

West, C. (2016). *Goodbye, American neoliberalism. A new era is here*. https://www.theguardian.com/commentisfree/2016/nov/17/american-neoliberalism-cornel-west-2016-election

WHO. (2020). *New WHO estimates: Up to 190,000 could die of COVID-19 in Africa if not controlled*. https://www.afro.who.int/news/new-who-estimates-190-000-people-could-die-covid-19-africa-if-not-controlled

Whyte, D. (Ed.). (2015). *How corrupt is Britain?* Pluto Press.

Wilpert, G. (2019). *Over 40% of US households are one paycheck away from poverty*. https://therealnews.com/over-40-of-us-households-are-one-paycheck-away-from-poverty

Winlow, S., Hall, S., & Treadwell, J. (2017). *The rise of the right: English nationalism and the transformation of working-class politics*. Policy Press.

Wolf, M. (2009). *Is America the New Russia?* https://www.ft.com/content/09f8c996-2930-11de-bc5e-00144feabdc0;

Wolf, M. (2020). *The world economy is now collapsing*. https://www.ft.com/content/d5f05b5c-7db8-11ea-8fdb-7ec06edeef84

Wolf, M. (2021). *Larry summers: I'm concerned that what is being done is substantially excessive*. https://www.ft.com/content/380ea811-e927-4fe1-aa5b-d213816e9073

Wood, Z. (2020). *Tesco defends £635m dividend payout after coronavirus tax break*. https://www.theguardian.com/business/2020/apr/08/tesco-sales-up-30-per-cent-because-of-pre-lockdown-stockpiling-coronavirus

Wren-Lewis, S. (2020). *Who still thinks austerity was a good idea?* https://mainlymacro.blogspot.com/2020/04/who-still-thinks-austerity-was-good-idea.html?m=1

Wright, B. (2020). *U.S. accused of stealing ventilators from Barbados as coronavirus spreads in the Caribbean*. https://newsone.com/3924158/barbados-accuses-us-ventilators-seized/

Yadav, P., Mehndiratta, A., Chalkidou, K., Rupani, S., & Reddy, K. (2020). *India's COVID-19 testing capacity must grow by a factor of 10: Here's how that can happen*. https://www.cgdev.org/publication/indias-covid-19-testing-capacity-must-grow-factor-10-heres-how-can-happen

Youn, S. (2019). *40% of Americans don't have $400 in the bank for emergency expenses: Federal reserve*. https://abcnews.go.com/US/10-americans-struggle-cover-400-emergency-expense-federal/story?id=63253846:~:text=Almost%2040%25%20of%20American%20adults,a%20Federal%20Reserve%20survey%20finds

Younge, G. (2020). *We can't breathe*. https://www.newstatesman.com/politics/uk/2020/06/we-cant-breathe

Zahoor, B. (2020). *Health: Why new viruses continue to spread*. https://www.dawn.com/news/1546447

# Index

A




A. Saad-Filho, *The Age of Crisis*,
https://doi.org/10.1007/978-3-030-81608-7

## G

## H

## Q

R

## S

The manufacturer's authorised representative in the EU is Springer Nature Customer Service Centre GmbH, Europaplatz 3, 69115 Heidelberg, Germany. If you have any concerns regarding our products, please contact ProductSafety@springernature.com

Printed and bound by CPI Group (UK) Ltd, Croydon, CR0 4YY
30/09/2026
02225701-0004